BECOMING A
SOMEBODY

Steven Nyczyk with Anna-Maria Kaneff,
Kristina Maria Kaneff, and Didi Kaneff

BECOMING A SOMEBODY

The Biography of Ignat Kaneff

DUNDURN
TORONTO

The Kaneff family will be donating all of their proceeds from the sale of *Becoming a Somebody* to charity.

Publisher: Scott Fraser
Editors: Cy Strom and Michael Carroll
Designer: Laura Boyle
Cover image and interior images: Courtesy of the Kaneff family.
Printer: Friesens

Library and Archives Canada Cataloguing in Publication

Title: Becoming a somebody : the biography of Ignat Kaneff / Steven Nyczyk with Anna-Maria Kaneff, Kristina Maria Kaneff, and Didi Kaneff.
Names: Nyczyk, Steven, author. | Kaneff, Anna-Maria, author. | Kaneff, Kristina Maria, author. | Kaneff, Didi, author.
Description: Includes index.
Identifiers: Canadiana (print) 20189067780 | Canadiana (ebook) 20189067799 | ISBN 9781459743786 (hardcover) | ISBN 9781459743793 (PDF) | ISBN 9781459743809 (EPUB)
Subjects: LCSH: Kaneff, Ignat, 1926- | LCSH: Real estate developers—Ontario—Biography. | LCSH: Philanthropists—Ontario—Biography. | CSH: Bulgarian Canadians—Ontario—Biography | LCGFT: Biographies.
Classification: LCC HD319.O5 N93 2019 | DDC 333.33092—dc23

1 2 3 4 5   23 22 21 20 19

We acknowledge the support of the Canada Council for the Arts and the Ontario Arts Council for our publishing program. We also acknowledge the financial support of the Government of Ontario, through the Ontario Book Publishing Tax Credit and Ontario Creates, and the Government of Canada.

Care has been taken to trace the ownership of copyright material used in this book. The author and the publisher welcome any information enabling them to rectify any references or credits in subsequent editions.

The publisher is not responsible for websites or their content unless they are owned by the publisher.

Printed and bound in Canada.

VISIT US AT
🌐 dundurn.com | 🐦 @dundurnpress | 📘 dundurnpress | 📷 dundurnpress

Dundurn
3 Church Street, Suite 500
Toronto, Ontario, Canada
M5E 1M2

To my father, who was my greatest influence and inspiration in life,
and always will be

Contents

1

The Nest

Looking back on everything now, I should have been afraid. That is not to say I was fearless; not knowing enough to be frightened need not be confused with bravery. It was through no grand display of courage that I left home at the age of fourteen — a mere boy by today's standards — to find my own way in the world, to live and work by myself in a place that was literally foreign and unfamiliar in every way. I did not speak the language of this new place, nor did I possess much formal education. What I did have was boundless optimism and ambition, as well as faith in God and myself. As it would turn out, that was enough: not just once, but twice in my life.

After a childhood during which I experienced nothing but closeness with my large and loving family, I suddenly found myself alone in the world. No longer could I go to my father whenever I needed guidance or support. No longer could I turn to my mother for a hot meal or a warm hug. I was removed from everyone and everything I had ever known or loved, forced to draw upon the lessons I learned during my childhood — and my own wits — for survival.

At first I believed my departure was temporary, a brief window of opportunity to scrape together some earnings for my family before heading back home. But shortly after leaving, I saw that returning would not be an option for me; for many years I could not safely return home.

Before leaving, I had received many important teachings, but truthfully it was those things I did not yet know that served me so well. I was unprepared for the loneliness I would face, and I knew little about the real danger that would soon surround me. Had I even possessed an inkling of what was happening in the world, I probably would not have left home in the first place. I would have realized that mankind was about to slip still deeper into what would prove to be the most destructive war in its history, and that I was walking straight into its heart. Like anyone else, I would have quivered at the notion of sleeping beneath a night's sky filled with falling bombs. Had I known any of it, I would have stayed close to my childhood home, clinging to the only known safe place in a world gone mad.

Of course, I did not realize that I would have nightmares for the rest of my life, often afraid to sleep for fear of what haunted me when I closed my eyes. I embarked upon the adventure of a lifetime without knowing enough to realize that I should have feared for my life. I was filled with the inexperience of youth and the young man's thirst for adventure.

At the time, I was just an innocent farm boy travelling beyond the borders of my small village, hoping to make my mark on the world. I did not know how I would do it, but more than anything I believed that things would somehow fall into place if I worked hard and tried to do right by those around me. There was so much that should have paralyzed me with fear, but none of it was ever so much as a thought in my mind. I was not afraid because I was not aware of all that should have frightened me. By the time I figured it out, I had passed the point of no return.

Even if there had not been a war, it was apparent that life on my own would be challenging. I may not have known about world affairs, but even then I was no fool. My upbringing had taught me that life as a rule was hard, leaving me with no expectation for anything to come easily. I had also learned to listen to my inner voice for guidance. I never doubted my decision to leave home because I trusted my intuition. My heart said to go.

As I saw it at the time, the world outside my village held the possibility of finding fortune and opportunities not otherwise available to me. Staying home meant becoming, at best, a big fish in a small pond. Perhaps I could even become a respected man like my father. But I knew the opportunity to test the limits of my potential was to be found elsewhere. I craved the chance to discover my true worth.

Since before I can remember, I have been compelled by a singular desire that has stuck with me: I wanted to be a somebody. (This is how we say it in Bulgarian; much later I learned that English speakers use the same expression.) As I left the only home I had ever known, I had only a vague notion of what being a somebody meant, yet the words echoed in my mind. "I'm going to be a somebody," I said to myself again and again, even — or especially — during the darkest of times, repeating this to myself until I believed the words to be as true as the rising sun. Becoming a somebody was everything to me.

As the years passed, I learned more and more what it meant to be a somebody. I also learned what it did not mean. Being a somebody was not about acquiring money. Like most people, I prefer having money to not having it, but I have always known that being a somebody has nothing to do with the numbers printed next to one's name on a bank ledger. My father was never a wealthy man, but he was most definitely a somebody. By that, I mean he was a respected businessman who was sought out for his advice. To me, being a somebody means positioning myself to help others; it means being respected for virtuous qualities; it means doing the right thing, even when it is easier to do otherwise. Being a somebody means doing my best to improve myself and my community. In my opinion, being a somebody means being able to reflect on my actions and know I have done my best to help others while striving to achieve my full potential. That was the kind of person I always wanted to be.

In many ways, my life was tough. It was nothing like a stroll through the rose garden, as an old Bulgarian expression goes. My life's journey was often fraught with danger, tragedy, and misfortune. There were times when it seemed I might not make it. There were times when I overcame hardship through my sheer force of will, and there were just as many other times when I survived by pure luck. Over the years,

I learned not to worry about what I could not control; I focused on giving myself a chance to succeed.

Some people meet me today and assume I was born with a silver spoon in my mouth, as if success had somehow been bestowed upon me as a birthright. Nothing could be further from the truth. It was only through experiencing loss, hardship, and heartbreak that I also came to experience success. I have had my fair share of triumphs, but I have also known failure.

The reason I am writing this book is to share my story, which is both unlikely and incredible, set during the most tumultuous century in recent history. I believe that others can benefit from my experiences while also learning from my mistakes, of which there have been many. More than anything, I simply wish to share the journey of a young boy who emerged from a tiny farming village and set forth in the world, desiring nothing more — and nothing less — than to become a somebody.

MY COUNTRY

The story of my life begins in Bulgaria, a fact that would prove to be of critical importance in shaping me as a person. I was born on October 6, 1926, a time in which Bulgaria was struggling to re-establish its identity following centuries of social and political unrest. The Bulgaria of my childhood was a place in which the people were highly protective of the right to their continued existence as a sovereign nation-state. Such a right had been taken from us before.

I was raised to be a proud and loyal Bulgarian. I have lived outside Bulgaria far longer than in it, but one of my defining characteristics has been my pride in my roots. Those who know me well know that I consider myself Bulgarian first and foremost. Even when I was not living there, my heart always remained in Bulgaria.

Of course, despite my great love for the country, I cannot say that being Bulgarian has always been easy. The Bulgaria of my childhood was a grief-stricken nation mired in poverty and perpetually beleaguered by its neighbours. Yet, after so many years of existing as little more than an extension of the Ottoman Empire, the Bulgaria of the late 1920s and early 1930s was fiercely proud of having regained its independence.

An old saying goes: "A bird should never be ashamed of its nest. Any bird ashamed of its nest doesn't deserve to be there." I heard these words many times as a boy, and they perfectly capture the warm feelings I have for the place in which I was raised. Bulgaria was my nest, and I was proud of it. When I close my eyes and recall the happiest and most golden moments of my life, many images hearken back to Bulgaria. I experienced a simple childhood, free of worry or pressure. I would not recognize this until later, but my Bulgarian village childhood was a sort of oasis.

It was also in Bulgaria that I was taught the foundational lessons that would carry me through the rest of my life. I learned to love and care for others, to be an active member of my community, and to take pride in being part of something bigger than myself. There is so much of Bulgaria inside me.

THE COURSE OF MY COUNTRY'S HISTORY

Bulgaria is a breathtaking land with many rivers and beautiful mountains. Our village was located in the broad Danubean Plain in the country's northeast; far away to the south, the Balkan Mountains form the backbone of the country.

I was told that the Bulgarian people began to settle these territories in ancient times. In school, we were taught about the First and Second Bulgarian Empires and their spread throughout the Balkan region to encompass Thrace, parts of Romania, and other regions. We learned about the importance of these two kingdoms to the cultural growth of the Slavic peoples. Our tsars fought many battles against the neighbouring Byzantine Empire — some were great victories, others ended in defeat. In 1205, Tsar Kaloyan crushed the invading Crusaders from Western Europe in the Battle of Adrianople.

But other invaders, including the Mongols, weakened the Second Bulgarian Empire in the late thirteenth century. By then, it was also threatened by Serbia and Hungary, and parts of the kingdom even came under Serbian rule.

When my father was a young man, the oldest men and women could still remember the Turks ruling our country. The Ottoman Turks made incursions into Europe in the 1340s and 1350s and captured Sofia in the 1380s. In 1393, they took Veliko Tarnovo, the Bulgarian capital at the time, and three years later seized Vidin, the last Bulgarian stronghold, bringing a complete end to the Second Bulgarian Empire and ushering in five centuries of Ottoman rule.

The years of Turkish occupation marked our people deeply. The roots of Christianity run deep in our country; in fact, Bishop of Alexandria Saint Athanasius (ca. 296–373 CE) built Europe's first Christian monastery in Bulgaria in 344. But now Bulgarian Christians were in danger of vanishing. A few clergymen toiled in remote rural areas; without them Bulgaria's history and traditions might have been forgotten.

We were also taught in our history classes about how Bulgaria rose again. The European Enlightenment and the French Revolution brought to the Balkans ideas such as liberalism and nationalism, inspiring Bulgaria's National Awakening. The sixteenth and seventeenth centuries had seen several major revolts against Ottoman rule, but it took Russia's declaration of war on the Ottoman Empire in 1877 in aid of the Bulgarian liberation movement — inspired by the famous Vasil Levski and other leaders — to finally defeat the Turks in Bulgaria. Then, in 1878, Russia and the Ottoman Empire signed the Treaty of San Stefano, which allowed the Bulgarian people to establish a large, independent principality of their own. The agreement brought tremendous joy to Bulgarians everywhere.

Sadly, the treaty was never put into effect. The great powers replaced the Treaty of San Stefano with the Treaty of Berlin later that same year.

This new treaty carved out a much smaller territory for Bulgaria — mostly the southern bank of the Danube and the region of Sofia — and gave it only limited independence. Many of our people suddenly found themselves living outside the borders of their own country. A series of wars of unification soon followed. Bulgaria recaptured Eastern Rumelia during the Serbo-Bulgarian War of 1885 and then attempted to unify other territories with Bulgarian populations, including Macedonia and Thrace.

On October 5, 1908, with the backing of Russia and Austria-Hungary, Prince Ferdinand — soon to be known as Tsar Ferdinand I — formally proclaimed Bulgaria's independence in Veliko Tarnovo. Then Bulgaria joined a series of disastrous conflicts. Bulgaria was one of the victors in the First Balkan War in 1912 against the Ottoman Empire, but it was still dissatisfied with the revised borders that left a large percentage of Bulgarians outside the new state. The disagreement led to Bulgaria's calamitous involvement in the Second Balkan War. This was the war in which my grandfather fought.

Serbia and Greece turned back the attacks from Bulgaria, which suffered damaging human and territorial losses. Yet despite its weakened condition, Bulgaria, under its new king from an old German dynasty, soon found itself fighting alongside Germany, Austria-Hungary, and Ottoman Turkey on the losing side in the First World War. The results this time were considerable territorial losses and the deaths of nearly two hundred thousand Bulgarian soldiers, nearly 4 percent of the country's population.

The Treaty of Neuilly-sur-Seine of 1919 required Bulgaria to cede Western Thrace to Greece, cutting off its direct access to the Mediterranean. Bulgaria also lost much land along its western borders to Yugoslavia, and also surrendered Southern Dobruja on the Black Sea to Romania. The treaty also demanded that Bulgaria reduce the size of its army and pay heavy reparations in cash and goods to its former enemies. These reparation payments were still being made when I was a child — they lasted until 1932.

Bulgaria's economy was in ruins. The period between 1912 and 1929 also saw more than a quarter of a million refugees immigrate to Bulgaria following the loss of Macedonia, Thrace, and Dobruja. This placed an even greater burden on the economy. The result of the Treaty of Neuilly-sur-Seine is referred to as the Second National Catastrophe, only a few years after the First National Catastrophe in 1913 following the Second Balkan War.

This was the Bulgaria into which I was born, a place where nearly everybody was penniless, and collectively, the nation was heavily burdened by tragedy, as almost every family had lost at least one of its beloved members to a war.

MY VILLAGE

I was born and raised in the tiny farming village of Gorno Ablanovo, located in Bulgaria's Ruse Province in the northeast of the country. Our home was situated in the scenic Danube Valley a couple of miles from the Danube River and about 185 miles from Bulgaria's capital city, Sofia. This village, as I remember it from my childhood, was a beautiful place.

My family was part of a tightly knit agricultural community made up of what we would now consider smallholder farmers. Unlike the peasant farmers elsewhere in Europe who were required to pay rent and offer services to a landlord, smallholders differed in that each household owned a parcel of land — in our case, twenty-five acres — which the farmer operated largely without outside interference. During the early part of my childhood, we grew crops mostly for our own consumption.

Established while Bulgaria was under Ottoman rule, our village was named after the daughter of a Turkish sultan. Translated into English, *gorno* means "upper," while *Ablanovo* derives from the daughter's name. There is also a "lower" Ablanovo named after the same girl, but I never visited it. I was told that it was quite similar to our village.

Gorno Ablanovo's picturesque landscape possesses a great deal of natural beauty with its lush, rolling hills, farmland, and trees lining the roads. However, our closeness to the Danube River is the village's defining characteristic. The waters of the great Danube, which travel almost eighteen hundred miles through ten European countries, rush by relentlessly. As a child, I looked at the river as a symbol of strength and determination, and always stood in awe of it.

While the ever-powerful Danube posed a constant threat, the ground beneath our feet provided for our survival. Gorno Ablanovo — like much of Bulgaria — possessed rich, nutrient-dense soil that was dark, heavy, and perfect for farming. Almost anything grows there: wheat, corn, barley, grapes, peaches, plums, watermelon, sugar cane, and nearly any other European vegetable or fruit you could name. Our barns were always well stocked with fresh produce.

Of course, we needed to harvest all we could to ensure our survival during the harsh Bulgarian winters. The climate in our region was oppressively hot in summer and unbearably cold in winter. Given our position on the Danubian Plain, the coldest months in Gorno Ablanovo brought with them a chilling, unrelenting wind. The temperature often dropped to twenty-five degrees below freezing with the wind chill.

Keeping our bodies warm and our bellies full during the deep freeze of winter was an ongoing challenge while living so close to the shores of the Danube. And an even more alarming problem appeared in our neighbourhood every winter: as soon as the river's ice became solid enough to support their weight, wolves began creeping over from Romania. They threatened our livestock, sometimes our lives.

The people of our village looked out for one another. Fortunately, Gorno Ablanovo was designed with mutual defence in mind. Unlike the majority of agricultural communities found throughout Europe, Bulgarian farming families did not live near their fields. In settlements established during the days of Ottoman rule, the farming people preferred to cluster together in small communities as a means of protecting one another from Turkish bandits. Bulgarians knew only too well the unspeakable tragedies that could befall their families if they chose to live on the open fields, which they toiled in isolation.

Under Ottoman rule, it was against the law for Bulgarians to assault a Turk under any circumstances, justified or not. The bandits were permitted to do as they pleased without fear of retribution. In order to protect their families, farmers would take their dogs out nightly for moonlight patrols, pretending to check for fire hazards while they actually conducted a neighbourhood watch.

Gorno Ablanovo was born out of this need for togetherness, and working co-operatively was ingrained in us because we relied on one another to survive. I witnessed this sense of community many times throughout my childhood. When somebody in the village decided to build a house, others were always ready to lend a hand with its construction. If a young couple announced their intention to get married, the entire community came together to prepare for the wedding before joining in on the celebration, contributing what they could to help the new family start out on the right foot. This spirit of togetherness was not lost on my impressionable young mind. I witnessed the harmony in which a community could exist when all of its residents worked for the betterment of the collective.

Our tiny village was hardly more than a speck on the map, but to me it seemed like the whole world. For much of my childhood, I had only a vague notion of places outside Gorno Ablanovo. It was only when I grew older that I began to realize there was a vast expanse beyond my village. I began to see photographs and film clips of cities like Paris and Berlin in school, and slowly my imagination took over. But until I was seven or eight years old, Gorno Ablanovo was my only reality, and its borders represented the limits of my imagination.

Amenities were scarce. There were a few small food stores and a pub for drinking, but there was little room for frivolity in our rustic lives. The people of our village were focused on farming. Not working meant not eating. The adults worked endlessly, and the children helped with select chores as soon as they were able. Everybody worked, as there was no other way.

Still, my life in Bulgaria was more than just chores and drudgery. I also spent much of my time playing in the fields of Gorno Ablanovo with my friends. In fact, it was around the age of six that I discovered a love and passion for playing soccer. I would often surprise myself with what I was able to accomplish on the field. I was one of the smallest boys in the village — the smallest for my age, in fact — but I was an excellent player, relying on my quick feet to great advantage. It was on the soccer field that I first learned that quick feet and even quicker wits were more important than muscles or height. I learned to never accept my size as a disadvantage. If anything, being underestimated by opposing players worked in my favour. This would become a recurring theme in my life.

We also played other sports such as *chilik*, or *gilli*, a game consisting of two sticks, one long, one short, with the object being to hit the short stick, which was sharpened at both ends, with the long one. The "batter" took up position at a hole dug in the ground or at a circle drawn in the dirt, struck the small stick with the large one so that it popped into the air, then tried to hit the small stick as far as possible. *Chilik* is very ancient and has deep roots in similar Central Asian and Indian pastimes that date back thousands of years. I remember many enjoyable hours playing it with my friends, which no doubt helped improve our hand-and-eye coordination as well as being a lot of fun.

Beyond sports, distraction came in the form of the rare car or ambulance that passed through the village. There were no cars or trucks in Gorno Ablanovo. The only modes of transportation we had to get around during my childhood were horses or our own feet. However, we would occasionally see an automobile travelling on the dirt roads cut out of the forest for the farmers' wagons. My friends and I would chase the cars as they drove past, hoping against all odds that the motorist might stop long enough to give us a closer look at the incredible machine. Most of the time the car would simply speed up and race away from our simple lives, its appearance like the flash of a comet across the sky. Seeing a car filled me with wonder, along with excitement for all that was possible beyond the boundaries of Gorno Ablanovo.

Besides the daily work that had to be done, whether at home by our mothers or our fathers in the fields, life in our village centred around church, the farmers' co-operative, and citizens' meetings. For me and my siblings, as with all the other children in Gorno Ablanovo, school was our primary focus in the fall, winter, and spring. Next to the school was the co-op store, and often after my day's studies I would help out in the shop, stocking and dusting shelves or undertaking any other necessary work I was called upon to do.

The auditorium in our school was where village meetings were held, as were occasional stage comedies by actors from Ruse. I recall one particular production in the 1930s when a troupe from that city put on a play that made fun of villagers like ourselves, portraying country folk as oafish and boorish and mocking the way we talked and behaved. My father took exception to the actors' condescending, sarcastic, and completely distorted view of rural people, so much so that he halted the performance and made sure those performers never returned to our village. As always, he stood up for his fellow citizens.

In my childhood, Gorno Ablanovo did not have electricity, something the village only got after the Second World War. Lighting before that was provided by gas, both in the home and in the streets. One day our teachers brought a film projector into our class to play us American movies. It was at this point that my imagination about the world beyond Gorno Ablanovo expanded. The movies opened up my mind to the possibilities that lay outside our village.

Of course, in those days screening a movie was not as easy as just flipping a switch. In order to power the projector — a monstrous contraption that needed to be wheeled into the classroom — our teachers had to haul a large generator in behind it. As the silent images flickered on the screen, my classmates and I would listen to the generator chugging away. Exhaust would seep into the air, sometimes causing us to cough. But it was all worth it, since those films provided the most amazing images I had ever seen.

I remember looking up and seeing Charlie Chaplin dancing on the screen, wearing the most elaborate clothing I had ever seen. In Gorno Ablanovo, everybody wore homemade clothes. America, in sharp contrast, was a world filled with colour, even when seen in a black-and-white film. For the first time in my life, the thought of someday exploring different parts of the world crossed my mind.

The village I grew up in was small, but we were strong and proud, steadfast in our beliefs, and loyal to one another and to God. In my opinion, Gorno Ablanovo is one of Bulgaria's hidden jewels, and in no better place could I have hoped to be raised. Within its confines, I experienced nothing less than full security and pure happiness.

2

The Family

Like all Bulgarian families of the time, my family was poor. Fortunately, the soil beneath our feet was among the best in the world, and the men in my family — like most in Bulgaria — were skilled farmers. The Bulgarian economy may have been in ruins, but we never had to worry about starving. In terms of cash, we were dirt poor, but I always liked to think of my family as "dirt rich"; we had more than enough to eat, thanks to everything we were able to grow in our region's lush soil.

An old Bulgarian expression explains: "When you have meat and vegetables, you have everything." As far as I was concerned, we had everything.

I never felt poor. Our primary needs were always met and my family never seemed to have less than any other family did. At the same time, of course, we had very few possessions. All of our clothes were homemade, as were our shoes. Everything I wore had already been worn by one of my siblings. In fact, I did not own a pair of shoes that were not homemade until after I left Bulgaria.

That is not to say that things could not have been better. My family lived in cramped conditions — up to eighteen people sharing a tiny house of no more than twelve hundred square feet. This structure, nothing more than sticks and logs held together by dried mud, was primitive, even for its time. But it kept us warm during the winter, dry from the rain, and safe from prowling wolves. It was home, and it was all we needed.

In addition to my father and mother and us six children, and my aunt and uncle and their seven children, my grandmother also lived in our three-bedroom house. Despite the sheer density of Kanevs per square foot, privacy was never an issue because I was simply unaware that such a concept existed. My parents, siblings, and I shared one of the bedrooms, while my aunt, uncle, and their children lived in another. Growing up, I became accustomed to sharing a straw bed with at least two of my siblings. It was good and comfortable until I came to learn that some beds were not made from straw.

The last bedroom was the domain of my grandmother — or Baba, the Bulgarian word for grandmother — though she seldom slept alone. Every night my siblings, cousins, and I would race to Baba's bedroom to see who would sleep with her, with the first two or three children to arrive claiming a warm spot next to our cherished grandmother for the night. I loved sleeping in Baba's bed. It was always so warm and welcoming. Whenever I heard wind whipping outside the window or wolves howling at the door, I always felt safe and secure if I was tucked in next to Baba.

Living in such cramped accommodations might have led to problems, but not in our family. We loved one another and appreciated the time we spent together. In a way, having so many people sharing such a small space was integral to our survival. Bulgarian winters were cold, and my family kept warm by huddling together in the front room of our house, an area that served as both our kitchen and dining room. Combining the body heat of nearly twenty people with our wood-burning stove that blazed throughout the winter — in addition to the extra insulation from livestock pressed against the side of the house — was the only way we were able to stay warm. We literally had to stick together to survive.

My greatest influence and inspiration in life was, and always will be, my father. To say that I admired him would be an understatement; I worshipped my father. In my eyes — and the eyes of many others, as I came to learn — my father was a great man, principled and fair-minded. He was at various times a soldier, a political organizer, a community leader, an influential speaker, a farmer, and a builder. Seen through my loving eyes, my father could do anything.

I tried to learn from him as much as possible. With his words and his actions, my father taught me about setting goals and achieving them. He taught me about loyalty, dedication, and morals. I trusted my father completely, and so we formed a deep and lasting bond.

Hristo Kanev, my father — the spelling of my last name changed later when I came to Canada — was born in July 1894, also in Gorno Ablanovo. His own father — my grandfather — lived until 1929, when I was only three years old. Sadly, I never came to know my grandfather. My grandfather's death was a tremendous blow to our family. Fortunately, my grandmother was the ultimate survivor, weathering not only these but many other hard times during her life. Baba was our family's spiritual leader for the duration of her life. She remained vital until the very end of her eventful life, reaching the age of 105.

After my grandfather's passing, my grandmother began to rely on my father as the leader of our family. Even in his young manhood, my father had gravitated naturally to a position of leadership. By the time I was old enough to understand the dynamics at work in our family, he had already grown accustomed to his position at the family's head, deferring only to my grandmother. Even when he might have been unsure of himself, my father projected confidence, always willing to take responsibility for his choices. He dedicated himself to the cause of furthering his family's lot in life and, when possible, doing whatever he could for the betterment of the community at large.

As a boy, I always considered myself to be a committed student and an avid reader. As I reflect on it now, however, my real education came to me from my father. As often as possible, I joined him on his horse-drawn wagon rides to and from our fields during which he would teach me about our family's and our nation's history, war, peace, love, and respect for our fellow men. To me, there was no smarter man, and nobody from whom I would rather learn life's most important lessons. My father managed to teach me something new whenever we spent time together.

In the spring, summer, and fall, as I accompanied my father to our field to work by wagon, he would share stories with me. The road stretching from our house to the field took roughly one hour to travel, and I always wished the trip had been longer. My father was a skilled storyteller, elegant with words and generous with insight. He spoke with passion, and I considered it a privilege to listen to him as I hung on his every word. It was during our wagon rides that my father first began challenging me to think critically about all that I encountered.

Although he drew from a never-ending supply of anecdotes, it was my father's war stories that transfixed me the most. Some of my clearest memories from childhood came from listening to my father telling stories from the First World War. Whenever he spoke of it, it felt as though I was there by his side.

My father was sent to Macedonia after being conscripted into the army as part of the Red Cross. He was deeply affected by war and never quite recovered emotionally. The experience haunted him for the rest of his life. I will never forget the first time my father told me about his time at war. We were riding home around dusk following a productive day on the farm. My father and I were alone on the wagon, and as we rode along, I began to notice that he was saying very little, as though he was deep in thought. I do not know why he chose that particular day to share his experiences with me. Holding on to the reins in his left hand, my father put his right hand on my shoulder, turned his head to me, and began to speak.

"Gatyu," he said, "it's time for you to learn about the war. It will be difficult for you to hear what I'm about to say, but it's something you need to know." Gatyu was what my family and friends called me in Bulgaria in those days.

My father began telling me all about his recruitment and training, leading up to the eventual deployment to Macedonia. I was just a boy, maybe twelve or thirteen years old at the time, and I knew nothing of war. I had only experienced the lasting peace of our village. There was no television at the time, so images of violence and destruction had yet to make their way into my consciousness.

He explained. "In Macedonia, we would fire at one another with rifles and cannons. There would be hundreds of men lying on the field, dead or injured. But at this point the real carnage had only just begun."

A distance crept into my father's eyes, and his voice began to crack. It suddenly felt as though he was somewhere else, far away from me. He continued to describe the horrors of war.

"Once they ran out of bullets," he continued, "the soldiers would charge at each other with knives and bayonets. They would use their weapons — or, in some cases, even their hands — to tear at each other's flesh as they fought to stay alive. In those moments, there were no heroes. Nobody cared about fighting for a 'cause.' As blood spilled and limbs were torn from bodies, the fields of Macedonia became littered with young men just coming to realize they had been sent to die.

"It's impossible to understand true fear and desperation until you've held a man facing his own grim death. The once-dry field would slowly become a patch of mud, soaked with blood from the dead and wounded as it flowed from their bodies and into the ground over which they had battled only moments ago."

My father went silent for a few moments. Even years later, the memories of battle shook him to his core. He lowered his eyes, and I watched a tear roll down his cheek.

"It was so senseless," he said softly. "It was all so very senseless."

As a member of the Red Cross, a battle's end only brought my father to the beginning of his own wartime nightmare. His unit lay in wait while bullets flew through the air, but as soon as the fighting stopped, the Red Cross took over.

"We charged into the field in the hope of saving as many lives and limbs as possible, but there just wasn't much we could do. We were given bandages to wrap wounds and chamomile tea to clean them, but that was far less than most of the men needed. So many soldiers died cold and scared as I raced from one man to another, trying to help anyone I could. At the end of the day I saved too few soldiers and watched far too many die."

The unfortunate responsibility of providing a dignified burial for the dead also fell to the members of the Red Cross.

"The dirt in Macedonia was so thin and shallow," my father recalled. "It was sun-baked and war-scorched. We never had enough soil to fully bury the dead soldiers. Far too often only a man's head could be fully covered by the dirt, leaving the rest of his body exposed. After fighting for their country, the soldiers were reduced to nothing more than food for crows and buzzards."

My father gazed straight ahead, pausing for a moment before finally continuing. Tears were now streaming from his eyes as I sat in silence and listened.

"I watched as hungry birds picked at the dead, some of whom were my dearest friends. Bodies were stripped of flesh until almost nothing remained. Men who had fought bravely were reduced to a mere pile of bones, one of many, and unrecognizable from the rest. I saw with my own eyes that there was no glory in war. There was only anguish and suffering."

At the war's close my father received his discharge and promptly returned to Gorno Ablanovo. Physically, he remained unscathed; his two arms and legs were in perfect working order. Emotionally, however, he was all but destroyed. Beyond his own horrible experience, two of his brothers — uncles I would never meet — were killed in Macedonia. Our family, like so many others in Bulgaria, was grief-stricken and devastated. Psychologically, my father was permanently scarred.

However, my father was also a strong man, and damaged as he might have been, he was not broken. On leave from the war in 1917, he married my mother, Mita Simeonova. Both were in their early twenties. He had begun formally courting my mother a short time before he was conscripted into the army, and he had left for the front with a promise to marry her if he managed to survive. They had both been raised in Gorno Ablanovo — meaning they knew of each other — but did not become better acquainted until early adulthood.

When my father returned from the war in 1918, he helped his parents and remaining siblings while also working the fields. He made certain that our entire family remained strong and unified, even after suffering the loss of my uncles.

In the years following his return from Macedonia, my father came into his own as a husband, parent, and pillar of our community. It was around this time that he also became interested in politics, joining the Bulgarian Agrarian National Union. Politically, the Agrarians represented Bulgaria's peasantry, emphasizing their interests over those of industry and factory workers. My father identified with the Agrarian cause as a way to enrich the lives of his fellow Bulgarians.

This movement started out in Bulgaria in 1899 as the Agrarian Union. It became a national political party in the lead-up to the National Assembly elections in 1901. After making an early impact, though, the Agrarians began to lose momentum until Aleksandar Stamboliyski came to lead the party. Stamboliyski was a charismatic leader and political thinker. I have already described the terrible social and economic crisis that followed the First World War. In the 1920 elections, Bulgarians reacted to this crisis by electing the Agrarian National Union as the first — and, to this day, the only — peasant party to win a majority government in a European nation. Aleksandar Stamboliyski became Bulgaria's new prime minister. It was an amazing victory.

But Stamboliyski's government soon fell from favour; there were concerns over corruption and his increasingly oppressive rule. The new prime minister also made tactical errors that included neglecting the military and the popular policy of territorial expansion. Instead, he pushed for a regional alliance of agrarian parties beyond Bulgaria's borders.

On June 9, 1923, a *coup d'état* deposed Stamboliyski, with a conservative militarist alliance immediately taking power. A rising in late September 1923 by communists in co-operation with Agrarians was put down within days. The Agrarian Party remained in existence for several decades, but it never again approached the influence it had under Stamboliyski. When communism fell in 1989, the Agrarian Party was also quietly dissolved.

My father's commitment to the Agrarian movement reverberated throughout my childhood. He believed in it deeply, viewing it as our country's only political party with a platform that helped ordinary people. The Agrarian agenda slowly seeped into my consciousness, with many of its ideals becoming my own. I saw my father put his heart and soul into the Agrarian cause, and his commitment to the ideology was an inspiration.

He was always looking out for the peasants — his people — and using every resource at his disposal to fight for the interests of the non-ruling class. More than for any other reason, my father participated in politics because he believed it was his duty to do his part to prevent his friends and countrymen from being killed in wars that exclusively benefited the ruling class. He aimed to protect those who could not protect themselves.

Although he identified as an Agrarian, my father's political leanings could be described as anti-communist above all else. After the Communist Party's takeover of the country in 1944, he became disillusioned with the lack of integrity and transparency in the Bulgarian government and did not hesitate in voicing his displeasure. The new government expropriated his horses and two cows. It requisitioned all property and farm equipment, as well as seeds, promising the peasantry they would be equal partners with the state. Needless to say, the promises were not kept. My father began speaking before the people of our village at every opportunity, spreading his own political beliefs throughout our community.

My father was an elegant and impassioned public speaker. He possessed confidence and charisma and spoke with conviction time and again during town council meetings. When he stepped to the podium at a public gathering, the crowd's murmur would dull to a hush. My father was able to change how the people of our village perceived the government and how they participated in it. He spread a great deal of knowledge, which created new ways of thinking.

Not only was Hristo Kanev the leader of our family, he was also a father figure to many in Gorno Ablanovo. My father was always prepared to offer friendly, well-reasoned advice or encouragement. It brought him great joy to help others in this way.

I remember an occasion during which one of our neighbours stood at the podium to speak at a town hall meeting for the first time. I was about eleven years old, and I recall watching as I shuffled through the assembled crowd. The man trembled with nerves, stumbling over his words like a petrified child called to the front of the classroom by his teacher. Just as this man began to give up on himself and started to edge away from the podium, my father intervened. Watching from the crowd, he gently approached the podium to offer his assistance.

My father calmly pleaded with the audience for its patience, all the while assuring the man that those in attendance would wait for him to regain his composure. The nervous speaker took a moment, cleared his throat, inhaled deeply, and finally opened his mouth to deliver an impassioned speech. So many years later I have no recollection of the topic about which the man spoke, but I clearly remember the beaming pride I felt after watching my father treat another person with such kindness. Throughout my childhood, I was always aware that my father was a special person.

Over the years, my father achieved even more recognition within our community for being something of a village sage. Drawing on his wisdom, he became an unofficial — and unpaid — therapist to the people of Gorno Ablanovo. It became common for members of the village vexed by personal problems — most often marriage-related — to be advised to seek out my father.

"Go talk to Hristo," they said. "He will tell you the truth."

There was nothing particularly analytical about the manner in which my father dispensed advice. He would listen carefully as the person in need of help aired his or her grievance. His counsel, however, was always the same. When it came to marital problems, my father always advised couples to work through their difficulties. He believed in compromise and compassion, and that the vows of marriage were to be honoured always. My father believed strongly that a husband and wife were always stronger together than they would be apart.

"You think you have problems now?" he would ask the couples that came to him for help. "Wait until you're separated from each other. Then you'll really have problems."

Sadly, even as my father continued to give so much of himself to our family and the village, his faith in God evaporated. Raised as an Eastern Orthodox Christian, Hristo Kanev possessed a fervent belief in God throughout his childhood, adolescence, and early adulthood. Like most Bulgarians — including myself — he regularly attended prayer services with his family, served as an altar boy, and sang in the church choir. Religion was one of the cornerstones of my father's life. It was only after returning from war that his attitude began to shift. While religion remained an important part of his family's life, for all intents and purposes, my father's relationship with God was over.

Out of respect for those around him — and because he believed the Church provided much-needed structure to our lives — my father continued to follow the religious traditions in which he had been raised. His children were to be brought up as members of the church, but it was, in effect, a hollow gesture. My father's faith in God was gone. It was not that my father had stopped believing in God, exactly. It was just that he no longer trusted Him.

"Where was God when the soldiers were being slaughtered like pigs in Macedonia?" he would ask me. "How could He allow the birds to pick at the bones of the dead? How could He allow the lice to cluster in their hair, thick as beehives? How could He let them starve and die in agony?

"It was the most vicious combat imaginable, worse than my worst nightmare. Where was God when He was so desperately needed by so many? Why didn't He answer our prayers?"

I could not answer my father's questions. Maybe I would have felt the same way, given a similar experience. He believed that God had failed him and many others. Try as I might, I could not fully place myself in my father's shoes, leaving God as the one topic upon which he and I would never agree.

As I saw it, my father turned away from God because men — his friends — suffered and died. That much I could understand. But as my father turned away from God because of what happened in war, I turned toward Him for the same reason. Amid the chaos, carnage, and destruction of war, my father's life had been spared. And for that I would be forever grateful to God.

My father fascinated me, and I did everything I could to emulate him. However, everything within my power amounted to very little, because people have always told me that I am much more like my mother. According to friends and family, she and I had nearly identical temperaments and very similar senses of humour. We even looked alike.

As the years passed, I grew to understand and appreciate the many qualities and attributes possessed by my mother. However, as a boy, I could not recognize all these apparent similarities because I only ever saw my mother do one thing: work.

Maria Simeonova, known to all as Mita, was born on June 6, 1895. As far as I could tell, she was the hardest-working person in the world. She ran our household with incredible efficiency despite lacking resources like electricity and running water; my mother's every chore had to be done the old-fashioned way. She spent the bulk of her time cooking and cleaning for our family, a significant undertaking, given that there were so many of us. When I think back to my childhood, it is astounding to consider how much she did for us all.

Even a normal, everyday task like preparing a meal was a monumental challenge in our house. Preparing a good meal takes time and effort even today. Back then my mother had to feed nearly twenty people three times daily, and she could not simply turn a knob on the stove or pull a carton of eggs from the refrigerator. Every step of the process required her to walk to the barn, start a fire, or kill a fowl. It was nothing short of laborious. However, my mother was fortunate to have all the raw materials to cook within easy reach. She had access to the meat of animals such as pigs and cows, which were slaughtered annually and preserved, while in the spring and summer, fresh vegetables were pickled for use in the fall and winter.

My mother operated her kitchen with military precision, relying on a strict routine to keep everything on schedule. She served every meal to a hungry crowd that made food disappear in the blink of an eye. Despite the pleasure I felt from having a full belly, there was often a twinge of sadness and guilt at the end of a meal when I looked toward my mother. She slaved away for hours, yet at the end of it all there was nothing left but some crumbs, dirty plates, and a new mess for my mother to clean.

In addition to all the work my mother did in the kitchen, she had to prepare food for school lunches, which usually consisted of bread and cheese along with two eggs she boiled the night before. Often, when she made lunch for me, she put together extra food for Mahmud, the boy who sat next to me in class. He was one of the poor children the school supplied lunch for, as well as breakfast and snacks sometimes. Back then there were already programs in place to deliver meals to needy children.

At home our table was always packed with hungry mouths to feed, but our meals were always orderly. My mother never had to ask her children to come to the dinner table. When it was time for the evening meal, my grandmother was always the first to sit, followed by my father, my mother, uncle, and aunt. The children were placed at a separate table, since there were too many of us to fit around one. Everyone was quiet, polite, and civilized.

Before we ate, we took the time to give thanks to God for the food we were about to enjoy. Throughout the prayer, my father remained silent. My grandmother was the first to take her meal. It was clear who was in command — our family was a true matriarchy.

In Bulgaria, we took nothing for granted. Our experience as Bulgarians made us appreciate life's simple joys. My family had suffered tragedy and endured deep sadness, but like Bulgaria, we had survived. Each meal was a celebration of our continued existence.

Unlike the wagon rides I shared with my father, I was almost never able to spend time alone with my mother during childhood. She was preoccupied with her many chores, forever milking cows, chopping vegetables, or working at any number of other household tasks.

My mother was so busy partly because she held our family to such high standards. The house and her children always had to be spotlessly clean. At school, discipline was very strict. We all wore uniforms with white-collared shirts and black pants, and every morning our shirt collars, hands, and fingers were inspected for cleanliness. My mother would not allow any of us to be seen by a teacher at school with a dirty collar or wrinkled slacks. She wanted us to always be presentable — and that was true also for the four boys in our family.

Everyday clothes were washed by my mother at home. Several times a day my father would bring old wine barrels, each filled with more than one hundred gallons of water, from the local spring that constantly flowed out of a hill through a pipe about a half-mile away. We used this cold, clean water for cooking, cleaning, and laundry, though for drinking we had a well that was closer to our house. Once a week washing was done at the spring for special items such as coats and sheets. My mother would slap the laundry against stones until it finally came clean, then hauled everything back to the house to hang on a line to dry. The entire job took the better part of a day.

There simply was no small task. Even bathing her children was a major production. Back then you could not run hot water from a faucet to draw a bath. Like the other houses in Gorno Ablanovo, ours lacked indoor plumbing, turning bath time into a major challenge for my mother.

By the time I was ten years old, getting water from the spring had become my job. It was my first true responsibility in life, and I took it seriously. Up to four times a day I pulled a small wagon holding two large wine barrels down to the spring. I used a smaller bucket to scoop up the running water. Then I lugged the heavy wagon back up the gently sloping path to our property. My father or an uncle would take over and push the wagon up a steep ramp onto the roof of a small structure attached to our house. There we set down the buckets and attached them to hoses that let us have running water below in the house. This process was only possible during the warmer months of the year, since the water would quickly freeze if left outside in the winter.

Fetching water from the spring became a big part of my life. It was a task that I performed countless times. It was a lot of work, but it made me feel important, giving me a sense of accomplishment.

My first sign that the time had come for a bath would be hearing the back door creak open on Saturday night. It meant that my mother was heading outside to collect firewood. She would make several trips, loading her arms with logs and then arranging them in a neat pile beneath a large black cauldron that hung from the ceiling in our main room. Striking a match, my mother lit the fire under the cauldron.

Once the water in the big cauldron had reached the proper temperature, she would pull out the old wooden bathtub my father had bought from travelling Gypsies many years before. To those children who had not heard the creaking of the back door or the crackling of the fire, my mother's call of "bath time" sent a chill down the spine.

Her first call was often ignored, as her children tried to make themselves invisible, hoping she might forget about bathing us, if only just this time. A few moments later she would call to us again, and once more we pretended not to hear. Finally, she would loudly threaten to punish us, at which point we would line up to be bathed, resigned to our miserable fates.

There was a good reason none of us wanted to be bathed by my mother; she insisted on using scalding hot water. Some winter nights she would add handfuls of snow to make it easier to bear, but even that did almost no good. Summer baths brought no such small mercies. For the first years of my life, I saw the bathtub strictly as an instrument of pain and suffering.

"Mita, let the water cool," my father would say. "You're burning the children!"

"If the water doesn't burn my hands, it can't burn the children," my mother retorted every time.

My mother insisted no harm would come to us, but I knew how it felt to be scalded. Bath night was Saturday, but it took until Monday or Tuesday for the burning redness to vanish from my skin.

Only many hours after I first heard the back door creak open would my mother finally finish bathing her children. She put up with kicking and screaming to get us clean. I cried as loudly as anyone, but even I can understand my mother's reasons — and I know that it could not have been enjoyable for her, either.

With the respect she received from her children, my mother was the unchallenged disciplinarian in our household. Even my father openly recognized that fact. "Mita, never let the children tell you what to do," he told her. "You are the true boss of this house."

With just one notable exception, my father never spanked me. My mother, on the other hand, did not hesitate to tan my backside whenever I stepped out of line. I quickly learned that when my mother told me to do something, it was best to just do it, immediately and without question.

This is what often kept me from misbehaving. I loved my mother, but at times I feared her.

More than anything, I wished to please my mother. I could plainly see that her life was often a grind of work, morning and night. Adding to her burden was the last thing I wanted to do. I wanted my mother to be proud of me, and for me to be the last of her worries. I wished to lighten her load as much as I could.

Of course, my mother did not live only to work. She was a social person who craved stimulating conversation and the company of others. Whenever she could, my mother enjoyed sitting in front of our house to chat with the neighbours as they strolled past after dinner. My mother was an intelligent woman with many interesting things to say. A warm summer's evening brought with it the opportunity to express that side of her personality. When given the chance, my mother possessed a special kind of warmth.

As she cleaned the kitchen after yet another big meal, I remember my mother saying the same words time and again as we ran around the house: "If only I could teach you all to stop eating, I could finally take a vacation. I wish I could take a break from cooking and cleaning for just one month. If I was able to stop just for a little while, it would make me so happy."

Later in life I would be in a position to help ease my mother's load, but as a child I could do precious little. Her contributions during my childhood were endless, selfless, and generous. She gave all of herself every day to care for our family. I have always considered myself to be a hard worker, but I do not compare to my mother. I cannot imagine where she found the strength and energy to do what she did.

Thanks to my mother's strength and dedication, I have always held a deep respect for women. She set an impressively high standard for a work ethic, against which I have always measured my own efforts.

As the parents of six impressionable children — along with being aunt and uncle to many others — my father and mother understood the importance of setting a good example. They knew it was impossible for them to watch their children at every turn, so they focused on teaching us right from wrong, giving us the tools to make our own decisions. It is not uncommon for children to pick up bad habits from their parents; many of my friends learned to smoke or drink from watching their mothers or fathers. But it never happened in our house. My parents went out of their way to teach us how to be good citizens. They understood that just telling us was not enough; we needed to be shown.

For example, never once did I hear my parents utter a swear word. Bad language was not tolerated in our family, and you would not hear a curse word from anybody. To this day, I never use coarse language, and I believe it is especially bad to swear in front of young people. My parents got along well, engaged in productive discussions — not loud arguments — and always supported each other in front of their children. They shared a tight bond of love and trust with no shortage of respect, compassion, and admiration. Their strong relationship was the linchpin that always kept our family together.

In our house, nothing was ever hidden from the children. For instance, we all knew where my father kept the household money. It was in a small briefcase whose location was known to us. Our parents trusted us implicitly.

Back in those days, young Bulgarian couples were expected to produce babies — and lots of them — to strengthen the country and their village. My parents began having children immediately after their marriage, with my mother giving birth to their first baby — my brother, Kanu — in 1918, with another one of us coming along just about every second year after that until 1932. After Kanu came my brother, Lambi, and then my sister, Kuna. I came next in 1926, followed by my sister, Maria, and my brother, Simeon. My parents had one more baby after that, but sadly, my youngest brother, Peter, died when he was three years old.

In our family, it was customary for the older children to participate in raising the younger ones. For example, Kuna always looked after me, often behaving more like a second mother than a sister. I was generally well behaved, although that is not to say I did not make her life difficult on occasion. Specifically, I remember having a toothache that ended up giving my poor sister a headache.

It was the early part of June and I was about ten years old, enjoying yet another beautiful day in Gorno Ablanovo. I began to feel a dull ache in the back of my mouth while eating breakfast, with the pain gradually intensifying throughout the day. By nightfall, it was too much to bear. I was in the grips of the first — and most agonizing, as time would prove — toothache of my life.

As I often did when faced with a problem outside my field of expertise, I went crying to my sister. "Kuna," I whined, "my tooth is killing me. Please help me. I don't know what to do."

My sister was a true sweetheart, and I loved her dearly. As always, she took pity on her crying brother, tenderly laying me down to bed, a damp cloth pressed upon my forehead. She assured me that she would take me to a man who could help with my pain first thing in the morning. I closed my eyes tightly, clutched my sister's hand, and tried my best to fall asleep.

Gorno Ablanovo was not exactly on the cutting edge of the latest advances in dentistry. If you had a serious problem — something like a bad infection or needed surgery — you had to travel to one of the bigger towns in our region, like Ruse. There you could see a real dentist. As I was soon to find out, when you had a run-of-the-mill toothache, you went to see a dentist on the other side of the village.

Following a night of restless sleep, I was gently woken in the morning by Kuna. I was groggy and still in tremendous discomfort. We skipped breakfast and left home immediately. My sister took me by the hand and led me to a house on the far side of the village, about a mile or two from our own. It looked no different than any other house in town, and I began to wonder about my sister's intentions.

Kuna knocked loudly, and we waited on the stoop until a man who appeared to be in his late fifties came to the door. He had no hair on the top of his head and was missing several teeth; those that remained were stained and ugly. He wore a white lab coat splattered with small drops of blood. An unkempt moustache drew some attention from his shifty eyes, but not enough to keep me from being intensely distrustful of the man.

In times of distress, I looked to my older, wiser sister for guidance. Kuna assured me that letting the man help me would make the pain in my mouth go away. So when this bald, toothless, shifty-eyed mustachioed man instructed me to sit back in his old leather chair, I could only place my trust in Kuna and do as I was told. As I reluctantly eased into the chair, the man reached into a drawer. He turned to face me, revealing the biggest pair of gleaming metal pliers I had seen in my entire life. Instantly, I saw this man for who he truly was: a puller of children's teeth and a collector of their tears.

I might have only been ten years old, but I was smart enough to know how he intended to use those pliers. This man was not planning to fix a wheel on his wagon, I can assure you. As I imagined it, he was only offering a different form of pain. I wanted nothing to do with him.

Without so much as looking back at the man or my sister, I shot out of the chair and darted from that house as if my life depended on it. I sprinted through the streets of Gorno Ablanovo as fast as my feet could carry me, and then into the forest. Then I ran even farther. I ran until I could run no more.

At last I stopped running. Doubled over, panting for breath, and drenched in my own sweat, I made a startling realization: in my terror, the pain in my mouth had somehow disappeared. It was a miracle. Even more amazingly, my toothache never came back. To this day, that once-agonizing tooth remains in my mouth as free of pain as the rest. It was as if the pliers man had scared the ache from my tooth. Fear proved to be the only cure I required.

Happy as I was to be freed from the pain in my mouth, I felt horrible about disobeying my sister. I had come to her for help and then refused it. Fortunately, my loving sister found it in her heart to forgive me, which is part of why I always held Kuna in the highest regard. Following her example, I took on a similar caregiver role in the life of my little brother, Simeon.

I considered myself to be mostly well behaved as a youngster. The same, however, could not always be said about Simeon. Although I believed him to be a good boy at heart, my brother had a rebellious streak and a penchant for mischief; he liked doing things his own way. I knew that he respected me, but I could never count on him to do as I said, even when it might have been in his best interest. For example, much as I instructed him to leave the bigger boys alone while playing in the schoolyard, Simeon insisted on taunting them. The furious boys would chase my brother through the dirt field in hopes of revenge. Simeon, of course, ran straight to me. Even though I knew that my brother probably deserved what was coming to him, I still could not help but play the role of his protector. As I saw it, if anybody was going to teach Simeon a lesson, it would be me. I felt it was my duty to protect and help him.

Every now and then, my brother caused trouble that could not go unpunished. It was during these times that I put him across my knee and spanked him. As one of his primary guardians, I considered it my duty to help teach Simeon right from wrong. Of course, I did not enjoy spanking my brother, but to let Simeon get away with misbehaviour would be to do him a disservice. I never spanked him with any great force, only enough to make my point. I wanted my brother to understand that his actions carried consequences.

I was still just a boy myself, perhaps possessing a slightly inflated sense of my own moral superiority. In my young mind, I believed Simeon should have thanked me for teaching him a great and valuable lesson, upon which he could draw for the rest of his life. My little brother, unsurprisingly, saw things a bit differently.

From an early age, my brother was crafty. Simeon never cried when I spanked him. Not once. Instead, he would wait until my father got home in the evening before bursting into tears and carrying on about how viciously I had treated him. I considered my father to be the smartest man I knew, but I could not understand how, when it came to my little brother, he was so blind to deception.

Whenever this scenario played out, my father would get angry with me. It never occurred to him that his sweet, innocent Simeon could be capable of such manipulations. He would warn me — loudly — not to treat my brother with such roughness, a rule I would strictly follow until the next time Simeon tested the boundaries of my patience. My little brother was the kind of boy who simply needed to be spanked sometimes, if only so he knew that you knew what he was up to. If being yelled at by my father was the price of teaching my brother right from wrong, I was willing to pay it.

Incredibly, that was about as tense as it ever got in our house. Even with so many people sharing a small space, my family got along harmoniously. And even those who did not share my blood felt like family. Our village was a tight-knit community in which everybody knew everybody. There were no strangers and even fewer enemies. All the children called the friends of their parents "aunt" or "uncle," as if we were all related. The togetherness we felt was special, and I have never again experienced a community in which the people possessed such a deep commitment to one another.

My family, my village, and my country shaped so much of who I would become. My childhood often seemed like a series of lessons meant to teach me how to be part of something bigger than just myself. Through daily life, I was taught that being kind and generous to others was not a choice but a responsibility.

Growing up in Gorno Ablanovo offered the best childhood I could have ever hoped for, and I thrived within a cocoon of safety and contentment. I lived in a house filled with people I loved, and beyond my door was the boundless Bulgarian countryside. My life was simple, and it felt perfect.

3

Tragedy

My childhood ended on May 24, 1936. Before that day I had known nothing but joy and happiness. I would grieve deeply for the very first time that day.

I can easily remember the exact date because May 24 was the national Culture and Literacy Day in Bulgaria. It was a major event in our village — as well as throughout the country — since everybody was excited to celebrate and honour the Bulgarian language and the Cyrillic alphabet. To the people of our village, it was a special time that allowed us to feel good about a defining aspect of our identity and cornerstone of our society: our language. Bulgarians valued literacy and knowledge, viewing education as a way of advancing ourselves as a people.

Bulgaria's written language goes back to the ninth century with the Greek Byzantine brothers, Cyril and Methodius. Born in Macedonia, the brothers became missionaries in their homeland and elsewhere in the Balkans, with a goal to spread Orthodox Christianity among the pagans. Cyril and Methodius created the Glagolitic alphabet — later renamed for

Cyril by his early followers — as a means of propagating the Bible and other important documents of faith.

The Cyrillic alphabet eventually provided the framework for Old Church Slavonic, which would come to be known as Old Bulgarian, in use during the First Bulgarian Empire. However, our country's non-Slavic neighbours would also influence the Bulgarian language, most notably the Turks living within our borders during the days of Ottoman rule. Bulgaria's mother tongue splintered into several distinct dialects. For many years, there was no official Bulgarian language, only variations of Old Church Slavonic spoken in and around our country.

It was only after the National Awakening of Bulgaria that an effort was finally made to codify a standard language to use throughout the country. In 1899, Bulgarians voted to select one of the various dialects to be our single official language. As it turned out, the variation of the language spoken in our region won the vote by a slim margin. Therefore, through no doing of my own, I can truthfully claim to be fluent in Bulgaria's first "official" language.

Given everything that we had experienced as a country, Bulgarians took a deep sense of pride in maintaining our traditions and heritage. Over the centuries, Bulgaria was nearly driven into extinction on numerous occasions. We always persevered. In addition to being critical to our continued development as a civilized people, the Bulgarian language was also a powerful symbol of our determination. Culture and Literacy Day on May 24 was an opportunity to celebrate everything Bulgaria had survived, all it had become, and what it might become one day. Bulgarians suspended every type of work. Farmers stopped farming, cobblers ceased cobbling, and storeowners closed up shop.

The people in our village had no choice but to enjoy themselves, if only for just one day. Even my father, dedicated as anyone to strict routine, might nip off to his barn and grab a bottle of homemade plum whisky to drink with his friends.

That year May 24 began as festively as ever. We would go to the centre of town to participate in the traditions honouring Saints Cyril and Methodius. I was nearly ten years old, but I had already grown familiar with these yearly customs: the morning consisted of a prayer service along with other presentations, and the afternoon was wide open for play.

As usual, I chose to spend time with my cousin Bozin Jordan Kanev. My cousin went by two names because there were so many people with the surname Kanev scattered throughout our village. Bozin and I were in the same class at school and we were best friends, truly inseparable. In the village of Gorno Ablanovo, if you saw Bozin, chances were good you would also see Gatyu.

Bozin was the son of Denko, one of my father's four brothers. My cousin and I did not live together, since Uncle Denko's family had their own house. Most mornings I rushed to see Bozin as soon as I was excused from the breakfast table. We might have only been cousins, but Bozin and I were closer than most brothers.

While our parents enjoyed a leisurely afternoon with their own friends, Bozin and I decided to get away from the village to graze our horses down by the river. As we rode down to the Danube, it was shaping up to be an ideal afternoon.

These days a ten-year-old child is considered by many to be something of a baby, afforded no responsibility and even less freedom. However, life was different while I was growing up in my village. Not only were children given important responsibilities around the house and farm but we were also trusted to go off on our own. Taking horses to graze by the river without adult supervision was no rare occurrence.

My cousin and I sat together on the shore, telling stories and using sticks to draw pictures in the dirt. Time seemed to pass slowly, and then not at all, as it often does for children with nowhere to be. Together we enjoyed a final, seemingly endless moment of blissful childhood.

Bozin positioned himself near the edge of the riverbank. My cousin liked to get as close to the river as he could. He did not know how to swim, but he was always drawn to the water. I was sitting beside him as we dangled our feet in the water.

Then, suddenly, everything changed forever. Like a bolt of lightning in an otherwise clear sky, tragedy struck from out of nowhere. The ground beneath my cousin began to break away. Squinting through the sunlight, I glanced over to see Bozin slipping from the shore and into the water. A look of terror washed over my cousin's face as he fell helplessly into the Danube River.

Before I could even stretch an arm in his direction, the rapids carried Bozin away. He gasped for breath while struggling to keep his head above water, trying in vain to grab a branch, a stone, anything that could prevent him from being sucked into the river and pulled under. It was no use. I watched as his head bobbed above the water once or twice more until he finally disappeared below the surface. As a ten-year-old boy, I understood very little about death, but in that moment I knew that never again would I see my cousin alive.

I stood alone on the riverbank, not moving a muscle. I did not twitch, I did not breathe, and I dared not blink. My mind could not process what my eyes had just seen. Mere moments ago my cousin was a happy boy sitting on a riverbank. Now he was dead, swallowed up by an angry river without warning. I saw what had happened, but I could not believe it. I could not understand.

As I regained my senses, I began to feel heavy with an unfamiliar, overwhelming sadness. I started to cry. I continued to sob before realizing that now was not the time to indulge my sorrows. I needed to tell my family about Bozin immediately. I could not keep this to myself. Some burdens are too big for little boys to carry alone.

I raced back to the village on my galloping horse. The closest house to the river belonged to my Uncle Denko and his family — that was my first stop. As I approached their home, I readied myself to break the news to my aunt and uncle that their cherished son had drowned in the Danube River. Mere moments ago I would not have believed that anything could possibly be worse than watching my cousin struggle and die. But I was mistaken. Telling my cousin's family was torture.

I jumped off my horse and ran as fast as I could to the back of the house. My aunt and uncle were turning earth in their flowerbed, spending their holiday afternoon doing what they most enjoyed. My uncle looked at me with concern as soon as he saw my face. It was obvious that I had been crying: my eyes were puffy and red. He moved toward me, and our eyes locked. I could not hold my uncle's gaze long.

"What happened to Bozin?" Uncle Denko demanded. "Gatyu, where is my son?"

"He's gone," I could barely whimper.

My uncle dropped to his knees as my aunt ran to him. I caught my breath and began to tell them everything as they cried and held each other. I was only ten years old, but this would prove to be the worst moment of my life. I felt the searing pain of an entire family in my heart, and it was unbearable. Before long the words would no longer leave my mouth. I sat on the ground and cried with my family.

Word of Bozin's death passed through the village. Within hours, everybody knew that my cousin had drowned, and a cloud of darkness soon hung over all of Gorno Ablanovo. It might have been a member of the Kanev family who drowned in the river, but the whole village cried for my cousin. Having the support of our community provided desperately needed comfort to my family — but it did not ease our pain.

As the shock of Bozin's death began to wear off, the gravity of the situation settled in. Not only had I lost my closest friend but I also knew that it just as easily could have been me swallowed up by the river. My mind ran in circles. I understood that Bozin's death was not my fault, but I still suffered the pangs of guilt for being the one who had survived.

I plunged into despair. The entire village existed in a suspended state as we waited for my cousin's body to be recovered. For more than a week, dozens of volunteers from all over the village searched up and down the Danube River for any sign of him. It would be ten torturous days before Bozin's body was finally recovered. When my father told me they had found him, I remember feeling great relief, as if a part of my nightmare had mercifully come to an end.

When Bozin was returned to Gorno Ablanovo, a large memorial was planned in his honour. We all gathered in the town's centre to pay our respects to my cousin. As a family — and as a village — we would mourn him together.

On the day of the memorial, I was shocked to see my cousin's dead body laid out for all to see. His corpse was bloated and blue, hardly recognizable. One by one every boy and girl in our village was marched past Bozin's body.

When I look back now, I see that the adults had decided my cousin should be displayed for all the children to see, to warn us to stay away from the ever-dangerous Danube River rather than teach us to swim. Today I consider Bozin's memorial to be a disgrace. Instead of honouring him, his memorial was used to prove a point about the river. For years, instead of remembering the lovely boy that he was, children grew up haunted by nightmares of my cousin.

In the days that followed Bozin's death, I lost my appetite and enthusiasm for life. Finally, after weeks of hopelessness, I began to see that my crying served as a release for sadness too intense to keep inside. The more I cried the less I found that I needed to cry.

What happened to my cousin was a crushing tragedy, bringing the fragility of life into sharp focus. Only ten years old, I became acutely aware of my own mortality. I suddenly understood that someday I would be the one to die, but instead of filling me with crippling fear, this realization liberated me. As a result of this terrible heartbreak, I realized I possessed the strength and resilience to carry on. Bozin's death could have destroyed me and left me a pessimist, but somehow it made me stronger. It matured me, forcing me to grow up much more quickly than perhaps I otherwise would have.

I was a young boy, but already filled with the ambition to become a somebody. I had believed that I would have a long lifetime to accomplish my objective. Now, however, I saw that the duration of one's life was uncertain — and a new sense of urgency and purpose filled me.

There was no time to waste.

4

Onward

In the days, weeks, and months following Bozin's death, I felt sad and confused as never before. I was disconnected from everything as I learned to live without the companionship of my best friend. I tried to cope with a great loss while feeling lost myself. With my parents distracted by their own pain, I drifted off to find trouble: I found myself running around with the village bad boys.

TROUBLE

Throughout my childhood, I always considered myself — and strived to be — a well-behaved boy. My parents made the rules, and I did my best to understand and follow them. I vied for my parents' approval and was never without their attention and affection. My mother and father did not provide me with a pretext for acting out, because I always felt loved.

But now, as a ten-year-old boy, I got involved in an act so senseless and destructive that it nearly ruined everything.

It was the middle of the summer of 1936, and I was slowly emerging from my family's protective cocoon following Bozin's death. When I was not attending school, I was spending my time hidden away at home. But now, as the weather improved and class let out for the summer, I wanted to go outside more and more. This brought a new problem: without Bozin I had no one to play with.

Then, one day, I stumbled upon a group of older boys kicking a ball in an empty field. One of the boys was a distant cousin of mine from the other side of the village. He called me over and introduced me to his friends. The boys struck me as funny and tough, and they immediately welcomed me into their group. I knew that they could not replace Bozin in my heart, but it was good to make new friends and feel something other than sadness.

As I spent more time with my new friends, I noticed that their idea of fun differed from my own. While Bozin and I generally played soccer, chased butterflies, or grazed horses, I watched from a safe distance as these boys engaged in petty theft and vandalism. To their credit, the boys were smart enough to avoid getting in trouble for their misdeeds — their offences always went undetected. They laughed and crowed upon returning from each act of senselessness, making it all seem like nothing more than a bit of good fun.

I did my best to remain detached. I knew the boys liked and accepted me to an extent, but it was probably hard for them to trust a quiet ten-year-old boy who mostly watched them from a safe distance. My parents, though, had taught me the difference between right and wrong, and I wanted to remain on the side of right.

Still, I was just a little boy hanging around with bigger boys, and I craved their approval. I saw the older boys as adventurous, daring pranksters, and that was more than enough to impress a kid like me. If I intended to become a true member of the group, I knew that eventually I would have to prove myself to them.

My day in the limelight came on a fateful summer's morning. Everything seemed normal, but I could sense they were studying me with suspicious eyes — the boy who watched everything they did but never participated. Maybe they thought I would snitch on them. Whatever the reason, there was no mistaking it: for the first time I felt the effects of peer pressure. Distrust was in the air, and their doubtful stares came at me like knives.

We stood around a grassy field, trying to pass the time. Some of the boys occupied themselves by throwing large clumps of dirt at one another, laughing like hyenas around clouds of dust that went up like little explosions. A hunk of earth landed by my feet as one of the boys spoke up. "Why don't we pick some watermelons?"

His words hung in the air like the early-morning haze. I glanced around and saw several of the boys smiling devilishly. A voice inside my head alerted me to trouble, but I ignored it. After all, we all liked eating melons. Why not pick a few? What could go wrong?

I should have known something was wrong from the beginning. There was only one farmer in the area who grew watermelons so early in the season, and he would surely not want to give them to us. We had no money to offer, and watermelons were not free. But to this group, anything was free if you could steal it.

There was no confusion in my mind; I knew that stealing was wrong. My father had told me so in no uncertain terms. I also reasoned that stealing was no way to become a somebody. But, as the youngest boy in the group, I felt it was not my place to oppose a scheme the group had decided to pursue. I also realized that if we were careful, our plan would likely go off just fine. Our bellies would soon be full of watermelon, and nobody would be the wiser. In just a little while, I imagined, I would share a victory with my new friends. They would slap me on the back as we all laughed and wondered how they could have ever doubted me.

To this day, I still believe that if we had stuck to our original plan, we would have gotten away with the whole thing. As we arrived at the field, however, and stood amid row upon row of meticulously planted watermelons, I began to notice a crazed look coming over the faces of my new friends. Without warning, they transformed from boys looking to eat a melon or two into wild animals bent on destruction.

They began kicking at the melons and tearing viciously at the vines. I was stunned. This was not what we had discussed. Even more shockingly, I found myself joining them in mindless destruction. We stomped watermelons with the heels of our shoes and watched as their sweet pulp spilled across the field. We lifted them high above our heads and slammed them on the ground, just to watch them explode. The older boys and I howled with delight.

In that moment, I completely abandoned my inhibitions. I pummelled the watermelon patch with everything I had. As I smashed away, all the feelings of anger, pain, and guilt — the lingering emotions stemming from my cousin's death — poured out through my hands and heels. As I slashed away at the tall vines, I unleashed my pent-up feelings on the poor farmer's watermelon patch.

Our manic grunts and screams alerted the farmer to our presence. The experienced fieldsman moved quietly, circling the field from his barn until he had us cornered.

"Hey, you kids!" he hollered. "What are you doing to my watermelons?"

I froze in mid-stomp. My heart skipped a beat as I looked at the other boys for reassurance. I soon realized that my new friends had no backup plan — the boys offered me nothing but heightened anxiety as I watched them scatter in different directions. Following their lead once again, I darted from the field, scrambling out of the farmer's view.

The plan called for us to meet up back at our horses, so that was where I went. I was certain I had outrun the farmer with ease. But he was too smart for that. He understood that he had little hope of chasing down and corralling a group of energetic young boys, so he took the more tactical approach of simply locating our horses. To this day, I do not know how he found our secret location. Obviously, the man was no fool. He crouched in the bushes where he could not be seen, lying in wait for our arrival.

I came to the meeting spot, thinking we had outsmarted the farmer. Just as I readied myself to swing a leg over the back of my horse, the farmer popped out from the shadows and grabbed me by the shoulders.

"I've got you!" he yelled, tightening his grip.

Everybody froze. There was no getting away from this farmer now. He studied each of our faces, then seized the leather satchel I had borrowed earlier from my father to carry my lunch. Immediately, he noticed the two letters burned into the cowhide: H.K.

"Oh, I see that you're Hristo Kanev's son," he said to me as the blood drained from my face. "I'm going to have a talk with your father right now."

With that, I knew I would soon be in more trouble than I had ever been in before. My friends and I had caused a massive amount of damage to this man's watermelon patch. My father was a patient and understanding man, but he would not tolerate theft or vandalism by one of his children. To make matters worse, my father was particularly sympathetic to the plight of local farmers, given his role in the Agrarian Party. In my father's eyes, destroying another man's crop was a sin.

The farmer let go of my shoulders but hung on to my bag as evidence, then marched straight into the village to see my father at the town hall, where he worked as a member of our village's council. As I watched the man leave the field, I began to realize what I had done and the consequences that were sure to follow. In a moment that was far from my proudest, I decided to do as any young boy might do in such a predicament: I ran and hid like a coward.

I rode home as quickly as my horse would carry me. I meant to return the animal to my family's stable and take off for my grandfather's house on the other side of the village before my father could make it home from work.

My mother's father, Simeon Simeonoff — considered, at the time, our village's finest horse trader, supplying the highest quality of stock — was a very generous man; he always had a few leva in his pocket to give me. As soon as I arrived on his doorstep, my grandfather could tell that something was amiss. Never before had I come to see my grandfather on my own, nor had I ever insisted on staying so long. But my grandfather was sympathetic, so he let me stay and did not force me to reveal my reason for hiding.

Having granted me sanctuary, my grandfather made sure my parents knew the whereabouts of their missing son. Still, he welcomed me into his home as if nothing was amiss. As far as my grandfather was concerned, my visit was an opportunity to spend time with his grandson.

Rationally, I knew that I could not stay hidden at my grandfather's house forever, but I was not thinking rationally. I had no intention of returning home anytime soon. It was clear that my father already knew what I had done and was simply choosing to leave me to stew in my own fear. But I could wait. I was willing to do so for as long as it took for my father to forget the matter entirely. I was prepared to wait and wait.

One thing, though, prevented me from living with my grandfather indefinitely. To that point in my life, I had never eaten a meal that was not prepared and served by my mother. She might pack me a piece of fruit to take for lunch, but I almost always ate at home. I was convinced that eating at my grandfather's would be a betrayal of my mother and would only add to my mounting list of misdeeds. Every time he sat down to eat, my grandfather invited me to the table, and every time I refused.

By the second day at my grandfather's house, I was feeling the pangs of hunger. My stomach rumbled like thunder. Finally, I made an agreement with myself: the very next time my grandfather offered to feed me, I would eat. I was practically starving, and I could hold out no longer. To my great disappointment, by that point my grandfather had given up on offering me food. He figured that I was determined not to eat, and he would only be contributing to my problems by continuing to tempt me.

Hours passed as my stomach growled and my resolve weakened. Just as I was beginning to think about finally trying to make my way home, there was a sudden knock at my grandfather's door. After three agonizingly long days, my father had finally sent my sister, Kuna, to bring me home. I had reached the end of the line.

I was resigned to my fate. To that point in my life, my father had never laid a hand on me, but those days were coming to an end, I was sure. Through my actions at the watermelon patch, followed by my refusal to face the consequences with even the slightest degree of dignity, I had forced my father's hand.

My sister led me back home, keeping me in her sight the entire way, in case I attempted to sneak away once again. But I had lost the will to continue hiding. Kuna and I both knew that the time had come for me to face the music. A torn-up field of melons would not go unpunished.

As we walked, Kuna told me how the farmer had gone straight to my father, yelling and screaming while he described the damage we had caused to his precious watermelons. The farmer demanded retribution, and my father and the fathers of the other boys were forced to pay the man fair value for his losses. Money was always tight, and buying a farmer's entire harvest of watermelons was not in our family's budget. The total cost was close to the amount a farmer from our village might earn in an entire year. As Kuna told me, my father was livid.

The sun was beginning to set as we finally made it home. I ran through the front door and straight into bed as the last glimmers of daylight peeked through the window. I buried myself beneath the covers, closed my eyes tightly, and waited for my father to come home. I had disappointed and enraged a man whom I had always placed upon a pedestal of admiration and respect. The time was almost at hand for me to face him. The clock ticked slowly, as each second felt like a minute, every minute, an hour. Light finally gave way to the darkness as I continued to cower beneath my covers.

At last I heard the front door squeak open. From the sounds of his heavy steps, I knew that my father had entered the house. Unlike most days, he did not stop by the kitchen to greet my mother, nor did he take the time to address any of my brothers or sisters. Without a word he marched straight to the bedroom in which I was waiting. I was shaking like a leaf.

He stood at the foot of the bed, towering above me, still saying nothing. There were no words to speak. He simply removed the covers from the bed, freed his belt from the loops of his pants, and turned me over, exposing my backside. Then he lashed me with the strap five times.

As I endured the leather striking my skin, I thought about the series of events that had led me to this point. I had allowed myself to follow the lead of boys who held no regard for my interests. I had simply lacked the courage to oppose them. It had brought me to the point of disappointing the person I most wished to please. I promised myself that I would always consider the consequences of my actions in the future. If I did not, it would only be a matter of time before I found myself across my father's knee once again.

After he finished disciplining me, my father walked toward the bedroom door. He stopped and turned around to face me. The anger I had seen in his eyes mere moments ago had faded away. Once again, he looked at me as a loving parent.

"Son, you must never damage another person's property again. You need to treat what belongs to others with respect."

My father's words resonated. I knew that I would learn from this experience, and I vowed to him and to myself that I would exercise better judgment from now on.

It was pointless to follow others if doing so brought me nothing but trouble. I stopped spending time with those older boys. In order to attain success and become a somebody, I would need to think for myself.

The incident at the watermelon patch taught me that simply knowing right from wrong would do me no good; I would need to act accordingly.

THE NEW HOUSE

To my father's credit, he did not hold the watermelon misdeed against me for long. He punished me, yes, but he quickly forgave. My father recognized that even good boys were capable of making big mistakes, and thankfully, he did trust me again.

Later that summer my father made a big announcement to the family: he and my uncle, Teodor Kanev, had decided they would move their families to separate residences. The first order of business would be a fair division of mutual assets. The house, livestock, and any equipment needed to be split evenly. Ever the fair-minded man, my father came up with a process that would prove beneficial to all.

"We'll write down words representing each of our assets on a piece of paper," he told his brother. "Then we'll take turns choosing the slips of paper. Even though I'm the older brother, I'll let you choose first."

The selection process would be determined by the luck of the draw, and if things did not break evenly, my father and uncle would surely have worked it out so that both families would have all they needed. My father prided himself on his fairness; he was considered a role model and an elder in the village.

The entire family gathered around the kitchen table to see who would come away with what. One after the other my father and uncle selected slips of paper with words like *plough, animals with horns*, and *animals without horns* written on them. Finally, my uncle chose *old house*.

That meant that he, his wife, and my cousins would stay put. But, more importantly, it meant that my parents, siblings, and I would move into a brand-new house.

In other families, the division of property can sometimes become contentious, but, due to the respect my father and his brother had for each other, the separation went smoothly. Both men always showed regard for the family as a whole, not just for their own wives and children.

One of the main reasons my father set out to separate the families was because he had recently gained the skills necessary to build a house. A few years earlier my father and one of his cousins had started a small contracting business, working around the village as needed. They specialized in building additions to homes. My father had no formal training, but his cousin had attended carpentry school outside the village and apprenticed under a skilled tradesman, eventually bringing the skills to Gorno Ablanovo. My father — always handy with tools — had done his own repairs on our house and the farm for years, but it was not until he began learning the trade from his cousin that he acquired building expertise.

Along with his increasing responsibilities as one of the chairmen of the farmers' co-op, my father's new business was also growing. Before long my father and his cousin were building small- and medium-sized structures. His cousin taught him everything he knew. When the time came to build a house of his own, my father was ready.

As an impressionable boy of eleven, I watched the building process with amazement. I was there when my father purchased his blueprints from an architect on the outskirts of town, and I quietly observed as he and my uncle examined them, studied the details, and made modifications.

A few weeks later they broke ground. I was fascinated to see an entire house being built from nothing but empty land. Before they even began framing the structure, I was captivated, and most of all, I was *excited*.

Of course, I was not free to simply stand around and watch others work. My responsibility of fetching water from the spring for my family extended to the job site. Once again it filled me with pride to be able to contribute in some way. I may have only been helping as a small child helps adults at their work, but assisting my father in building our house remains one of my happiest childhood memories.

Unlike our old house, which was made of wood and dried mud, the new one was made of brick and mortar, and would be considered a modern home for 1936. My father had saved money for years to build a new house, and he used much of it to buy and transport a massive pile of bricks from a nearby town. Along with his cousin and a few other friends, he laid them down one by one, taking great care to do the job right. Once in a while my father called me over to show me his workmanship, occasionally letting me lay down a few bricks of my own. With each brick laid, I felt a sense of fulfillment in knowing that I had a hand in building a structure that would provide shelter for my family for decades to come. Our house still stands in Gorno Ablanovo to this day.

From that very first experience, construction made sense to me. Unlike Bulgarian grammar, which took so many twists and turns, building a house was as simple as making a plan and following it. My father showed me how to look for mistakes and weaknesses before they became a bigger problem. It would be many years before these lessons proved applicable to my own life, but I received a valuable foundation of knowledge about building as my father laid the foundation of our house.

My father, his cousin, and their rotating cast of assistants built my family's new house in a year. While they worked on the house, the rest of the family helped in the fields, allowing my father and his cousin to devote much of their time to the construction.

Compared to our old dwelling, the new house was pure luxury. We had previously shared twelve hundred square feet with as many as eighteen people; now our immediate family of eight occupied more than twice that amount of space over two floors. For the first time, we had a flight of stairs in our house. The lower level contained the kitchen, bathroom, living room, and dining room, and the upper floor held three bedrooms. To us, it was a palace.

In addition to the heightened comfort we experienced with the additional space, there was another luxury that my family would enjoy for the first time: genuine, modern beds.

Like the rest of my family, I had always slept on a bed of straw covered by a sheet. To the best of my knowledge, this was how everybody slept. That is, until I experienced an alternative.

My brother, Kanu, had recently returned from school, where he had made a great discovery during his time away. Having slept on a real mattress at school, Kanu could no longer rest comfortably on our primitive straw beds. So he brought home a spring mattress.

My father, after trying the mattress out himself, decided he wanted the rest of the family to enjoy the same comfort. So he commissioned a local carpenter to build a number of bed frames for our new house before travelling outside our village yet again to acquire the mattresses. With new beds to go along with our new house, it felt as if my family was really coming into its own.

MY EDUCATION

In the aftermath of the watermelon incident, the summer holidays soon ended. I was going back to school, and I focused only on being a good student. I was now about to turn ten years old and start school for another year, hoping only to do well enough to earn back some of the trust I had lost from my parents.

In the classroom, I was a bright and enthusiastic pupil, thirsty for knowledge. Unlike some other children in my class, I truly enjoyed learning, considered it a privilege, not a burden, and applied myself to schoolwork with dedication. As I later came to realize, education is one of the cornerstones to a better life.

Math, history, geography, and science were all subjects I enjoyed. It fascinated me to learn about our world and everything in it. I received top marks in nearly every class and considered myself to be quite the young scholar. It was important to me to do well in school, and I tried my hardest to excel.

There was one subject I could never seem to grasp, and it plagues me to this day. For whatever reason, I have always struggled with Bulgarian grammar. Even later in life, after learning how to speak half a dozen different European languages, speaking and writing proper Bulgarian continued to be problematic for me.

I even remember my teacher, Mrs. Ksanta Kabaivanova, teasing me about my lack of aptitude.

"Kanev," she would call to me from across the room as I struggled to fill out the answers in my Bulgarian language workbook, "you will never be a good Bulgarian."

My teacher would laugh while gently teasing me, but I knew that if being a good Bulgarian depended on speaking and writing the language properly, Mrs. Kabaivanova would be proven correct about me. I continued to struggle with Bulgarian grammar even as I excelled in all of my other subjects. Try as I might, I could not raise my grade.

Yet, despite my poor grammar skills, I always seemed to have luck on my side when it came to passing the course. The first evidence of good fortune came at the end of grade six when I was all but sure to fail my Bulgarian grammar exam. Through a stroke of sheer serendipity, the Bulgarian monarch, Tsar Boris III (reigned 1918–1943), celebrated the birth of his son, Simeon, on June 16, 1937. To mark the occasion, he raised every child's grade in school by one full level. Strictly owing to the ruler's joyful caprice, I managed to pass my Bulgarian grammar class.

TSAR BORIS III AND HIS FAMILY

In Bulgaria, Boris III is still a revered figure. Back in the 1930s, with Nazi Germany's Adolf Hitler on one side and the Soviet Union's Joseph Stalin on the other, it was extremely difficult to find a path that would keep Bulgarians safe. Earlier, in 1934, another military coup overthrew the government and abolished political parties, reducing the Bulgarian tsar to a puppet. However, Boris launched a counter-coup in 1935 and assumed personal control of the nation, ushering in a period of remarkable prosperity until the early days of the Second World War.

At first, Bulgaria was neutral in the war but was soon put under unrelenting pressure by Nazi Germany to move into its orbit. By spring 1941, the country allied itself officially with the Axis Powers, received back territory lost after the First World War, and avoided invasion by Germany, which now occupied Greece and Yugoslavia. Despite such co-operation with the Nazis, Boris refused to contribute Bulgarian troops to fight alongside German soldiers on the new Soviet front and would not deport Bulgaria's Jews to death camps in Poland and Germany.

At the end of March 1943, Hitler invited Boris to Wolf's Lair, the Fuhrer's eastern front headquarters near Rastenburg, East Prussia. No doubt the issue of Bulgaria's non-compliance with the deportation of its Jews came up once more. Throughout the spring and early summer of 1943, German demands for Bulgaria to send troops to the eastern front escalated, leading to Hitler summoning Boris once more to Wolf's Lair, this time in mid-August 1943 for what turned out to be an especially heated confrontation. Not long after his return to Bulgaria, Boris died mysteriously of apparent heart failure on August 23. Suspicions still circulate that the tsar was actually given a slow-acting poison by the Nazis that caused his death. All told, approximately fifty thousand Bulgarian Jews were saved by the heroism and courage of Boris III.

The tsar was succeeded by his six-year-old son, Simeon II, who was supervised by a Regency Council headed by Boris's brother, Prince Kiril. By the summer of 1944, Bulgaria announced its withdrawal from the war and requested all German troops to leave, but it was too late. On September 9, the Soviet Union declared war on Bulgaria, immediately invaded the country, and soon set up a shadow communist regime. Show trials were staged in late 1944 and early 1945, leading to the execution of Prince Kiril, the other royal regents, twenty-two former government ministers, and hundreds of others. It has been estimated that tens of thousands may have also been executed summarily without "trial." On September 15, 1946, a nationwide referendum was engineered by the Soviets, resulting in a 97 percent vote to establish Bulgaria as a republic and abolish the monarchy, officially deposing Simeon. Free elections were promised by the communists, but they never took place. In 1947, Nikola Petkov, the leader of the Agrarian Party, was arrested and quickly executed. Bulgaria was now firmly communist and would be so until 1990.

Before that, shortly after the "referendum" in 1946, Simeon II was forced into exile with his mother, Ioanna (formerly Giovanna), and his older sister, Maria Louisa. They first went to Alexandria, Egypt, where Ioanna's father, the former Italian monarch Victor Emmanuel III, was living in exile. In the early 1950s, the family moved to Spain. When Simeon married in 1962, his mother moved to Portugal where she died in 1999.

In 1957, Princess Maria Louisa married Prince Karl of Leiningen, a great-great-grandson of both Britain's Queen Victoria and Russia's Tsar Alexander II. She had two sons with the prince, Boris and Hermann, both of whom were born in Toronto after the couple immigrated to Canada. Hermann is currently a managing director at the Royal Bank of Canada in Toronto, while Boris resides in Neptune, New Jersey, where he is director of business development at an architectural firm. The brothers are both in the line of succession to the British throne, though, of course, far down the list. Hermann and Maria Louisa, in particular, have become close friends of my family.

Simeon II's marriage to a Spanish aristocrat, Doña Margarita, produced four sons and one daughter: Kardam, Kiril, Kubrat, Konstantin-Assen, and Kalina. In 1996, a few years after the fall of communism, Simeon returned to Bulgaria where he went into politics, eventually becoming prime minister of the country from 2001 to 2005. During his term in office, Bulgaria joined the North Atlantic Treaty Organization (NATO), and Simeon received the Path to Peace Award, a distinction also bestowed on U.N. Secretary General Kofi Annan, Polish President Lech Wałęsa, and Philippines President Corazon Aquino, among others.

THE FARMERS' CO-OPERATIVE

At the end of the school year in 1938, I found myself once again struggling to pass my Bulgarian grammar class. Again I was in danger of being held back. Wanting nothing more than to avoid the humiliation of failure, I left nothing to chance. In addition to studying as much as possible, I hatched a plan that I hoped would put me in my teacher's good graces.

The day before the final examination I left the house and set out for the field, returning with a basketful of delicious cherries. Not only were these cherries perfectly ripe but I had also chosen only the most flawless ones. Normally, I would have eaten the fruit myself or shared it with my family, but this basket was earmarked for a more important cause. The morning of the test I presented the cherries to Mrs. Kabaivanova, just in case she could find a few discretionary marks to award my answers. I passed the exam by a mere few points. To this day, I cannot be certain if my gift provided the margin I needed to pass, but I had done what I thought I needed to.

Now that I knew I would not be held back, I prepared myself for yet another golden summer in Gorno Ablanovo. I was a couple of years removed from the tragedy of Bozin's death, and I felt as though I had finally regained my emotional equilibrium. I was looking forward to spending Bulgaria's warmest months playing with friends, kicking the soccer ball, and helping on the farm. What I did not know at the time was that my father, and perhaps destiny, had different plans for me.

Instead of drifting through another long and glorious Bulgarian summer, I was set up with my very first job, thanks to my father's professional connections. Back in 1923, my father — along with several other men — established our local farmers' co-operative, designed to be a meeting place for the people of our village to buy and sell produce, as well as a way for farmers to borrow the heavy equipment they needed to work efficiently. Few could afford to buy these machines on their own. The co-op provided great assistance to the struggling Bulgarian farmers.

I was just a boy and did not understand any of this yet, but I learned later on how the people of our village could set up a co-op like this one. The co-op's founders had to pledge their own money and personal property to the Raiffeisen Bank in Austria, after which our village's co-op store was named. It was part of a regional network of credit unions and co-operatives. Like most co-operatives in Bulgaria at the time, membership was completely voluntary and guaranteed each farmer a share of the profits. For the people of our community, the co-op was nothing short of a godsend. By 1944, communism would come to Bulgaria and the co-ops would gradually be exploited and dismantled, but throughout my childhood they benefited the whole agricultural community. During its first decades — before and after I worked there — my father always held an important leadership position at the farmers' co-op. Along with Luben Teodosiev, his good friend, he was a central figure involved in every important decision.

It was my father's urging — along with his stature within the organization — that landed me a part-time position at the co-op store. He wanted me to have a job because he believed it would keep me out of trouble by occupying my idle hands and reinforcing the value of hard work. As always, my father was right.

I began working at the co-op just as soon as school let out for summer vacation. Although it was meant as a part-time job, I found myself working something closer to full-time hours, spending as much time as I could at the store, working hard while soaking up as much knowledge as I could. My job consisted mainly of wiping the counters and stocking the shelves, but I was thankful for the opportunity. Having a real job provided me with a new sense of fulfillment that I had never experienced before. For the first time, I was beginning to feel like a somebody as compared to those around me — my classmates and siblings.

Every morning I raced to the store, eager to learn under the tutelage of Mr. Teodosiev, who was more than willing to teach me about business. He showed me the inner workings of the organization and soon saw that I was qualified to do more than just sweep floors. Although I started as an unpaid apprentice, within a few months Mr. Teodosiev gave me the chance to earn some money by selling produce in the store. Much to my own surprise, I took to this new task as a fish takes to water.

Immediately, I recognized a new talent in myself: I excelled in sales. For reasons I did not understand at the time, I was able to make sales that others could not. It was an incredible self-discovery. My strong math skills allowed me to amaze many of our clients with my ability to calculate their change quickly and accurately, seemingly without effort. Here I was, this little boy, doing math in my head that was tricky even for most adults. I felt that I had found my calling — I was born to make sales.

Everything about the new job excited me, and before long I experienced the bubbling of ambition to advance even further. Mr. Teodosiev quickly agreed to let me sell any eggs I could find around the village in the co-op store and keep a tiny percentage of the profit for myself. I soon found myself embarking on a new mission.

Every morning I woke with the roosters and headed to farmers' houses. Before the sun even rose I was knocking on their doors and pleading with their wives for access to the chicken coops.

"Do you have any eggs this morning?" I would ask, already knowing I was about to get the runaround.

"No, Gatyu," they would invariably say. "There's nothing here for you today."

As I quickly discovered, farmers' wives are generally not interested in opening up their chicken coops at the crack of dawn. They had more important things to do than to oblige a little boy, they thought. I knew that in most cases these women simply could not be bothered to check — but I was persistent.

"Do you mind if I go back there and have a look for myself?" I would ask. "Maybe I can find a hidden egg or two if I search around for a little while."

Exasperated, the farmers' wives would eventually relent. I like to believe they were impressed by my determination, but more likely they just lacked the energy to shoo me off so early in the morning.

My doggedness paid off. Without fail I would find at least ten — and often up to two dozen — eggs at each house I visited. There were eggs everywhere. I would emerge from these chicken coops with a basketful of eggs and a beaming smile.

"I guess I must've missed those," the women would say to me, laughing as I emerged from the coop.

I would pay for the eggs, thank them, and head back to the co-op to sell them at a markup. The more eggs I found the more money I made. The farmers' wives came to love me because I made them money, and they never had to lift a finger. My customers also came to love me because I would check my eggs carefully to ensure that each one was of the highest quality, with no cracks or blemishes. Between the farmers' wives, my customers, the co-op, and me, everybody was happy.

Soon enough I began making real money. Naively, I thought there was no limit to my earning potential, and at the tender age of thirteen I began producing more income than my father. It was unbelievable to everyone, but most of all to me. I gave every cent earned to my family, since the feeling of accomplishment in helping my parents make ends meet was more than reward enough for me.

Making money at such a young age could have caused my ego to swell. After all, I suddenly found myself in the position of being my family's primary breadwinner. Instead of boasting, I conducted myself carefully, making certain not to get ahead of myself. My father had warned me about the effects of greed and how it could change people. I wished to avoid that by sharing whatever wealth I was fortunate enough to acquire. The money was not my primary motivation. Certainly, I was proud to bring so much more in earnings to the farmers' co-op through my efforts, but otherwise I didn't care about the money.

One of my favourite things about working at the farmers' co-op was chatting with the customers. For the first time, I found myself mingling with everybody in the village and greatly enjoying the social side of my job. In the store, I interacted with adults, made jokes while I worked, and quickly became known around town as the little boy who sold the best eggs, cherishing the fact that people actually knew my name.

I began to develop immense pride in my work — and in myself. For the first time, I felt as though I might have a chance to become a somebody. Along with the ability to make sales, I also discovered my strong work ethic. I was willing and able to work long hours to accomplish my goals, a sacrifice that not everybody was willing to make, as I came to learn. From a very young age I saw that hard work brought positive results.

In the meantime, summer had come and gone and I had to return to school. Unfortunately, that meant cutting back on my hours at the co-op as, once again, I needed to focus on my studies.

FINAL EXAMINATION

Although I loved learning, my parents had made it clear that I would not be advancing to secondary school. There was no such institution in our village, meaning that a student had to move to one of the bigger towns nearby to further his education.

School was free for all in Bulgaria, but according to the custom of the day, only the firstborn son in a family would continue his education past grade seven. The rest of the children would remain home to help on the farm. Kanu was the oldest in our family, so he was the one to continue on to high school. My second-oldest brother, Lambi, was sent to learn the tool-and-die profession at a trade school, while my sister, Kuna, was enrolled in home economics courses. That stretched our family to the limit, meaning that my formal education would soon be coming to an end. Grade seven would be my last.

Kanu, though, was kicked out of school and sent home because of my father's Agrarian politics. After the Agrarian Party lost power in a *coup d'état* during 1923 — which resulted in the murder of Aleksandar Stamboliyski, alongside other Agrarian leaders — the party was split between an extremist left-wing group that rejected parliamentary democracy, joining communists in terrorist activities, and a more moderate group that continued to take part in the formal political process. The extremist group, in an effort to hurt those who continued to hold true to Agrarian ideals, used various scare tactics to sideline the families of known Agrarian Party members.

One day, in the winter of 1938, my father, who was in charge of entertainment for our village, brought in a theatre group from Ruse to put on a play at a new school that had just been opened. The production could not begin until the mayor arrived. Time passed, but still no mayor. Snow was falling and the storm had gained force. Finally, some of the villagers went out to find the mayor. When they located him, they put him in a cage and pulled him through the village to his immense embarrassment. The mayor was not a popular fellow in Gorno Ablanovo. He was a government appointee, as were provincial officials, while the village council was elected and dominated by moderate Agrarian Party members. The federal and provincial governments viewed our village with great hostility.

When the mayor was freed from his cage, he contacted provincial officials and told them that the citizens of his village were rioting against the government, which was completely untrue. The only protest in Gorno Ablanovo was against the mayor. Nevertheless, provincial police were sent to our village in the early hours of the next morning to quell the "riot." My father was dragged in the deep snow for twelve miles by the police as part of their campaign to suppress the imaginary Agrarian uprising.

Another tactic used to attack Agrarians, as mentioned earlier, was to remove their children from school. My brother, Kanu, was one such victim. Therefore, even if I had been the one in our family sent away to school, I most likely would have been expelled, too, for the same political reasons. It seemed that higher education was, in my case, not meant to be.

Even though I knew I would soon be finished with school whether I liked it or not, I applied myself every bit as much as I had in the past. It only heightened my resolve to learn. To this day, I value education highly. The fact that I was unable to receive a proper education by today's standards, meaning finishing at least high school, caused me to treasure the opportunity for others who work hard to complete their schooling. I have never forgotten this ideal: later in my life I supported many universities and places of higher education in both Bulgaria and Canada through numerous donations.

The school curriculum had advanced from the previous year, and again I struggled to keep up in Bulgarian. I continued to work in the store part-time after school before racing home to study and practise my grammar, but no amount of effort yielded improved results. As the year progressed, my disappointment mounted. Soon I would face my final examination in Bulgarian grammar, and this time I had no doubt I would fail. All the studying in the world would not help me, and this year the tsar had no reason to rejoice and raise my mark; I was doomed to fail.

The day of the exam finally came, and I walked into the classroom like a boy facing his own execution. My chin nearly dragged along the floor in sadness as I made my way to the front of the room. Adding to my impending humiliation was the fact that, for this test, I would be made to write my surely incorrect answers on the blackboard at the front of the room for all to see.

The questions were written out clearly, but I had no answers to give. The words seemed to jumble up in my mind. I looked to the heavens for help, and as I braced myself to write an answer that had no hope of being correct, I heard the voice of an angel. As clear as day, I could hear all the answers. It was a miracle.

I scribbled down what I was told, realizing that the angel in question was my teacher, Mrs. Kabaivanova. With saintly mercy, Mrs. Kabaivanova had decided that she did not want me to fail. I cannot say what made her do it, but I was so thankful. Unfortunately, not everyone saw her act as one of kindness.

"We can hear you, Ksanta!" yelled one teacher from the hallway. "The boy won't learn anything if you just give him the answers."

But that teacher was wrong. That day Mrs. Kahaivanova taught me something even more valuable than proper Bulgarian grammar. By saving me from an unnecessary and otherwise unavoidable humiliation, my teacher taught me about compassion, kindness, and mercy. I never forgot the lesson I learned that day, and pledged to treat people with the same kindness.

FASCINATION WITH GERMANY

In addition to learning important skills like reading, writing, and arithmetic, my time in school also impressed upon me the importance of Germany in Europe and beyond. Gorno Ablanovo, at the time, was very limited in its communications with the outside world. When I was very young, I remember seeing the newspaper. Only later on did I first hear broadcasts on the radio. All of these communications had one thing in common: an obvious pro-German attitude that spread into many aspects of Bulgarian life. Germany was the country that Bulgaria most tried to model itself after, the nation we most wanted to become.

From everything I had learned in school and heard through the media, Germany was a nation far greater than any other. I might see a car pass through our village a few times every year, but in Germany they filled the roadways. German buildings, as I saw them in photos, were masterfully built towers beyond anything Bulgarians would even attempt. Germany was at the height of modernity during the late 1930s, while Bulgaria lagged behind.

The German propaganda machine was such that I viewed the country as the only bright shining star of Europe, as did almost everybody in Gorno Ablanovo. Since the liberation from the Ottomans, Bulgaria's fortunes had been closely linked to those of Germany, so it was important to us to see Germany succeed, given that every Bulgarian monarch was of German descent.

When Germany's economy prospered, ours improved; when Germany's economy suffered, ours teetered on the verge of collapse. I often heard people around the village say, "When Germany has a cold, the rest of Europe has pneumonia."

In the years leading up to the Second World War, Germany and its allies began preparing for battle. With legions of German soldiers to feed, there was a greatly increased demand for produce down at the food terminal near the edge of town. Located at the intersection of Europe and Asia, Bulgaria was an ideal trading partner for Germany. We were able to sell all that our country produced for a fair price when otherwise it would have rotted in the fields.

I fondly remember making those trips to the food terminal with my father on our horse-drawn carriage. Our produce helped supply Germany before and during the Second World War. We did not know about the atrocities Germany had in store for its own population, Europe, and the rest of the world, evil that I now know began as early as the Nazi rise to power in 1933. All we knew then was that Bulgaria was starting to be a good place to live again. My family, like others in the village, enjoyed this increase in prosperity.

In those days, if a Bulgarian was lucky beyond his wildest dreams, he might be recruited to work at a market garden in Germany. In a few short months, he could earn enough money to buy and pay for a new house back home. This would be like working and saving in Bulgaria for over two years. Being selected to work in Germany was, to Bulgarians, like winning the lottery. Nobody turned down an opportunity to go there.

Furthering my esteem for Germany was an encounter I had with German soldiers as they passed through Obretenik in 1941 on their way to Greece. I was told they were coming to town, and along with a few of my friends, I went to observe them as they marched through. These men were unlike any I had ever seen; they were dressed in immaculate uniforms, precisely tailored for comfort, mobility, and even nobility, as it appeared to my young eyes.

The German soldiers always seemed to conduct themselves like gentlemen. They were always respectful to Bulgarians, and therefore were always welcomed warmly by the people of Bulgaria. In our village, they were treated like heroes. Wherever they travelled, the soldiers found a clean spring of water for drinking and bathing. When Russian soldiers came to Bulgaria in 1944, I was told that they only looked for vodka and women, tearing through the countryside like wild men, in stark contrast to the courteous behaviour of the Germans. Although, in retrospect, I now realize there was likely some anti-communist revisionism in such descriptions.

These soldiers, along with everything I had seen and read, caused me to form a fascination with the productivity, organizational skills, and modernity of Germany. Everything I knew informed me of one simple fact: Germany was the place to be.

BAI KOLYO

After passing grade seven, I began working at the co-op store full-time, making an ever-increasing amount of money that helped my family keep its head above water. I was happy to give my parents all I earned because I had no material wants of my own. I enjoyed working for the sake of learning how to work, learning how to sell, and for the accomplishment I felt; money held little importance to me at the time.

By 1940, as summer changed to autumn and then finally to winter, I found myself working less — stocks of produce and sales decreased in the colder months as most people lived off their preserves. I was just thirteen years old, yet I already felt that I was approaching the limits of my potential in Gorno Ablanovo. How much could I improve at selling produce? How many more eggs could I possibly scrounge from the chicken coops?

I was more focused on becoming a somebody than ever before and believed I had made considerable progress. But I could not see what was next in store for me in the village. And then, just as I might have reached the point of frustration, a visitor to our house changed my life forever. Nikola Parush Cholakoff — who would become known to me as "Bai Kolyo," a nickname that very appropriately connotes both intimacy and respect — would end up having a profound impact on my life. I did not know it at the time, but he would be a catalyst for so much of what would happen to me in the future.

I first remember meeting Bai Kolyo during the Christmas season of 1938. As old friends and fellow members of the Red Cross during the First World War, Bai Kolyo and my father shared an indelible bond. Starting that winter, Bai Kolyo would make an annual pilgrimage from his village, Draganovo, situated about sixty miles from Gorno Ablanovo, to visit my family at Christmas. It was a tradition between two old friends; they resolved to see each other at least once a year.

Draganovo, located near Bulgaria's northeastern tip, was perhaps the most prosperous village in the entire country in 1940. Many of its citizens were able to find seasonal employment in Germany, Hungary, or Czechoslovakia. They would return to the village in the off-season, building big, beautiful, and well-financed houses. When I visited the village later in life, I was struck by its incredible landscape and breathtaking architecture. Like many others in Draganovo's population of about four thousand people, Bai Kolyo's family owned several houses.

Each Christmas, Bai Kolyo would visit our home and regale my father with stories of Draganovo, while also providing updates about his new market gardening business in Germany.

An educated gentleman capable of speaking several languages — most notably Bulgarian, German, Russian, and Czech — Bai Kolyo came from a wealthy family and presented himself as a man of the world. As they sipped on my father's homemade plum whisky, the two men spoke of world politics, their families, and life in general. It was plain to see that Bai Kolyo held a special place in my father's heart. Yet my father and his dear friend held opposing political beliefs. Bai Kolyo was a Russophile — though not necessarily a communist — while my father, most decidedly, was not.

By 1940, Bai Kolyo's annual visit became an expected ritual around our house. My father's good friend arrived on our doorstep a few days after Christmas, as was his custom. This time, however, his visit held a purpose beyond the simple enjoyment of drinking whisky, holding spirited conversation, and reminiscing with my father. That night he spent much of his time watching me. He was aware of me mostly from my father telling him about my accomplishments at the co-op store. My father had spoken of my potential to be a fine businessman. I had only just turned fourteen, but I could sense from the way that Bai Kolyo was looking at me that I had been in his thoughts.

Bai Kolyo turned to me and then looked at my father. "Hristo," he said, pointing to me, "give me that little boy. Give me that little boy and I will make him a man."

I asked my father what he meant and learned that Bai Kolyo intended to recruit me for his market gardening business in Germany, with a promise that I would be able to resume my schooling there, as well. Given my fascination with Germany, the thought of such an opportunity filled me with excitement. All of a sudden I was being given the chance of a lifetime.

I was stunned by the development and overjoyed by the prospect of going to Germany. I did not yet know that with Bai Kolyo I would really be in Austria, which had been annexed by the German Reich in 1938. All I knew was that after years of fantasizing, I would be given the opportunity to see for myself all that Germany had to offer. It was a dream that had come true. I could hardly believe it was all happening to me.

My father and Bai Kolyo agreed that I would travel to Germany along with the rest of the recruits from Gorno Ablanovo to start my new job in the spring. I would be one of many working the fields for Bai Kolyo's market gardening business.

Later on I would discover that my father had encouraged Bai Kolyo to choose me. Normally, such an opportunity might have gone to my older brothers, but Kanu was already serving in the Bulgarian military, while Lambi was well on his way in a career as a tool-and-die tradesman. My father had long been observing me at the farmers' co-op and was impressed by all that I had accomplished in a short time. He could see that I was a born salesman with determination and persistence and that I was willing to work hard; he had no doubt I would achieve great things in Germany.

As winter melted into spring, signs of the great war that was raging over much of Europe made their appearance in Bulgaria, too. In the first week of March 1941, the German Army passed through our country on its way to Greece. These were the troops I watched marching through our village. The very next week my father began planning to send me to Germany. He understood that there I might be in harm's way. He knew war and recognized that bombers could soon be flying above me. Yet he also knew I would not be on the front lines fighting, but in the field, working the land. That was where my best chance would be to earn some money and get ahead in life. And now that the German Army was in Bulgaria, my chances looked even brighter — Germany was our ally.

My father also understood that in a mad world Bulgaria might be a less violent place than other countries, but staying home would in no way guarantee my safety. In a few short years, I would be old enough to be conscripted into the Bulgarian military. If my father chose to keep me at home out of fear for my safety, it was very likely that I would become a soldier. The opportunity to leave Bulgaria would likely not come my way again soon.

While my father knew he could not protect any of his children from the dangers of the world, he could do his best to help us along a path to success. He had done everything in his power to help my older siblings, and now it was my turn. My father would allow me to go to Germany simply because it was the best chance I would ever have at becoming a somebody.

Upon reflection, I believe that part of my father's reasoning for sending me away from Gorno Ablanovo stemmed from his own inability to leave for Canada years earlier. He wished for his son what he was not able to do for himself: to experience the vast world beyond the confines of our small village. He wanted me to test the limits of my own potential, and he knew such an opportunity was unlikely to repeat itself.

But my father kept his concerns from me until long after my departure. As far as I was concerned, Bai Kolyo's offer was nothing short of a godsend, the answer to my prayers. I was going to Germany, where I believed money would be easily earned, people were all well dressed and groomed, and every building was grand.

Following the discussions with my father, Bai Kolyo made his return to Draganovo and I was left to wait. My new job in Germany would not begin until April. The days could not have passed more slowly.

As much as I tried to enjoy the remaining days with my family in Bulgaria, Germany dominated my thinking. I thought I would only be gone for a short time, since most Bulgarians who worked outside the borders returned home in the off-season. My father, however, was living with the knowledge that these remaining days might be our last together. Bombs had been dropping over Germany for months already, and any one of them could bring death. Lacking faith in God, my father could not pray for my safety. He could only hope for the best.

DEPARTURE

At long last it was time for me to leave Gorno Ablanovo. As I readied myself to go, I noticed the long faces of my mother, aunts, and sisters. For reasons I did not understand at the time, they all wept uncontrollably.

"But I'll see you all in a few months," I reassured them. "You probably won't even notice I'm gone."

I hugged and kissed each of them goodbye. Years later my mother told me she could have filled a river with all the tears she had cried for me. But I felt nothing except excitement and could only wonder why she did not feel the same.

And so, at the tender age of fourteen, I watched as my father picked up my huge suitcase and potato bag and placed them on our horse-drawn wagon. Then he lifted himself onto the seat while I got in next to him. As he flicked the whip and shook the reins to get the horse moving, I found myself looking at our house, my mother, my sisters, and my aunts as I drove away with my father. I was leaving behind everything I knew and loved for a new adventure.

As we got farther from the village on our way toward the train station in Dve Mogili — about eight miles south of Gorno Ablanovo — I found myself in a quiet state of reflection. In my excitement, I had not fully processed what it would mean to be away from my family, my village, and my country. Now, as the horse patiently pulled us toward our destination, I found myself thinking about all the happy times I had enjoyed in Gorno Ablanovo. For the first time, I wondered how I would fare on my own.

I thought about Bozin, working at the co-op, my time at school, and even smashing those watermelons. The experiences of my childhood came flooding back to me, and the lessons learned filled me with confidence and enthusiasm for my next adventure.

My father was mostly silent throughout our ride, speaking only to point out various landmarks as we passed them. I could see that he was deep in thought, so I allowed myself to sink into my own daydreams.

Nobody had told me how much money I would earn in Germany, and it did not much matter to me. I saw my journey to that country as the next step on my path to becoming a somebody. I could not foresee how I would accomplish my dream, but I was certain I would somehow make it happen. It was just a matter of time.

When we pulled up to the train station, I hopped off the carriage. My father picked up my suitcase and potato bag and set them next to me. "Working men carry their own luggage," he said with a wry smile.

We walked to the platform. Having never seen a train station in anything but photographs, I marvelled at all I saw before me. It was amazing — so many massive machines, each one opening a path into a different world.

My father bought my ticket from a woman in a booth and handed it to me, instructing me to present it to the conductor when asked. I could hardly contain my excitement at the sight of the train I was about to board. I began drifting toward it before my father pulled me back by the shoulders. His eyes were glassy, his face strong and serious. After a long wagon ride in near silence, my father was ready to speak.

"Listen to me, son," he said. "This is the last advice I may ever be able to offer you."

I began to disagree, reassuring my father that I would be back home before he knew it. But my father ignored my remark, shook his head slightly, and looked deeply into my eyes. In an even more serious tone, he repeated himself. "Listen to me, son."

We faced each other, my father's left hand now resting atop my right shoulder, our eyes locking. Certain that he possessed my full attention, he continued. "Firstly, always work hard and be honest with those around you. You will earn people's respect by being honest and having integrity. You must always do what you say you will do." He paused to see that I had taken this in. "Secondly, do all that you can to help others. Someday you'll be the one who needs help. When the time comes, others will be there to help you."

I promised my father that I would follow his advice. I pledged to always be honest, to always work hard, and to do my best to help those in need.

"Finally," my father continued, "I have one last piece of advice."

I listened to my father more attentively than ever before.

He leaned into me, his forehead now touching mine. "This is the most important thing I can possibly tell you." He paused and wiped his eyes before continuing. "Always listen to Bai Kolyo. I won't be there to offer you guidance, but Bai Kolyo will never steer you wrong. Listen to him."

I nodded my agreement before my father pulled me in for one last hug. As far as he knew, this might be the last time we would embrace, the last time he could show love and affection to his son.

"Always listen to Bai Kolyo," he repeated softly into my ear, releasing me from his hug. I picked up my baggage from the platform and raced onto the train. It was time to go.

I found my seat on the train, overcome with excitement, emotion, and nerves. I glanced out the window to see my father standing on the platform, waiting for me to pull away.

The train began to move, and my father grew smaller in the distance until he was only a speck and then not visible at all. I remembered his words and swore to myself that I would do everything possible to follow them.

At last I was on my way. As I stared out the window, gazing at the Bulgarian countryside, I let out a long, self-satisfied breath. I was on my way to Germany. I was on my way to becoming a somebody.

5

Setting Forth

I did not know it at the time, but I was setting forth on an odyssey that would span the rest of my life. I was on my own: still a boy, but somehow a man on the move. Sitting on the train, destined for a new life, I found myself surrounded by the five other boys recruited by Bai Kolyo to work in Germany — four of them about the same age as I was, and one just a few years older. I was starting to feel that I was living my dream.

It was exciting enough to be aboard a train travelling all the way to Germany. The Bulgarian countryside flew past my window. The train ride marked the beginning of what would prove to be a wild ride — the rapid course of my life in the coming years.

As we rode the tracks, it took almost no time at all for my bubble of elation to burst. The journey to Germany took us through Serbia. As a Serbian customs officer approached me, I was introduced to the tensions that were overcoming Europe during the first years of the Second World War.

This customs officer came toward me with a very sour disposition and demanded to see my passport at once. His hostility, at first subtle, quickly turned into unmistakable contempt as he examined the document and realized I was just another Bulgarian on his way to work in Germany. To this man, my Bulgarian identity marked me as an indirect supporter of his German oppressors. For the first time in my life, I felt hated.

With my documentation clearly in order, the customs officer derisively flipped the passport back into my lap and walked away without a word. I was still unaware of the tensions boiling over in Europe. But at that moment it was very clear that, as a Bulgarian, I would not necessarily be received warmly everywhere I travelled.

I quietly looked out the window during the remainder of my trip, gazing on lands I had never seen before. The train chugged along all the way across Serbia, and then through Hungary, before crossing into German territory in what is now Austria, where we switched lines, finally stopping in Wels.

I had arrived.

NEW LIFE

The day was April 18, 1941. For reasons that remain a mystery, this day would hold significance for me again and again. Not only did it mark my arrival in Germany, but ten years later I landed in Canada on the very same day. Amazingly, it would also prove to be the date of my daughter Kristina Maria's birth in 1981. Needless to say, April 18 holds a special place in my heart.

As I stepped off the train, my hands trembled with excitement; I was entering a new world. My dreams of going to Germany had become a reality. My senses were overwhelmed by the surroundings and by all the new sights, sounds, and smells. On my first impression, the city of Wels — with its great churches, tall, impressive buildings, and bustling squares — exceeded the already lofty expectations I had for the world outside Bulgaria.

Located in the northern part of Austria along the Traun River, Wels is the second-largest city in the state of Upper Austria. When I arrived there in 1941, the population was roughly thirty thousand. It may have only been the eighth-largest city in Austria, which itself was then only a part of Germany, but to my naive and sheltered fourteen-year-old eyes Wels was nothing short of a great metropolis.

Bai Kolyo met his new employees at the train station and gave us a few moments to enjoy the city. But it would only be a few moments. As I stumbled through the streets in amazement, I heard Bai Kolyo calling us in the distance. Discovering Wels would have to wait for another day; all of Bai Kolyo's new recruits — myself included — were hustled away to our new home.

Along with Bai Kolyo and his other Bulgarian imports, I lived in a framed barrack-style building on the outskirts of town. Unlike Wels itself, the state of our living quarters did not impress me. During my time working for Bai Kolyo, I shared the house with twelve other employees — as well as Bai Kolyo himself — and we endured spartan conditions. There were many rows of identical metal-framed beds with thin mattresses spread across a cold wooden floor. In fact, my family's house in Bulgaria was considerably nicer than my new home in Wels.

Of course, luxury was the furthest thing from my mind at the time. I was part of a group of men, young and old, brought together for one purpose: to work. What we produced in the fields was directly related to what we took home in pay, motivating us to work as hard as possible. Our accommodations were strictly utilitarian. Therefore, as long as there was a roof over my head, I cared about little else.

The barrack had a small kitchen off to one side containing a wood stove and a few rudimentary cooking tools. There were wooden spoons, a cast-iron skillet, and a few sharp knives. As market gardening employees, we had access to almost unlimited amounts of fresh, beautiful produce, along with plenty of meat. As in Bulgaria, I found out — once again — that when you have meat and vegetables, you have nearly everything you need.

For some reason, I ended up doing a lot of the cooking for our group of young farmers. Since nobody else seemed to know how to cook, I applied what little I had gleaned from watching my mother make so many meals during my childhood and became the primary preparer of food for a large group of perpetually hungry Bulgarians. In learning by doing, I more or less taught myself the basics of Bulgarian cuisine. Every day I cooked up meat and vegetables, often serving them up in a goulash. With practice, I honed my culinary skills. Cooking became a source of enjoyment, and even pride. To this day, I still love to spend time cooking a big goulash for my family. My daughters say I am an amazing cook!

But while the kitchen in Bai Kolyo's barrack was functional, the bathroom was seriously lacking. Even my family's old house in Bulgaria had a makeshift shower; Bai Kolyo's barrack offered nothing of the sort. Unless you had the chance to go to one of the bathhouses in the city, you cleaned yourself in the most primitive way. Of course, Bai Kolyo still demanded that his workers maintain good hygiene at all times.

There was a stream that ran just steps from our door, but the water, while perfect for drinking, was too frigid for washing. We had to set it out in buckets before leaving for work in the morning, hoping the sun would warm it up enough to pour over our bodies in the afternoon. The only way for me to wash myself at Bai Kolyo's barrack was to have one of the other boys dump sun-soaked water over my head as I scrubbed myself with soap and a brush. If you put your mind to it, you will find a way.

Still, living and bathing facilities caused me no great concern, since I was just a boy and cared little about such matters. My greatest source of anxiety after moving away from home was simply being away from home. I began to feel homesickness almost immediately. Suddenly, I was living the life of a man, even though I was still hardly more than a child. My family was everything to me, and to be separated from them at such a young age was achingly painful.

So, while I was overjoyed to be in Wels, I also felt lonely. If not for the boys I lived and worked with, I might have run back home to my mother and father. Being surrounded by Bulgarians reminded me enough of my village to get me through some of the toughest bouts of homesickness.

There was a healthy camaraderie within our group: because of our shared nationality and nature, we had great loyalty and trust for one another in a foreign place. We looked out for each other, and I enjoyed living with the other boys and men as I myself began to change from a boy into a man.

Still, I had not left my home merely for the company of others; I was there to work. I knew that anyone in Gorno Ablanovo would have been tremendously grateful to have my job, and I cherished the opportunity. We were put to work from the first day, and we worked and worked, and then we worked some more. When we rested, it was only to regain the strength needed to do more work. It was hard work but that never bothered me. I truly appreciated the pulling, the watering, the cultivating, and the hulling. I relished every moment of it, since I viewed each act as a necessary step in becoming a somebody.

As well, it was the work that distracted me from my homesickness. Between the near-constant labour, the Bulgarians surrounding me, and the Bulgarian food I was eating, my day-to-day existence was very much like my life in Bulgaria.

A PROMOTION

I spent those first days in Wels doing my best to impress Bai Kolyo. It must have worked, because less than a week after my arrival, Bai Kolyo approached me to talk. I was hard at work, digging a trench. He grabbed my left arm and began to pull me away from my task.

I looked at him with a puzzled expression, unsure whether I had done something wrong. "What are you doing?"

"I'm taking you to see the market," he told me. "We're going into the city."

After spending several days with my head down, working away in the field, I had practically forgotten about the city I had passed through so briefly after stepping off the train. Bai Kolyo took me to the market, which I discovered was only a short bicycle ride from the barrack. I was immediately captivated by its bustle and electricity.

For the next hour, I wandered through the town market, soaking it all in. There were so many people making what seemed to be thousands of transactions, all of them at once; the energy of it entranced me. Without a doubt this was where I wanted to be.

I finally staggered back to Bai Kolyo's side, a huge smile on my face.

"Did you enjoy your time looking around the market?" he asked.

I assured him that I had.

"Gatyu, I want you to start learning German," he said. "As soon as you can pick up enough of the language, I'm going to put you to work in the market. Consider this a promotion."

After just a few days of work, Bai Kolyo was offering me advancement. I was overjoyed and thanked him for the opportunity.

Bai Kolyo handed me a sheet of paper with a list of German words for various fruits and vegetables. As soon as I could grasp this basic vocabulary, which required me to learn the Latin alphabet, I would start trying to make sales in the market, just as I had in Gorno Ablanovo. Given my experience at the farmers' co-op, I was more than confident that I could justify Bai Kolyo's faith in me.

For the next few weeks, I carried that piece of paper in my back pocket everywhere I went: *Apfel, Kartoffel, Kohl, Zwiebel* ... Before long I had the list of words memorized well enough for Bai Kolyo to put me in the market. German was a challenge for me, given that the alphabet was different from that of Bulgarian — Latin-based rather than Cyrillic. Nonetheless, as soon as I began interacting with the customers, I once again recognized the calling I had discovered back home: I had been born to make sales.

Although my German was still quite limited, I had enough vocabulary to get by in my new job. As always, I did all I could to learn quickly. On my first day, I listened intently to the customers for the keys words from Bai Kolyo's sheet of paper. In addition to my limited vocabulary, I relied heavily on eye contact, body language, a pleasant manner, and whatever natural charisma I possessed. Somehow that was enough, and I was a success right away.

In those days, every market gardening company had its own little stall at the market in Wels. I was taking over Bai Kolyo's stall from his brother, Constantine, who was returning to Bulgaria. In reality, I was working in a small wooden box, but at the time it seemed to me like the greatest store in the world.

Given that I was interacting with Germans almost every afternoon in the market — I still worked mornings in the field — I picked up the German language far quicker than my friends. This is a special talent of mine. I became the interpreter for our entire group anytime we ventured into the city, enabling my fellow Bulgarians to communicate with shop owners, bartenders, or anyone else.

My ability to speak German soon gave me a big boost of confidence during my early days in Wels. I also noticed a proportionate increase in my popularity. My father had advised me to help others as much as possible, and my grasp of German came to the aid of my Bulgarian countrymen on more than one occasion. As always, I enjoyed the feeling of helping others.

Often my language skills saved my friends from a case of mistaken identity. In those days, Wels was home to a group of foreign prisoners from German-occupied countries who were being made to build military aircraft. These men were permitted to walk through the city only during certain times of the day, meaning they were nearly as unfamiliar to the police as some of my friends were. Whenever a policeman saw one of my Bulgarian friends striding through the city, he would stop him in the mistaken belief that one of the market gardeners was a prisoner on the loose.

Being accosted by a police officer yelling in German was beyond stressful for my friends. On one occasion, I was at least a hundred yards away when I heard a friend yelling my name.

"Gatyu, come quickly!" he hollered. "I need your help."

I ran to the scene, arriving just in time to explain to the police officer that my friend was a Bulgarian market gardener and not an escaped prisoner. Fortunately, most of the policemen in this area had come to know me from the market, and they were quick to release my friends. Had I not been around to speak German on their behalf, some Bulgarians would have been terribly harassed.

WARTIME LIVING

As a child, I often rode with my father to and from our fields while he told me stories about the First World War. At the time I felt as if I was there with him; I could almost smell the fear in the air and see the blood on the ground. But hearing stories about war was far different than living through one, as I was now learning.

The Second World War was less than two years old when I arrived in Germany, and I still did not understand what it meant for us. That changed when I began working for Bai Kolyo in Wels. As the war progressed, the violence intensified, and soon Wels became another battleground. Mere months removed from living in rural Bulgaria, I now saw that my father's worst fears had become reality: I was living in a war zone.

The first time we came under attack I simply did not understand what was happening. I had never been anywhere near a bomb. I quickly learned that when a bomb hit the ground a thunderous sound could be heard even several miles away. Nothing was louder or more destructive than a bomb exploding nearby.

I was lying in bed one night close to midnight when I first heard the British aircraft flying overhead. This became a familiar pattern, since they never came before nightfall for the rest of the war. The engines buzzed louder and louder as they drew closer, reaching a crescendo before finally tapering off. In the distance, I heard the bombs explode. The ground shook beneath me.

Although the bombs landed somewhere far away from my barrack, it was still too close for me. I agonized that a bomb might kill me at any moment. Had I not been so exhausted from working all day, my fears would have kept me up all night. But, as it was, I almost always fell asleep as soon as my head touched the pillow. Now I drifted off, only to be awakened by the sound of attackers and defenders engaging in battle once again.

I cannot explain the terror I felt while sleeping under a night sky full of bombs, knowing that any breath could be my last. I would lie in bed, squeezing my eyes shut as tight as they would go, plugging my ears with my fingers in an attempt to drown out the booming noise. Still, I would hear nothing but explosions and air raid sirens as I prayed for my own safety and that of those around me. I could do nothing other than put my fate in God's hands.

Until 1943 we almost never left the barrack during a bombing. At the time British and American forces focused on destroying the military aircraft hangar in town. To counter this, the Germans set up a strong anti-aircraft artillery force in Wels, which generally prevented attacking planes from flying within five or six miles of our location. This left us with a sense of being ever so slightly safe, a feeling that would evaporate later in the war when the Allies intensified their attacks.

At that point I went from hearing bombs blasting in the distance to finding myself squarely within their range. The Allied Powers began to close in on the area where we lived, sending in a thousand planes at once to carpet-bomb an entire area no more than two miles or so away.

One aircraft would fly past us and drop a bomb, followed by another and then another. Previously, the largest bomber formations had flown past Wels and on to Vienna.

Although terror was constantly present in our barrack, some of the guys liked to act defiantly in the face of fear. I remember one in particular. My friend, Alexander, had served in the Bulgarian military and liked to tell the rest of us how — compared to what he had already seen in combat — the Second World War, as we knew it in Germany, was nothing.

"Conditions were far worse for us when I was serving in the army," he said. "Sure, there are a few bombs dropping around these parts, but it's nothing compared to what I've already been through."

His arrogance was laughable, but I understood that we all dealt with this ever-present anxiety in our own way. I tried to block out the fear; Alexander preferred to laugh in its face. My friend remained defiant in the face of fear until the moment a bomb blew off our roof.

That moment came months later in the summer of 1944. It was a night like any other. My Bulgarian colleagues and I had worked all day and were passing the hours between finishing our dinner and going to sleep. Normally, we left the barrack only on Saturday night when we went to watch a movie at the city theatre; on work nights we generally stayed put.

I was sitting on a stool around a small round table, playing cards with three other boys. One other boy was about five paces away, sitting on his bed and playing the flute. He filled the night air with a song we all knew as "Sad Mother." All the while, Alexander hovered around us and talked his usual nonsense about not being afraid, even though we all knew the bombers could be flying overhead at any moment. I tuned him out and tried to concentrate on my game.

As we played the first hand, I began to hear the whirring engines of bombers in the distance. As my friend continued to play his flute, the notes rang sadder and sadder, and the feeling came over me that these truly could be my last moments.

The planes were closer and louder than ever before. Somehow they had evaded the German anti-aircraft artillery and penetrated into our airspace. We kept going with our game, my friend continued to play the flute, and I began to think about the sadness my mother would feel upon learning of my death.

Before we knew it, bombs began falling everywhere. It felt as if the entire world was caving in around me. The ground shook violently, and our cards flew off the table before the table itself was knocked over. Each explosion was followed by another, every few seconds. After the second or third wave of bombs, I regained my composure and was able to run and hide under my bed.

I closed my eyes and waited. I could still hear the bombs dropping all around me and could imagine the fires and destruction. But all I could do was to wait until it was over.

Finally, I heard the loudest blast of all. It lifted my body from the ground. The next blast was even closer and blew the roof right off our barrack.

Exposed to the sky, I sprawled on the floor like a quivering mess, certain the next bomb was going to be the one that killed me. I waited for it and braced myself for my doom. I continued to wait. Nothing.

There was nothing but silence.

I looked across the room and saw Alexander. Our eyes locked. He was as white as a sheet, his face drained of blood, his personality sapped of bravado. Like the rest of us, Alexander knew we had just survived a brush with death.

Composing himself, he walked over to me, put his arm around my shoulder, and squeezed tightly, then leaned in and whispered in my ear, "That was nothing."

I laughed, and Alexander smiled. Then we both cried.

REBUILDING

As the war intensified, destruction became common in Wels. Houses and other buildings were blown up on a regular basis. Amazingly, the Germans were so efficient in rebuilding that it was hardly noticeable. Even buildings that appeared to be completely knocked down would often be repaired overnight, or so it seemed.

The morning after our roof was blown off I went to work, unsure of where I would sleep that night. It was my hope that Bai Kolyo could somehow find temporary housing for his workers. To my amazement, the entire structure was completely rebuilt by the time I returned home that evening. During the twelve hours I had been at work, the Germans had fixed our house to look like new. In fact, I rarely ever saw evidence of destruction in Wels for more than a day or two. Whenever there was a bombing the Germans made the wreckage disappear like magic.

The Nazi regime considered it to be of the highest importance that living quarters like ours should be rebuilt as quickly as possible. Bai Kolyo's company was a link in the food chain, making us important to the proper functioning of German society. If we were unable to work, nobody would have produce to eat. Our work in the fields was critical to the well-being of the Reich.

When the food market itself was bombed, the Germans always restored it by the next morning. On a good day, I could be back at work within a few hours of a bombing. Destruction and chaos became almost normal; these things were life as we knew it.

A BIG MISTAKE

Despite the war, I was enjoying my time in Wels. As I continued to work in the market, my German improved, as did my sales record. I became more communicative, gaining confidence daily. As I became increasingly successful, my relationship with Bai Kolyo flourished.

Just as my father had advised me, when Bai Kolyo spoke I paid full attention. If he offered advice, I followed it. My father was more than six hundred miles away in Bulgaria, but Bai Kolyo was a valuable surrogate. He was like a second father to me, and I was like a son to him.

After just a few months of working in the market, Bai Kolyo told me of his plans to expand the business and supply produce to other parts of Germany. The months passed and Bai Kolyo's plans matured. I had been in the country for less than a year before Bai Kolyo offered me an improbable second promotion. I would travel to other nearby cities to facilitate large shipments of fruit and vegetables, mostly to supply hotels and restaurants.

Bai Kolyo was showing a tremendous amount of faith in me, trusting me to make important sales that could make or break his company. My new responsibilities would see me travelling throughout the country to meet our shipments at their destination, making the exchange with buyers and ensuring that all transactions went according to plan. It was a big job for a little boy. But, despite my youth and diminutive stature, I knew I could do it.

Every morning I rose with the sun and rode my bicycle to the train station. By the time I arrived, there were several other people waiting for my instructions on where to send the produce. Each and every person in the chain of command had an important job to do, but it was ultimately my responsibility that the produce found its way to where it needed to go.

After sorting through the orders, I would ship the fruit and vegetables to their destinations and then hop aboard a train, travelling to various cities in my corner of Germany to finalize the sales and collect cash from our clients. I carried a briefcase full of cash. To this day, I continue to be amazed that Bai Kolyo trusted me with such an enormous responsibility. His faith in me gave me the confidence I needed to do business with men who might have otherwise tried to take advantage of a boy.

Unfortunately, I put Bai Kolyo's belief in me to the test right away, making the biggest mistake I ever made during my tenure as his employee.

Although I was just sixteen years old, I thought I was mature for my age. I had a great deal of confidence in myself and my ability to meet any challenge. Bai Kolyo trusted me with his out-of-town orders, and I had no doubt I could do the job as well as anyone. However, even though I had a basic understanding of the German language, I had not yet become a fluent speaker. I could easily get confused when this new language was spoken too quickly. And some of those German words and strange place names were long!

I arrived at the train station on a beautiful morning in July 1944, just before sunrise, accompanied by my good friend and co-worker, Bratoi Panayatov, another boy from my village in Bulgaria. In the early days of working for Bai Kolyo, I rarely travelled outside Wels without

Bratoi at my side. Bai Kolyo made us regular travel companions, and it worked out very well.

Bratoi quickly became my closest friend, the confidant I had lacked since the passing of Bozin. During our time off, Bratoi and I spent our hours together, going to one of the bathhouses, watching a film in town, or simply wandering the still-unfamiliar streets of Wels. It was good to have a true friend once again.

Although Bratoi was an excellent employee and an important helper in much of my work, he could not speak a word of German. Therefore, when we were in the train station that morning and I heard the announcement of departures and arrivals over the public address system, it was up to me, and me alone, to understand what was being said. But this day the announcer was speaking very rapidly.

I could not keep up with the announcements, and a feeling of dread descended on me. Disoriented, I led Bratoi onto a train that I believed was headed for our destination. I rushed to get on the train and climbed aboard with no real assurance it would take us in the right direction.

Bratoi and I sat down. Glancing around, I realized almost immediately that something was amiss. But the train was already moving. Instead of being on the way to our proper destination of Vöcklabruck, in the direction of Salzburg, to make a huge cash deal for Bai Kolyo's business, we found ourselves travelling the opposite way toward Passau in Bavaria. I quickly became aware of my mistake.

But even that was not the worst of my troubles. After looking around a little bit more, Bratoi and I saw that we were aboard a military train filled with German soldiers on their way back from the eastern front. Out of all the trains we could have possibly chosen by mistake, a military train was the worst option; it was illegal for civilians to travel aboard them.

Bratoi and I stuck out like beets in a cornfield. Uniformed soldiers surrounded us, and it took no time at all for them to notice that two of the passengers were unlike the others. Within moments a huge German policeman approached us. He towered above me like a bear casting his shadow over a mouse. I felt so intimidated that I could hardly breathe. My heart thumped loudly in my chest as I waited for the man to speak.

"What are you doing here, little boy?" he thundered.

I had no good answer, since there was no legitimate reason for Bratoi and me to be on this train. I cleared my throat and tried to provide an answer that would not anger this officer any further.

"We're headed to Vöcklabruck," I whimpered.

"Vöcklabruck? This train is headed for Passau and then Berlin. You have no business being here."

As the German police officer continued to tell me what I already knew, I felt my heart sinking. I swallowed hard and prepared to be arrested. The policeman was not mistaken; we had no right to be aboard a military train, and the Germans had every reason to suspect us to be their enemies. It appeared as though I would be unable to make any sales for Bai Kolyo, an unprecedented failure.

Thankfully, the officer sensed our innocence — or perhaps it was our fear — and chose not to prosecute two lost young boys. Instead, this intimidating policeman paused for a moment, examined me closely, and asked a question. "Where are you from, little boy?"

"I'm travelling from Wels," I answered. "But I'm Bulgarian."

"You're a Bulgarian?" he asked excitedly, now with a smile on his face. "Why didn't you say so in the first place? We love Bulgarians."

Suddenly, my feeling of terror changed to one of immense relief. Fortunately for us, the Germans had been treated with great respect and hospitality as they passed through Bulgaria on their way to Greece in 1941. They felt that they owed a debt of gratitude to Bulgarians, and this man chose to repay it to Bratoi and me. The kindness of Bulgarians before us had provided for our salvation.

The big German who seemed so frightening to me only a moment ago began treating me like a dear old friend. I explained to him that I had become confused at the station in Wels and boarded a train that was travelling in the wrong direction. The German officer spoke to Passau's railway commander on our behalf, and thanks to him, we were sent to Vöcklabruck immediately upon our arrival in Passau about twenty minutes later.

With the help of our new friends, Bratoi and I finally made it to our destination, although nearly four hours late. Without a doubt I had made a big mistake by boarding the wrong train, but I was not so late that I believed the day's sales to be lost. If I got to work immediately, I thought I could do all I had set out to accomplish when I left Wels that morning.

However, before I could begin crossing off completed tasks from my list, I had to deal with my supervisor, Bai Kolyo's brother and second-in-command, the angry and profane Constantine. He had recently returned from Bulgaria.

Despite his faults, I mostly considered Constantine to be a good man. Most people are, I have found, when you look deeply enough into them. Unfortunately, he lacked Bai Kolyo's diplomacy. When things went badly, Constantine found a way to make them worse. Forever suspicious of others, he did not trust those who worked beneath him. He went so far as to set up a network of spies throughout the cities to which we delivered produce. In Vöcklabruck, Constantine's man worked in a hotel across the street from the train station.

This hotelier was operating under strict instructions to contact Constantine at the very moment I set foot in town. When I arrived late that day, this man confronted me immediately, telling me that I was to speak to Constantine at once.

I walked with the man back to his office in the hotel, where Constantine was waiting impatiently on the telephone connection. Constantine's rage had been simmering for most of the past four hours and had now reached a fever pitch. The boss was furious.

I picked up the telephone and braced myself for Constantine's fury.

"You idiot!" he yelled. "How could you do something so stupid?"

I completely understood Constantine's anger, but I did not appreciate being called an idiot, or any of the even less flattering names he shouted at me. I knew that my job was critical to the success of Bai Kolyo's business, and I knew as well that I had made a big mistake. But, even as a sixteen-year-old boy, I was only willing to be chastised for so long. I had my pride. After several minutes of Constantine's abuse, I calmly placed the phone receiver onto its cradle and hung up on him.

I had no time to talk because I was planning to make up for my mistake and salvage the day. I said goodbye to Constantine's friend, left the man's office, and raced around Vöcklabruck for the next few hours, completing my day of sales in record time. Of course, none of my success was due to Constantine's tirade. I did it in spite of him, since I was deeply offended by his attempt to make me feel even worse than I already felt.

Luckily, the hoteliers in town knew I always came to Vöcklabruck on Wednesdays. They were always happy with the produce I provided, so every one of them decided to wait around for me. Had they not done so, I would have lost all the sales I was supposed to make for Bai Kolyo.

After several hours of working harder and faster than ever before, I caught the return train to Wels with Bratoi. My clothes were soaked in sweat, but I felt an overwhelming sense of pride and accomplishment. I was still just a young boy, and for the first time in my life I truly felt as though as I had risen to the challenge of overcoming a massive mistake.

Even with this sweet taste of success, bitterness lingered from my earlier conversation with Constantine. I was disgraced by his foul language, surprised by his anger over an honest mistake, and saddened by his unwillingness to treat me like a human being. I could think of little else as I rode the train back to Wels. The tables had turned, because now I was the one who was furious.

Finally back in Wels, I cycled from the train station directly to Constantine's office. Without a word I dumped a bag containing the money onto his desk. Momentarily silent, Constantine counted it and realized I had sold every last piece of produce. The expression on his face changed from one of contempt to shock and then finally to embarrassment.

Instead of profanity, words of apology began to flow from Constantine's mouth. Suddenly, he was treating me like one of his own, with the respect I felt I deserved.

As he continued on in this vein, Constantine practically jumped across his large mahogany desk to try to hug me, but I was having none of it. I might have been young, but I was not so naive that I was unable to recognize such insincerity.

He begged me to join him on a late-afternoon trip to the market, but I refused. I openly defied him for the first time. I told him I was going home for the day.

"If Bai Kolyo asks where I am," I said, "you can tell him exactly what happened."

I left Constantine's office, knowing I was making a statement that I would not be disrespected or mistreated. I knew myself well enough to know I was a good worker, one who had always been honest, forthright, and conscientious. Never again would I allow Constantine — or anyone else — to abuse me. In the days to come, I would forgive Constantine as we resumed our regular business relationship, and he never treated me poorly again.

In 1943, during my time in Wels, I began to take driving lessons. One day, after finishing my lesson, my teacher and I were motoring back to his garage from where he ran a business, and I spotted a policeman guarding someone digging at the side of the road.

"What are they doing?" I asked my teacher.

"The policeman's guarding a prisoner who's volunteered to defuse a bomb in exchange for his freedom," the teacher told me.

When we got back to the garage, we heard an explosion, the garage door blew open, and the next thing I knew we were both on the ground. Both of us rushed over to where the policeman and convict had been, but there was nothing left of them. That day and what I witnessed will always be burned into my memory.

THE FÜHRER

It was fair to say that I was naive to the ways of the world during the first part of my stay in Germany. The world was in the midst of war, and I could watch the destruction from my doorstep. But even so I knew very little about it. For instance, I knew the name Adolf Hitler and understood he was the leader of the Nazi Party, but like most Bulgarians and Germans at the time, I did not fully appreciate what he represented, nor did I have a good grasp of his political manipulations.

To a great many people in Germany during the early days of the Second World War, Hitler was like a saviour. Having overseen Germany's economic rise from the deepest of depressions, Hitler had given hope to many. Incredibly, it appeared that very few people understood the nature or the extent of the atrocities he was in the midst of committing. The people I met and spoke to seemed to have no knowledge of the Holocaust or the concentration camps. If there was talk of Hitler's true intentions at the time, it was no more than an occasional whisper or offhand comment.

As I would later learn, one of the concentration camps was actually located a mere ten miles from Wels, hidden behind ten-foot fences and branded with signs that read VERBOTEN, German for FORBIDDEN. I passed the camp many times while driving a truck filled with produce throughout the country, oblivious to the horrors taking place behind its walls.

In February 1943, Hitler came to Wels on a tour celebrating the anniversary of his National Socialist Party taking power in Germany. Every citizen in town was made to line the streets. A "great hero" was coming through, and we were to greet him with enthusiastic appreciation. By this point, though, the war had been going on for more than three years. People in Germany were tired of living in wartime conditions, the violence, fear, and adverse living conditions having gradually taken their toll.

The streets were lined with citizens as we waited for the exalted leader. When Hitler appeared, his soldiers circulated through the crowd as every person in attendance raised his or her arm in salute. Unfortunately, the Bulgarians with whom I worked did not understand the German language, and therefore could not comprehend that they, too, were expected to raise their right arms. One of my friends failed to salute the Führer as he appeared before us. It was nearly a fatal mistake.

Before I had the chance to translate the orders, one of Hitler's henchmen stormed toward my friend. The soldier screamed right in my friend's face as spittle flew from the corners of his mouth. "Get your arm up right now, you pig!"

My friend still did not understand the command but raised his arm ever so slightly.

"Raise it higher, swine!"

He finally brought his arm to a suitable height for salute. Had the German concluded that my friend was being intentionally defiant he could have suffered a far worse fate.

It was the first and last time I would see the Führer in person. Frightening as that day might have been, eventually the day came when I learned, to my horror, much more about the terror he had brought upon Europe and the secret world he had created to enslave and exterminate "non-Aryans" and other so-called undesirables, including Slavs, a group to which I belong.

COMING HOME

The longer I stayed away from Bulgaria the more homesick I became. I was about to turn seventeen, but regardless of my maturity and self-sufficiency I could not stop thinking about my family. Day after day I found myself wishing that I was riding our horse-drawn carriage next to my father or enjoying a meal with my brothers and sisters, lovingly prepared by my mother. I was excelling in my new life in working for Bai Kolyo, but there was no substitute for the family life that I so cherished.

My time away might have been easier if I could have written or spoken with those back home. In the early 1940s, though, private citizens in Gorno Ablanovo did not have telephones; they were only found in public institutions such as the post office. I could not simply dial up my family for a casual conversation. My homesickness was made worse by the fact that I was unable to receive letters from my family through the mail service. I did not know that the Bulgarian government had been intercepting the letters that my father tried to send me, as well as the ones I had been sending home. Therefore, I had almost no communication with my family during the first part of my stay in Germany.

Night after night I lay in bed thinking about my family, wondering what they were doing, imagining myself happily reunited with them. On the surface, I presented myself as a confident young man, proficient in my work and ambitious about my future; in reality, I was just a boy who wanted nothing more than to hug his mother and father.

Finally, I reached a breaking point. I could stay away no longer. After clearing it with Bai Kolyo, I took a leave of absence from work on October 6, 1943, on the occasion of my seventeenth birthday. I would return to Gorno Ablanovo for a visit. Unlike most of the Bulgarians working in

Germany, I had not been returning home during the off-season because travel was too expensive for me.

With no way of letting my family know, I made my way home completely unannounced. I booked a train ticket and travelled by myself, bubbling over with excitement that I would soon be face to face with all the people I most loved. Following an uneventful trip by train through Serbia and Hungary once again, at long last I was back in Bulgaria.

It might have been a case of the heart growing fonder with absence, but my visions of the Bulgaria I left more than two years before hardly resembled the place to which I returned. As I walked the streets of Gorno Ablanovo, the state of the village was much worse than I remembered. The buildings looked dilapidated and the people appeared tired, hungry, and downtrodden. I wondered if the beautiful little village that I left behind had only been a figment of my youthful imagination. Compared to what I had come to know in Germany — or even my childhood memories of Bulgaria — my hometown seemed nothing short of dreary.

While supplying produce and other goods to power Germany's war machine had at first been a boon to the Bulgarian economy, it had brought with it a terrible downside: along with the extra cash that now lined farmers' pockets, so, too, had come shortages and inflation. Bulgaria had been forced to provide Germany with more than it could comfortably afford to sell, leaving precious little remaining for Bulgarian consumption. This caused the price of almost everything to skyrocket. The average Bulgarian farmer now had a few extra dollars in his wallet, but he also had even less purchasing power than before. As my father would explain to me later, having money was worthless if it could not be used to buy a coat to keep you warm in the winter. Once again my beloved Bulgaria was struggling.

After my nostalgic and somewhat disheartening stroll through the village, I finally came to my family's home. I passed through its front doors like a prodigal son. There stood my mother, my father, and several of my siblings, with expressions of shock painted across their faces. My mother dropped what she was doing and rushed over to greet me. Her eyes welled with tears.

"Gatyu, you've come home," she cried. "I was worried I'd never see you again."

My mother embraced me tightly, reminding me why I had come home in the first place. I had missed her terribly.

My brothers and sisters followed, hugging and kissing me. Only my father waited until the commotion died down. When it finally did, he slowly approached me.

My father and I shared a special bond, and I fully expected him to greet me with love, happiness, and excitement. It had been so long since we had last seen each other. But, as he slowly approached, my father cocked his head to the side, squinted, and addressed me with words I did not expect.

"What the hell are you doing here?" he asked.

I was shaken for two reasons. First, my father never swore, and second, why would he see my visit home as anything less than a blessing?

He furrowed his brow, wearing the worried look I knew well. "Son, you should have stayed away."

My father understood that it was much easier to enter Bulgaria than to leave. He explained to me that although I was still too young to join the military, the government would want to keep me in the country until I was old enough to serve Bulgaria. That explained his puzzling greeting; he was thinking ahead and looking out for me.

Just as I had dreamed it, my first night back home was the joyful family reunion I so desired. Word of my return soon trickled through the village, drawing a mass of visitors to come knock on our door. I saw everybody and talked about everything. I was so happy to be home again.

But these good feelings would not last long. There were new problems on the horizon.

RETURNING TO GERMANY – MY NEW HOME

The very next morning I went to the Regional Government Police Department headquarters in the city of Byala to ask for an exit visa. Unfortunately, the Bulgarian government saw me as a soldier of the not-so-distant future. It had every intention of keeping me in the country until I was old enough to serve in the military. And, as my father knew, the Russians would soon be in Bulgaria.

I had grown up listening to my father's war stories. These were not tales of glory but rather ones of horror and tragedy. I knew of some boys who craved the action and excitement of battle, but I was not one of them. I could only picture death and destruction.

First and foremost, I saw myself as a businessman, far more inclined to strike a deal than fire a gun. It was my intention to become a somebody, and I could not see myself ever receiving that opportunity if forced to join the Bulgarian military.

After my first request for an exit visa was denied, I found myself trapped in Bulgaria indefinitely. Like all boys my age, I was subjected to a battery of tests to determine my eligibility for the military. After being poked and prodded by a doctor, I was deemed to be of sufficient fitness to fight for my country. In one year, I would be forced to enlist.

The officer explained the terms of my eligibility, and I waited for him to finish before asking if there was any way to leave Bulgaria from now until my eighteenth birthday. After all, I saw no sense in staying around the village when I could be making far more money for my family — and the Bulgarian economy — by working in Germany for Bai Kolyo.

The officer could not grant me permission on the spot. He seemed skeptical that I would receive it at all but advised me to come back the following day to apply for my free release. Heeding his instructions, I woke up early the next morning, mounted one of the family horses, and trekked the twenty-five miles or so to Byala.

Upon my arrival, I walked into the military office and asked for a free release to get myself out of Bulgaria. I was not the first person to make such a request, nor would I be the last. The man working in the office hardly looked in my direction before giving me his answer.

"To gain your free release," the uniformed man said, "you must give the government 17,000 leva as a deposit to guarantee you'll return to Bulgaria when you turn eighteen."

To me, 17,000 leva was an astronomical sum. I had done well in Germany, but nearly everything I earned had been sent home to help my family. I had no bank account of my own from which I could withdraw the funds I needed to get out of the country. At that moment the unthinkable seemed possible for the first time: I could be stuck in Bulgaria for good.

Once again I turned to my father for help and put my fate in his hands. As always, he rescued me. Incredibly, he had saved nearly every penny I had sent to my family from Germany.

"Son," he said, "I knew the day would come when you would need the money you've earned."

Unfortunately, getting myself out of Bulgaria was not as easy as just handing over a pile of bills. After receiving the money from my father, I once again travelled the twenty-five miles back to Byala. I arrived at the office and was met by a bureaucrat who promptly gave me the runaround, saying there was a backlog in paperwork and it might take quite a while for my application to be processed.

"So when can I get my free release?" I asked the bureaucrat.

"You can try again tomorrow."

The next morning I woke up and made the same journey to Byala on horseback. Once again I stepped to the counter with my money and requested my free release. And, once again I was told to come back another day; today was not a good day to process my application. No further reason was given. After several other attempts, it was becoming apparent that the reason I was unable to leave Bulgaria had little to do with paperwork. I was being held in the country against my will.

Day after day I did the same thing: I woke up, ate breakfast, and rode to Byala. Every day I returned home disappointed, and with the same 17,000 leva in my pocket. Time after time I was denied free release due to dubious technicalities. I finally deposited the money with the regional government in Byala, but this act in no way guaranteed I would receive a free release from the country.

Despite the lack of co-operation I received from the government, I never allowed myself to believe I would be permanently stuck in Bulgaria. Had I lost faith in getting back to Germany, I would have started looking for a job. But I never did. I simply returned to Byala day after day, week after week, in the hope of being granted my free release. I never gave up, even when the situation appeared darkest. I felt in my heart that I was destined for big things and knew those big things awaited me in Germany. I would get back there somehow.

After months of frustration, my prayers were finally answered. In a stroke of sheer luck, my father bumped into an old friend with whom he had served on the Macedonian front during the First World War. My father's old friend had a son working with the Thirty-First Infantry in Svishtov. I was told to go to this military office for my free release. It was a long shot, but the man told my father that he would ask his son to do all he could to help me find a way out of Bulgaria.

The next day I rode my horse twenty-five miles to the Thirty-First Infantry office. This would mark my best chance at getting out of the country, and I felt the tension in the pit of my stomach. If this man's son could not help me, I might be at the end of my rope.

I arrived at the military office and quickly identified the son of my father's friend. He was a tall man dressed in an impressive military-green uniform. Unlike most soldiers with their stoic bearing, this man wore a warm smile. He and I quickly bonded over the fact that we both spoke German before briefly discussing our fathers. With that, the ice was broken. Mere minutes after meeting him, my mind was finally at ease; I knew this man would help me get back to Germany.

I handed him the receipt for the warranty money I had deposited in Byala, and he stamped my passport with an exit visa. Before I left, the man offered me a parting piece of advice. "Get out of Bulgaria as fast as you can. The Russians are coming. You don't want to be around when they get here."

I trusted this man and would heed his warning. I walked out of the Thirty-First Infantry office, went straight home, and made plans to leave the country at once.

My quick visit to Bulgaria in October 1943 ended up lasting more than five months. By the time I was able to leave the country, it was already February 1944, and I was itching to get back to Germany to work.

I would be gone within days of gaining my free release, and this time even I knew it would be many years before I would see my family again. I had no intention of returning to serve in the military when I turned eighteen, which meant I would soon be considered a criminal in my own country. Saying goodbye was even more agonizing, given the knowledge I might never be able to return.

The night before I left Bulgaria my family threw a big farewell party in my honour. Nearly everybody I knew from childhood was there, and they filled our house to eat, drink, and offer me their best wishes. It felt as though I had all of Bulgaria cheering me on as I prepared to return to face my future in Germany. As always, my tight-knit community gave me strength. Bulgaria would always remain a part of me.

I rose the next morning, my heart full with love. After I said goodbye to my weeping mother and sisters, my father took me to the train station. This time he did not attempt to conceal the truth from me, since my experience in Germany had exposed me to the realities of the world. My father and I both understood that we would not be able to see each other again for many years, if ever.

Any hope I possessed of becoming a somebody was entirely due to his influence. He had taught me well, and I attributed all of my success to him. I tried to speak, but the words would not come. I wanted to tell my father what he meant to me. I wanted to tell him he was my hero. I wanted to tell him I loved him.

Instead, through teary eyes and a hoarse voice, I could only muster the faint whimper of two words. "Thank you."

My father started to cry and pulled me into his arms. Hugging me, he offered his own parting words. "Son, I wish you nothing but the very best."

I was leaving Bulgaria once again. This time there was no going back.

6

Independence

My journey toward independence began in earnest when I left Bulgaria for the second time on February 8, 1944. Until the moment my father and I parted ways at the train station near Gorno Ablanovo, I had felt very connected to my family; I felt as though I was part of something special even when I was far away, knowing I could go back at any time. But those were my feelings during the first trip to Germany; this time returning to Germany was different. I had paid a steep price for my free release, and there was no going back for me. I was completely isolated from my home, and for the first time in my life I was truly on my own.

For better or worse, I was forced to stand on my own two feet, depending only on myself as a seventeen-year-old boy. I should have felt overwhelmed, but I was so blinded by enthusiasm about returning to Germany that I did not even consider the dangers of the path I was taking. I could only see my bright future on the horizon. More than ever I believed I could become a somebody.

JOURNEYING BACK

I had little time to ponder my new independence, since I was forced to make critical decisions for myself right away. After a brief train ride, I arrived in Sofia, only to learn that the city had been bombed the night before. This was the first attack on Bulgarian soil during the Second World War, leaving the city's residents in a panic.

Although it had not been damaged during the attacks, Sofia's train station was operating in a state of chaos. Everyone was running around manically, trying to find a train amid a general feeling of aimlessness. Thanks to my experiences in Germany, I was in a better position than other Bulgarians in Sofia to process the violence that had just struck.

I did all I could to keep my fear in check. I needed to ensure that I made it back safely. I understood by now how to remain calm and focused in the attack's aftermath, and I knew a wrong turn could prevent me from getting to where I needed to be.

Fortunately, among all the confusion, I ran into my Uncle Kris at the train station. He was my father's cousin and a soldier in the Bulgarian Occupational Army, stationed in Serbia. I had never seen him before in uniform. If he had not stopped me, I might have walked right past him.

"What are you doing here, Gatyu?" asked Uncle Kris. "Where are you going?"

"I'm going to Germany," I told him.

"How do you plan to get there?" he asked.

"I'm going through Serbia and Croatia."

Uncle Kris shook his head disapprovingly and told me I could not go through Croatia. It was an unsafe place for travellers. He advised me to change my plans immediately.

"Every train in Croatia has been knocked down by Serbian partisans," he reported. "Don't go through Croatia. Go through Romania and Hungary."

I took Uncle Kris's advice. The route through Romania and Hungary was a longer one, but it offered the best chance of making it safely to my destination.

Uncle Kris and I hopped aboard a train and rode together to Ruse, nearly two hundred miles to the northeast. When we arrived at the Bulgarian-Romanian border, there were customs officers conducting baggage checks. Before I left home my father had given me more packs of cigarettes than allowed. They were quickly confiscated by one of the officers. I did not smoke in those days, but my father wanted me to use the cigarettes as a form of currency if the need arose.

Coincidentally, the head border officer was a man from my village. In fact, he was my elementary school teacher's husband and another old friend of my father's. He recognized me immediately.

"Gatyu, if I'd known you were coming, I could have turned a blind eye to these cigarettes," he said. "Unfortunately, I can't let you cross the border with them now, but I can return them to your father the next time I see him in the village."

Travellers were only allowed to carry five packs of cigarettes across the border, so I stuffed those packs into my coat pockets and gave up the rest. As I found out much later, my teacher's husband did give the cigarettes back to my father when they ran into each other at the farmers' co-op the next day. When he saw my father, the border officer said to him, "I have your cigarettes. I grabbed them from Gatyu when I ran into him at the train station in Ruse."

My father stared at his friend blankly, taking a moment to process what had been said before replying. "You couldn't have seen Gatyu in Ruse. I just dropped him off on his way to Sofia yesterday."

My father did not understand how or why I could have made the long trip from Sofia to Ruse in such a short time. He could not believe it, but the fact that this man had the cigarettes proved his claim to be true.

The man explained to my father that I was crossing into Romania through Bucharest, but that I had not told him my reasons. I did not mention anything about the bombing in Sofia, nor did I reveal any of my other travel plans.

Years later, when we could finally communicate, I told my father about the situation in Sofia and my chance encounter with Uncle Kris. At the time my father could only guess why I ended up in Ruse. All he could do was hope and pray that I made it back to Germany safely.

When I arrived in Bucharest, I used the few words of Romanian I knew to let the baggage handler know I was travelling to Germany. All the trains arrived at the same time in one area of the station, just as in Budapest, Hungary, and Paris. This made for a confusing scene. I asked the baggage handler, "Where's the train going to Germany?" Without answering me, he picked up my two heavy bags and placed them on the steps of a train just as it began to move. Had I arrived even a minute later, I would have missed the train.

I boarded a train that was already moving, hoping the baggage handler had understood me when I told him I was going to Germany. If my spoken Romanian had let me down, who knows where I might have ended up?

Once aboard the train, I hauled my luggage into the cabin. Immediately, I noticed all the passengers were German military men, just as on my trip to Passau when I was working for Bai Kolyo. While I was relieved to confirm that this train was, in fact, going to Germany, I swallowed nervously as I felt them eyeing me suspiciously. Who was I? And why was I aboard their train? Once again I was a mouse among men.

Just then one of the brawny military men approached me. "What are you doing here, little boy?" he asked as he towered over me.

"I'm travelling to Germany," I squeaked.

"And where do you come from?"

"I'm Bulgarian."

His eyes lit up. "Bulgarian? Why didn't you say so?"

This man and his fellow soldiers had been in Bulgaria en route to Greece in 1941. He had had a great time in my home country, reporting that everybody in Bulgaria had treated him with kindness and respect. Right away they welcomed me into their group, made room for me to sit, and helped me lift my heavy bags into the overhead rack.

The soldiers brought a festive atmosphere to our ride. They were playing instruments and singing as if they were going on vacation, though they were simply heading to Berlin for a weekend off before being sent to a different front. Still, the train was filled with merriment, and I felt a tremendous sense of relief knowing I could relax and enjoy this leg of my journey.

Sometime into our trip the train staff began serving food to all the passengers. They fed us little sandwiches of bread, meat, and cheese. I was so elated that I asked one of the soldiers to reach up to the overhead storage and pull down my luggage.

I opened one of my bags on a little table next to the window, pulling out a big jug of wine and an entire smoked ham, one of four I was carrying with me. My father had given them to me to share with my friends in Wels. But since these soldiers were being so nice to me, I chose to share my gifts with them. I passed around the wine, and the soldiers all took big gulps straight from the jug. Then I pulled out my pocket knife and began slicing off pieces of the delicious ham.

"Come here, guys," I called to them. "Come and eat with me."

We ate, drank, and sang for most of the forty-hour trip. It was only just before our train could pass into Germany from Hungary that I was jolted by one last bump in the road.

Upon reaching the German border, a Hungarian customs officer stepped onto our train, scanning around for any non-military personnel. This was a military train, after all, and as a civilian I had no authority to travel on it.

"Are there any civilians on this train?" the officer asked.

"None," answered one of my new German friends.

The customs officer continued to look around the cabin, eventually zeroing in on me, surely suspicious of my presence. I was not dressed like the others, and I certainly did not look like a military man.

"Who is this little boy?" he asked.

Without prompting, one of the Germans rose from his seat and spoke up on my behalf, assuring the customs officer that I was part of the group.

"He's with us," said the soldier. "He's one of us."

Had they not counted me as one of their own, I would have likely been made to leave the train. I had acquired a Hungarian transit visa in Sofia, so the border officer would have eventually had to let me go, but thanks to my German friends he did not even ask to look at my travel documents.

After that one stop, our train went straight into Vienna. From there I split off from my German friends. They went to Berlin and I headed to

Salzburg. My train came to a stop, and I took one step off the car only to find myself overjoyed by the ground on which I stood. After many agonizing months of uncertainty, I had finally made it to Germany. At long last I was back.

UNCLE GEORGE

Upon arriving in Salzburg, I quickly realized the violence had not quieted since I had been away. If anything, it was worse. From the moment I left the train, I noticed the huge anti-aircraft artillery guns mounted on all the tall buildings. I had never seen such a thing before my visit to Bulgaria. This was a clear sign the war had escalated in danger.

Finding myself in Salzburg, I decided to visit an old family friend, Uncle George Davidoff. Uncle George's family lived in a small wooden house near the back of a large piece of land. I arrived at their home in the early evening, only a few hours before the air raid sirens began to wail at eleven o'clock. The sound alerted Uncle George — like everybody else in Salzburg — to draw the blinds on his doors and windows. When the Allied forces flew over the area at night, the first wave of planes dropped flares that lit up the sky for the bombers.

The government instructed everyone in town to darken all the lights in their houses so that Allied bombers could not see the city from the sky. But even when we made the house as dark as possible, you could still thread a needle inside because of the flares. Uncle George's thick black curtains posed no match for the blinding lights criss-crossing the sky.

On that first night, only the damp weather saved us from destruction. The moisture in the air quickly snuffed out the flares. The bombers could not see their targets, so they dropped their loads on the outskirts of the city. The airport was damaged and a few farms were destroyed, but many lives were spared thanks to the fizzled flares.

Uncle George — with whom I would remain close until the time of his death many years later — knew about the work I had been doing in Germany before my arrival in Salzburg. His brother, Angel, owned a business in Wels and spoke about me to Uncle George. Being the owner of a market gardening business himself, Uncle George offered me a job doing work that was very similar to what I had done for Bai Kolyo: selling produce in the market every day. I accepted the position. With that, I settled in for an indefinite stay in Salzburg.

We survived many bombings during my time in Salzburg, often taking cover in a bomb shelter beneath the castle about three hundred yards from Uncle George's house. Amazingly, we were almost never scared of being killed. We always knew ahead of time when the Allied bombers were coming in. The air raid siren would blare out in increasingly longer spurts as the threat got closer. By the time the bombs started dropping, we were already safe inside the shelter.

I liked working for Uncle George and enjoyed living with his family. My original intention had been to visit Salzburg only briefly, but the time slipped by so quickly. I ended up staying in Salzburg for many months, finally leaving at the end of September 1944.

After so long in Salzburg, I decided finally to make my way back to Wels to resume the life I had unintentionally left behind so many months earlier. I was returning to the city I had come to consider my new home.

BAI KOLYO GOES HOME

I finally got back to Wels on September 30, 1944. To my surprise, Bai Kolyo was already gone by the time I had returned. He had been notified that the Russians would soon be at the Bulgarian border, so he had hopped aboard a train and snuck back into Bulgaria. He never returned to Wels.

To me, Bai Kolyo's departure meant the unmistakable loss of a mentor. I was left to fend entirely for myself in Germany. He had served as a father figure in the absence of my actual father. Now, for the first time, I would be forced to rely on my own wits and best judgment for survival.

As I would only come to learn many years later, Bai Kolyo was appointed mayor in his hometown of Draganovo as soon as he returned. A village of about three to four thousand people, Draganovo was among the richest places in Bulgaria, considered to be our country's answer to Paris or Bavaria. Nearly every household had someone making a living in Germany or elsewhere in Western Europe. Therefore, just about everybody in the village had money, as evidenced by the many beautiful homes lining the streets.

In addition to its wealth, Draganovo was also naturally beautiful, and the architecture was unlike anything else you would find in Bulgaria. From the perspective of a child growing up in Gorno Ablanovo, Draganovo was one of the best villages in the world.

Before I left for Germany for the first time, Bai Kolyo took me and his other new Bulgarian employees to visit his house in Draganovo. It was massive and breathtaking, far beyond anything I had seen in Gorno Ablanovo. The rest of the village was just as impressive. From that memory alone I could understand why Bai Kolyo would leave a successful business in Wels to go back home. Additionally, being appointed mayor of Draganovo must have been a great honour for him.

I would not see Bai Kolyo again until 1968, and it was only then that I learned his biggest secret: Bai Kolyo was a communist, or at least he was during the time I worked for him. Unknown to me, Bai Kolyo was pro-Russian, even though he presented himself as the opposite. A wealthy man, he was far from the sort of person one might expect to side with communism's ideals. But, for many reasons, he believed that communism would benefit Bulgaria.

Looking back, I should have probably suspected that Bai Kolyo was a communist based on what I saw while working for him in Wels. He liked to listen to Radio Moscow, which was strictly forbidden. Bai Kolyo would get a few of his employees to line the street while he listened so that they could give him a signal to change the channel if they saw somebody coming. In those days, I was too naive to understand what listening to Radio Moscow meant about Bai Kolyo.

Although the Russians directly appointed him mayor in Draganovo, Bai Kolyo would have been a strong candidate even if there had been an election. He was a rich, intelligent, handsome gentleman, capable of speaking German, Russian, Czech, and of course, Bulgarian, all fluently. Given his abilities as a leader and a businessman, he was nothing short of the ideal choice for mayor.

Unfortunately, it was not long into Bai Kolyo's mayoral term that he caught his first glimpse of communism's dark side. It was then — and only then — that he finally realized the political system implemented by the Russians did not live up to the ideals of equality and egalitarianism that it claimed to espouse or hold up. After witnessing a bone-chilling act of violence, Bai Kolyo turned his back on the Russians then and there, returning his Communist Party membership card right away. Almost as quickly, he was removed from his position of mayor. Bai Kolyo was no longer Russia's chosen man in Draganovo.

From there Bai Kolyo's life took a difficult turn. Unwilling to support communism in his hometown, he became outspoken in its opposition.

Bai Kolyo was now *persona non grata* in his own village. Once mayor, he was now a second-class citizen. The Russians took away his telephone and his other privileges, too. They made his life uncomfortable in every possible way.

Of course, I knew nothing of Bai Kolyo's life in Bulgaria until many years later. In the autumn of 1944, I was far more concerned with my own situation in Wels. I was told that Uncle George's brother, Angel Davidoff, was now running Bai Kolyo's business. I worked under Angel for about a year, thinking all the while of starting my own venture. I knew I had the experience, the relationships, and the skills to do well for myself in market gardening. With Bai Kolyo back in Bulgaria, I began to consider my future. For the first time, I contemplated life as a self-employed man.

MARISHKA

Despite Bai Kolyo's absence, life went back to normal as soon as I returned to Wels. I worked for Angel Davidoff now, but I did the same job I had always done for Bai Kolyo, toiling away for long hours. As always, I spent most of my evenings in the barrack with the other Bulgarians, eating, resting, and generally passing wartime as one did — making the best we could of a difficult situation. It was only on Saturday nights that we had time to enjoy some fun and recreation in the heart of the city.

Almost every Saturday night a group of friends and I went into town to watch a movie. At this time, when I was just eighteen years old, some of the boys in my group had girlfriends. Others, like me, did not.

Isolated from my family, I found myself longing for the closeness I felt when surrounded by my loved ones. More than a girlfriend, I wanted a close friend, somebody to whom I could talk. Marishka, the daughter of a Hungarian general, came into my life at just the right time.

I was working in the market on the day we met. The crowd of people buying produce was thinner than usual on a crisp autumn afternoon until a big group of Hungarians — including Marishka's family — flooded the market with their booming presence. I noticed Marishka immediately, trailing behind as her mother approached my stall to buy vegetables. She was a very pretty girl and impossible not to notice in her traditional Hungarian embroidered shirt and long skirt. Although I was not struck by love at first sight, Marishka definitely caught my eye.

After buying fruit and vegetables, Marishka's mother asked me if she could also purchase a few pounds of flour. I had no flour, but luckily I did know someone who worked at a flour mill near the market, and I offered to escort the entire group of Hungarians to see him. It was a thinly veiled scheme to spend more time with Marishka, hoping she would notice me. Incredibly, it worked. We had a chance to speak and made plans to see each other again in the coming days.

As I got to know Marishka, I learned about the way she and her family had come to live in Germany. In those days, many Hungarian military officers and their families lived in Wels and throughout the rest of the country. They had left Hungary for Austria during a six-month-long fight along the eastern front during the Second World War. Once the war ended, many of them stayed put, having grown accustomed to the German lifestyle. Hungarians were familiar with the German language and culture from before the First World War, given their many years of integration in the Austro-Hungarian Empire.

Over the next year, Marishka and I spent a considerable amount of time together and became close friends. I never considered what we had to be a serious romantic relationship, but my friendship with Marishka was very important to me. She was my primary source of companionship, comfort, and warmth in Germany. She was my best friend.

Sadly, Marishka and I were never given the opportunity to see where our friendship might lead. In November 1945, the American occupation forces rounded up all the Hungarians they could find in Wels and shipped them out of town on a cattle train. The Americans had made an agreement with the Soviets to return expatriates to their countries of origin. The Hungarians — predominantly soldiers and their families — were told they were being sent back to their home country.

Not only was I devastated by the loss of Marishka, I was also heartbroken to lose her parents, to whom I had grown very close in the absence of my own mother and father. Marishka was my first close female friend, but now she was gone and I would never see her again. Sadly, I only knew her for one year.

The whole family disappeared, vanishing from my life as if they had never existed. It would be a long time before I was able to find out what had happened to Marishka. In the meantime, I was left alone, depressed, and confused.

Many years later I learned that the Americans had handed over the Hungarians to the Soviets, who promised to return them to their homes. However, the Soviets did not hold up their end of the bargain. Instead of sending some forty thousand Hungarians home as promised, they were transported to Siberia where most of them eventually died.

I never heard from Marishka again. It is my hope that she survived her time in Siberia and eventually settled in Russia like some of the more fortunate Hungarians, but I will never know what became of her and her family.

I had lost Bozin, and now Marishka was gone, too. Through these painful experiences, it was becoming clear to me that life could often be unfair and very cruel.

RUN FOR THE FIELDS

The sight of lit flares, the rumble of falling bombs, and the sound of air raid sirens became an all too common part of life in Wels toward the end of 1944. The Germans had substantially built up their anti-aircraft artillery in Vienna; British and American planes were now being shot down with ease. Unwilling to risk further casualties, the Allied forces were compelled to redirect their aircraft to Wels.

For those of us in Wels, the war intensified greatly at this time. The bombings came closer and were now far more frequent. In the barrack, my friends and I had our own ritual for the attacks: we might be sitting down, playing cards, taking a nap, or even eating, but when we heard that alarm wail, every one of us got up from whatever we were doing and ran a mile into the fields.

We felt safe out there. "Nobody is going to bomb us in the fields," we told ourselves. My friends and I believed the Allied forces would surely focus their bombers on the airport in Wels, ignoring the few of us hiding among the vegetables. And for a time we were right. Again and again we dashed to the fields when the planes flew over Wels, and each time they passed us by to focus their fire on the nearby airport, only a few miles away.

Then, one day, we were not so lucky. The air raid siren rang through the city, and as always we dropped whatever we were doing and raced to the fields. I remember being out of breath as we arrived, assuming my normal position within a crop of corn, hoping to find safety there once again. I sat quietly until I heard a dull hum slowly grow into a loud buzz. Finally, I peered up into the sky and saw a fleet of planes heading straight for us. This was not what I had come to expect.

I dropped to the ground in fear. The Allied pilots were supposed to be carpet-bombing the airport, but the Germans had started to retaliate and protect it with increased vigour. As a result, the Allied pilots were instructed not to fly too deeply into the city. That was how our field became the dumping ground for their bombs.

As I glanced up from my position on the ground, a sheet of bombs filled the sky. I watched in horror as they tumbled to the ground and could only close my eyes in terror.

The gravelly soil made the blasts far louder than normal. It was the most fantastic sound, like nothing I had ever heard before, and it seemed to go on and on. The attack might have only lasted seconds, but it felt like an eternity.

Explosions went off all around me. I clenched my eyes shut, unsure if I would survive. Finally, the noise stopped. Silence. There were no more blasts on the ground or engines whirring in the sky. I opened my eyes, carefully, unsure whether this quiet meant the attack was over or if I had gone deaf.

I rose to my feet and dusted off my clothes, looking around to survey the damage, watching as my friends stood one by one. Miraculously, nobody in our group was hurt.

That was the first time we were bombed in the fields, but it was not the last. The Allied forces knew about our hiding spot, and our safety could no longer be assumed. Violence had become part of our daily existence, ever frightening but increasingly expected.

RECONSTRUCTION

By the beginning of 1945, Wels was getting hit with a regular onslaught of bombs. Every morning the city woke up to find more buildings blown apart in the previous night's attack. There was wreckage everywhere.

Wels was being steadily destroyed, but people still needed to live. Those who survived the war needed to have homes. That being the case, the local government went around and enlisted all the boys around my age who were not in the military to help rebuild the houses around town.

I was only too happy to lend a hand. I loved Wels, and the German people had always been good to me. It was my first adopted home outside Bulgaria, and I wanted to do anything I could to help out during these hard times. Of course, even if I had not wanted to help, the government would have forced me to do so against my will.

For the next year, I went out to help rebuild houses twice every week. I was a volunteer, and volunteers did not get paid, but we did get a free lunch. Regardless, I would not have accepted money even if they had offered it to me. I considered it to be my privilege to help rebuild the city.

As it turned out, I was compensated for my time and effort with valuable knowledge, receiving an education in the basics of construction. The Germans worked with remarkable quickness and efficiency. I had seen my father and uncle build my family's house when I was a boy, but the Germans took construction to another level.

I knew almost nothing about construction when we began the rebuilding. I had gleaned a little bit from watching my father and uncle, but back in those days at home I was often away from the job site fetching water. The process of building had always fascinated me, but I had almost no practical experience.

Fortunately, I was placed in a crew with some very skilled builders who eased me into the job gradually. At first I did nothing but sweep sawdust and pick up scraps of wood. But, after some time, I got to cut steel and even do some masonry work, learning the finer points of both from men who understood their trades. Even though I was not getting paid, I approached the job with enthusiasm, constantly asking questions and trying to soak up knowledge.

The Germans were ideal teachers. They applied diligence, order, and a system of hierarchy to the construction process, restoring the homes brick by brick, and doing so with incredible precision. I was amazed by their discipline and inspired by their intelligence and planning.

I began to discover my passion for building. I loved seeing the houses go up and was delighted by the feeling of creating something solid that came with it. I was also discovering that I possessed instincts and a good eye for construction, traits that cannot be acquired or taught. I was able to develop those instincts over the many years to come.

Restoring houses in Wels filled me with a feeling of accomplishment, but even that was less exciting than what I had discovered about myself: I had a passion — not to mention an aptitude — for construction. At the time I could only hope it would somehow figure in my future.

MY OWN BOSS

By May 1945, I decided the time was finally right to start my own business. Of course, there was a series of steps I had to follow to get my new company, which I proudly named Bulgarian Market Garden, up and running in Wels. There was much to do, but I was excited and happy to be calling the shots for my own enterprise.

First and foremost I had to rent a plot of land. German law of the day stated that to be eligible for a licence to buy and sell produce at wholesale, you had to grow at least a portion of your own supply. I searched around for a rental property before happening upon a nice plot of land equipped with a beautiful farmhouse. I inquired about the rental price and was amazed to discover that it cost almost nothing. I moved into the house immediately, since it had everything I needed.

After that I was the beneficiary of some major luck. By chance, I found out from a friend that the government was burning thousands of military vehicles in a nearby field. I rushed out, hoping to save one for myself. A vehicle of my own would mean everything to my new business; without it I would have to get around on horseback like all of my competitors. I made it to the field just in time to buy my first truck, a Steyr. I was proud to call it my own.

I got the truck for just 300 Austrian schillings, a small price to pay. The truck cost far less than it would have under typical market conditions. Normally, a man in my position could not have afforded such a vehicle. But now, due to the government's fire sale, I was suddenly a new business owner running circles around the competition. I had motorized transportation and my rivals did not. It provided me with a major advantage in the marketplace.

In those first days of running the business, my work was a labour of love. I continued to buy vegetables from the same suppliers I had dealt with while working for Bai Kolyo, and I planted my own fields, as well. My company was small at first, but I had clients who wanted to buy my produce right from the beginning. Between working in the market, checking my fields, and running around to buy and sell produce, I was incredibly busy. I worked every day to cultivate the business, and I could feel it growing all the time.

Although it was still only a small seedling I had planted, Bulgarian Market Garden was, to me, a big success from the start. Thanks to all the years I spent working for Bai Kolyo, Uncle George, and Angel Davidoff, I knew exactly what I was doing and had already formed important relationships. And, with my new truck, I was able to do my job very quickly, getting to and from the fields in about ten minutes, as opposed to almost an hour on horseback.

I was only nineteen years old, but I already had nearly five years of experience in the industry. I had shown myself to be a fast learner, and I was ready to be successful on my own. I knew all the buyers in and around Wels, I knew how to speak to them, and most important, I knew how to make sales. My clients always understood that I was telling them the truth, and I believe that earned me their respect. I was known around the city as a hard-working boy with a good sense of humour. Everybody seemed to like me, and I got the sense that they wanted to see me succeed.

I was mature, responsible, and ready for the challenges that awaited me as a business owner. Everything was falling into place.

THE WAR COMES TO AN END

During the spring of 1945, one of my favourite customers was a nice German man named Mr. Zwerger, a city councillor and the owner of a clothing store in town. Mr. Zwerger also had the defining characteristic of being more prepared for bombings than anyone else I knew.

My client had an elaborate bomb shelter built into the basement of his house. After I had been delivering groceries to this man every Saturday for months, he finally decided to show it to me.

The shelter had everything: comfortable beds and a bathroom, along with vast quantities of food and water. It was spacious and made out of heavy concrete, virtually indestructible. I had been in a bomb shelter before, but nothing that approached the level of comfort found in Mr. Zwerger's basement.

Over time, Mr. Zwerger and I became friends. He liked to talk and I was always happy to listen. Eventually, we became close enough that Mr. Zwerger told me to take shelter with him the next time the air raid sirens rang out over Wels.

However, before I ever had a need to use his shelter, Mr. Zwerger broke some major news to me during one of my Saturday deliveries.

"Wels has been declared a free city," he told me. "We still have the bunker in the basement in case we ever need it, but it doesn't look like we will. There won't be any more fighting here."

It was becoming clear that the war would soon end. Germany was under constant attack, and we could see that the Allied forces were only getting stronger. We were told the Americans would soon be coming into Wels.

Even though the war was at an end, I learned there had been a big disturbance in Passau during the past few days. The German Army was ordered to leave the city, but it wanted to cause any kind of damage possible before departing. In those last days, the German soldiers managed to destroy a large number of Allied tanks.

The next day, May 7, 1945, I heard that the Americans were entering Wels, something I wanted to see myself. As I pedalled my bicycle to Mr. Zwerger's part of town — he lived near the train station where the soldiers would be arriving — I could see the flares of rockets flying through the sky toward a three-engine plane. The aircraft was hit and caught fire in midair. It smoked through the clouds and was out of sight before it hit the ground. Later on I heard that the plane managed to land safely at the nearby airport. The rocket strike was quite a sight to behold!

As I approached the intersection near the train station, I noticed right away that American jeeps equipped with machine guns were all over the place. "Holy smokes," I said to myself, and continued to pedal.

I got to the train station and watched in amazement as all the German soldiers approached with their rucksacks in hand. In a very orderly manner, they were leaving the area to report elsewhere. The Americans were supervising their march out of town, simply instructing the Germans to throw their firearms into a pile before directing them onto a train.

It was about five o'clock in the afternoon when I arrived at the scene. I stood in awe with a large group of people as the sun blazed down upon us. We all spoke peacefully among ourselves, trying to make sense of the spectacle playing out before us. I understood that I was seeing history in the making, even if I could not fully grasp the huge scope of what I was witnessing.

It was still hard to believe that the war was actually ending. An official announcement had not yet been made to the public. Then, just as it was dawning on me that the violence and terror might be coming to an end, somebody pointed to the horizon and cried out, "The prisoners are coming!"

The Americans had opened the gates to a prison camp just outside town, and a horde of prisoners were descending onto Wels in a wild scene. These were not prisoners of war or political detainees, but actual criminal convicts being released for the simple reason that the Americans had no interest in upholding the punishments for their crimes. They were unwilling to pay to imprison these potentially dangerous men in a land not their own. Later on I found out that some of the released prisoners went straight to a local bank and tried to rob it. In that moment, however, their presence presented a far more personal threat.

As I watched wave upon wave of released prisoners flowing through, one of the men tried to grab my bicycle as I was holding it. Luckily, I was able to hang on. After a few moments of struggle, the man gave up, most likely so he could go off and try to steal something else.

Amazingly, just as the action of the day seemed to reach its highest pitch, all of the excitement ended. For all intents and purposes, the war had ended, not with a bang but with a whimper. There was nothing left to see. I never even made it over to Mr. Zwerger's house. I had seen what I had come to see and was satisfied to return home quietly. I was anxious to begin leading my postwar existence.

The next day, May 8, 1945, the Allies formally accepted Nazi Germany's unconditional surrender.

PEACETIME

The Second World War officially ended on September 2, 1945, with Japan's surrender. From that day forward I was able to focus entirely on building my new business. I had a truck, the needed skills, and a foothold in the industry. All I needed now was time to grow my company. I never expected the business to take off right away, but I knew that if I treated my company like a garden, planting the seeds of success and cultivating them with care, I would eventually achieve my goals.

During the early days of running my own company, I did not market to Graz because it was too far away, almost 250 miles. Toward the end of 1945, however, I became friendly with a neighbour who was also a big landowner in Croatia. He told me about his landowner friend who was doing big business as a market gardener in Graz. My neighbour believed that Graz was the perfect place for a young, ambitious man like me.

"Natzl, why don't you move to Graz and have a partnership with that landowner?" he asked. Germans and Austrians called me Natzl rather than Gatyu, Iggy, or Ignat. They derived it from the last three letters of my first name and added *zl* to it, a common practice with Germans when a name wasn't common in their language.

"He has all the equipment you'd need to do really well," my neighbour continued. "You could grow far more fruit and vegetables than what you're doing on that small plot of land you have now. You could be successful in a big way!"

I carefully considered my friend's suggestion. In a sense, it was the perfect time for me to make such a move: I was young, unmarried, independent, and ready to do what was necessary to become a somebody. I had already come so far in a short time; moving 250 miles seemed like just another step along my journey to success.

This man with whom I would enter into a partnership had everything I could possibly need: a few hundred acres of land, all the best farming equipment available at the time, and lots of money. I travelled to Graz to meet him and then quickly made the decision to join him in a business. He promised to give me a free hand to do anything I wanted. The offer was too good to pass up; I was moving to Graz.

In early 1946, the Russians left Graz, and I came into town. The Soviet Union had occupied the area until signing an agreement with the Americans, French, and British, at which point the land was turned over to the United Kingdom.

I brought along Bratoi and another acquaintance from Wels to be my employees in Graz. It was nice to have men I knew and trusted working for me in an unfamiliar city. Bratoi, in particular, was a long-time friend and ally.

As my neighbour in Wels described it, Graz was a place where a young man like me could really thrive. I had already left my home in Bulgaria for new opportunities in Anschluss Austria; now it was time to improve my situation by moving to Graz in British-occupied Austria.

During the occupation, I had two chances to see Kanu, my eldest brother. He was a chief mechanic on a Bulgarian boat that transported goods along the Danube River between Bulgaria and Austria. The first time I met him was in Vienna after obtaining the necessary permissions from the Allied Powers. Our second get-together occurred after I received a note from Kanu, saying that he was coming to the Soviet zone of Vienna again on a Saturday morning. By then, I was in a relationship with

Katarina Kern, whom I had met when she began working for me at the market garden. Katarina accompanied me on my second visit to Kanu, but for this trip there was not enough time to secure visas to enter Soviet-controlled Vienna.

At the checkpoint, I said to the Soviet officer in charge, "We're here to see my brother from Bulgaria and he's only here briefly. I know we don't have visas, but is there some way you can let us through?"

After mulling over my request for a moment, the officer said, "All right, but make sure you're back here at 2:00 p.m. I'll be on duty again and will waive you through to the British zone."

Katarina and I had a great time with Kanu, and on Sunday returned to the checkpoint, only to discover that the officer we had dealt with was not there. Despite our protestations, the fellow in charge arrested us and put us in a windowless room, telling us we would stay there until he figured out what to do with us.

I knew if I could speak with the officer who had allowed us to visit my brother I would be able to fix what was becoming an increasingly alarming situation. Over the next few hours, I continually asked to use the bathroom, hoping I might spot the officer in question. Finally, after an excruciating amount of time, I saw the man I was looking for.

"We've been detained," I told him.

"I'm so sorry," he said. "I meant to tell my colleagues about you when I knew I wasn't going to be here at 2:00 p.m., but I forgot. Don't worry. I'll straighten this out."

He was as good as his word. In fact, he accompanied us to the packed bus for Graz, pulled off two people on it, and installed us in their seats.

As always, I was guided by my ambition of becoming a somebody. I had moved to Wels to pursue success, and now I would move a little bit farther. Once again there was little hesitation; I instinctively felt that Graz was the right place for me.

The last few years had taught me a great deal about independence. I had gone through the painful experiences of separation from my family, the death of my best friend, and the sudden departure of my mentor. Through it all, I had endured the most dangerous war in our planet's history. It might have seemed that I was taking a big chance by moving to Graz, but after everything I had already been through, I was not scared in the least.

In my own mind, I was going to Graz to become a great success. I was going there to learn more about my industry, make money for my family, and continue inching toward my goal of becoming a somebody.

7

Graz

I made my way into the unknown yet again, heading to Graz in the early months of 1946 with nothing but my truck and my two employees. Even though I had a free hand to operate a successful business, being in a partnership felt restrictive. Almost immediately I began longing for the day I could become a sole proprietor once again.

I realized, for the first time, that I was at my best when I was the boss of my own business. This would prove true on many occasions throughout my professional life. I needed the independence to make decisions; I thrived on calling the shots and accepting responsibility for my company's fate.

Still, for the time being, I was comfortable in this partnership. It gave me a foothold in Graz, allowing me to start forming important business relationships I would need when the time came to strike out on my own.

Overall, life was pleasant in Graz under Allied occupation. But in the early weeks of the summer of 1946 I bore witness to yet another horrific tragedy. Having finally seen the end of the Second World War, I hoped that violence and heartbreak might stop being a part of my daily existence. Sadly, that would not prove to be the case.

It was a warm morning in Graz. The sun was shining on me through the early-morning mist as I made my way to the fields. I was still getting accustomed to my new surroundings, doing what I could to learn the lay of the land. My new job was similar to what I had been doing in Wels, but the environment was different, and so were all the people. I was trying to be observant, doing my best to quickly learn how business was conducted in my new city.

As I made my way around the fields, one of our employees, a Croatian man, was ploughing a field with a new tractor. I took a moment to stand and watch him operate this impressive piece of machinery.

Suddenly, the man rode over a land mine — it must have been left over from the war — causing a tremendous explosion. Man and tractor disappeared into a fiery blaze, followed by a cloud of smoke and dust. I had to wait for the dust to settle before heading out to look for our employee.

The poor man was nowhere to be found. Even the tractor and its massive rubber tires had been obliterated. For me, this tragedy offered yet another painful reminder of life's impermanence; as we were taught, no man knew his time on earth. I privately resolved to be ever more urgent in pursuing my dreams and thankful to God for my good fortune. How quickly things could change, how suddenly a life could come to an end!

With that in mind, I decided to start my own business once again at the beginning of 1947. During that entire first year in Graz, I could not shake the feeling that having a partner was simply unnecessary for me. If anything, it was holding me back. I wanted nothing more than to have my own business, even if it was just a small operation at first.

I was happy to regain my independence as a businessman and content in the knowledge that I was my own man once again. Amazingly, my new company made a profit right from the start. After just a few months, I was experiencing real prosperity for the first time in my life, selling produce in vast quantities to all kinds of hotels and restaurants in Graz. As it turned out, my new business was in the right place at the right time. I was just the man to be stationed at its head.

With serious income beginning to flow in, I quickly bought a house with a big barn to use for storing produce, which I was buying by the truckload from Vienna to sell in Graz for a tidy profit. The region around Vienna was an extraordinarily prolific agricultural area, known as Europe's breadbasket. Every day I was reaching into this breadbasket and reaping its rewards.

My life in Graz was unfolding better than I could have ever hoped. I had come to form a partnership but quickly realized I was happiest — and most successful — when running a business myself. Coming to Graz was turning out to be one of the best decisions of my life.

DIFFERENTIATING MYSELF FROM THE COMPETITION

In Graz, I was proving to myself that I could run a company that required timely and smart decision-making. It was a time of genuine growth for me. In business, I was learning how to tune in to and trust my instincts.

In the spring of my first growing season, my resourcefulness was put to the test. A terrible hailstorm wiped out nearly all the crops in my area. Like all the other market gardeners in Graz, I was forced to rely entirely on selling produce bought from outside sources.

Nearly every produce company in town — all of my direct competitors — completely gave up on the growing season. Their crops had been crushed beneath the heavy pellets of hail, and they thought it was too late in the season to replant. I, on the other hand, was unwilling to give up so easily.

If I plant some string beans now, I thought to myself, *they could be ready just in time for September when people are buying up vegetables for their winter preserves.*

With that in mind, I sowed a vast tract with string bean seeds and tended the plants all summer with loving care. Painstakingly, I attached a pole to each beanstalk, ensuring each one grew upward. In my first growing season as an independent business owner in Graz, I worked with enthusiasm, energy, and resolve to salvage a harvest.

My efforts paid off. The beans grew strong and true, and by the end of the summer I had a lot of them. Best of all, I was the only market gardener in town with string beans to sell. My competitors were forced to buy their beans wholesale, making their prices less competitive than mine.

When I brought them into the market, my beans caused a sensation. Customers clamoured to buy up my entire supply. I was new to the market gardening scene in Graz, and everybody was surprised that I, of all people, thought to grow beans so late in the season. It was not the first time — nor was it the last — that I would be underestimated as the little newcomer. I took deep satisfaction in defying expectations.

The next summer I had another opportunity to differentiate myself from the competition. This time it was onions that failed to grow in our area of Graz. Of course, every market gardener needed onions to sell in the market. They were always in high demand, since a single hotel usually went through about twenty-two hundred pounds of onions in a week. Like the rest of the farmers in my region, I would have to look elsewhere for my supply.

Fortunately, I had established a good contact in Vienna, a man well known for growing outstanding onions. I called him up and asked, "How are the onions growing in your area this year?"

"Fantastic," he said.

My man in Vienna arranged to bring me a sample of his onions. When they arrived, the strings were still attached to their sides. That gave me an idea. Normally, those little strings would be torn off before the onions were brought to market, but I wanted to keep them on. I thought I could use the strings to tie twenty or thirty onions into a chain, offering ten- or twenty-pound bundles for customers to hang in their houses over the winter. I was convinced my clientele in Graz would be excited to buy onions that I presented this way.

My supplier and I struck a deal for twenty-two thousand pounds of onions. However, when his delivery truck arrived at my house a few days later, it turned out that he had sent me twenty-four thousand pounds instead. I lacked the money on hand to pay for the extra onions, and since his truck driver worked strictly by rule of cash on delivery (or COD), I had to go to my Bulgarian next-door neighbour's house to see if I could get a quick loan.

I made the short walk and rapped on my neighbour's front door. After a few moments, he came outside.

"Listen," I said to him, "can you lend me a few thousand schillings to pay for some onions? The delivery man from Vienna brought me more than I ordered and now I can't pay for them."

Fortunately, my Bulgarian friend had the money in his house to lend me. However, after mulling it over, he was not interested in offering me a straightforward loan. This man had observed me in the market since I had arrived in Graz and had noticed my instinct for sales.

"Gatyu, you always seem to know what people want at the market. Instead of me lending you the money, how about I buy three thousand pounds or so of the onions to sell for myself?"

I agreed to my neighbour's terms without objection. After all, I was in no position to negotiate. We shook hands and he gave me the cash. With me, a handshake was as good as a signed contact. I went back to my barn and paid the delivery man.

My friend later took his onions to the market and put them out in a barrel, just as any other market gardener would do. While I was linking mine together and selling them in bundles of at least ten pounds, my neighbour was selling one or two onions at a time the old-fashioned way. By the end of the week, my instinct about tying the onions together was proven right; I sold every last one. My Bulgarian neighbour was not quite as successful.

I do not claim to be the first person to tie onions into a chain, but as far as I knew, I was the only one doing it in Graz. As always, I did my best to look for little innovations that could make my products stand out among the others. For me, being good was not good enough; I always wanted to be the best.

When I first made the deal with my neighbour, I assured him that if he could not sell the onions within a week, I would buy them back from him, no questions asked. The following Saturday I was driving past his stand at the market when he spotted me.

"Gatyu, come here," he called out. "I need to talk to you about the onions."

"What is it?"

"Would you mind buying them back from me? Nobody around here seems very interested in them."

I upheld my end of the agreement and bought back the onions. In fact, I was happy to do so, because I knew I could sell them in no time.

Backing up my truck to his stand, I then loaded the onions. My neighbour jumped into the passenger seat and accompanied me home to help unload them in my barn.

To be honest, I needed no help with the onions. But my neighbour liked to find any little excuse to visit my house because I always kept some liquor in the kitchen cupboard. I did not drink alcohol in those days, but I liked to have it around for guests. Since my neighbour's wife did not let him drink at home, he stopped at my place frequently.

We made the quick drive through town back to my property. I opened the doors to my barn and then looked on with delight as I watched my friend's jaw drop in shock.

"Gatyu," he stammered, "where are all your onions?"

My entire barn had been full of onions, but now it was empty. I had purchased twenty-one thousand pounds of them, and they were all gone. My neighbour was astonished. To him, the onions might as well have disappeared into thin air. It was like magic. Now, more than ever, he needed a drink.

He took a moment to think before reversing his course once again. "You know what, Gatyu? I think I'd actually like to keep those onions for myself, after all."

I could only laugh. My friend believed that an onion was just an onion, but I knew something different. To me, an onion was actually a commodity. Marketing was the difference between selling onions and having them rot in a barn. I would learn many such lessons about business during my time in Graz, and they would all serve me well in the future.

KATARINA

My first wife, Katarina Kern, was a displaced person from Croatia living in Graz with her family when we met in 1946. Before she and I ever dated, Katarina and her mother were my employees, working for me in the market garden.

Life was harsh in those days for Croatians living in Austria, which had separated once again from Germany in April 1945. Josip Broz Tito had gained control of Croatia and the rest of Yugoslavia after the Second

World War and had become a totalitarian leader, considering himself to be president for life. In November 1945, Tito's People's Front, led by the Communist Party of Yugoslavia, won the national elections by an overwhelming majority.

Tito enjoyed massive popularity because he was considered to be the liberator of Yugoslavia and was credited with uniting a country that had been devastated by war and ultra-nationalist violence.

Although she was born and raised in Croatia, Katarina was of Austrian descent. Before 1918, Croatia was part of the Austro-Hungarian Empire, and Katarina's family had opted to live in Croatia. Unfortunately, her family — like so many others — was kicked out of the country when Tito came to power. Katarina and her family wound up in Graz, where I met the woman who would become my first wife.

From the beginning of our relationship to its very end, I always thought very highly of Katarina. In those early days, she was a pretty young blond girl of about five foot five, the same height as me. She was highly intelligent, and we communicated easily in German, sometimes in Croatian. How did I know Croatian? Back when I was in Wels, I knew some Serbian pilots. We spent our nights together talking in Serbian (or Serbo-Croatian, as the common language of most Yugoslavs was called). It was not very different from Bulgarian.

Katarina reminded me of a typical Bulgarian farm girl, and after so many years away from home, I was drawn to the familiarity I saw in her. We were immigrants, people of the land, and had almost no one else in our new country.

As I came to know Katarina, I saw that she was a kind and good person. She respected me, and we almost never argued. Our relationship progressed quickly and easily. Being together felt natural. We dated for almost a year and a half before getting married in April 1948. At the beginning of springtime in Graz, Katarina and I wed in a small ceremony before a few members of her family.

Katarina was always very supportive of my career ambitions and helped in any way she could. Although our marriage did not stand the test of time, I never regretted the years we spent together. We shared a great deal of happiness, especially in those early days.

Although Katarina and I rarely disagreed, there was one instance in which we had a big argument. It was during the evening, after the market closed, when I was entertaining a few clients from the hospital at one of the hotel restaurants in town. These were important clients who bought quite a lot of produce from me.

Shortly after dinner, while we were still sitting around the table, Katarina suddenly got up and left. Without warning she went home, leaving me alone with my clients. I was stunned that she would desert me.

When I got home later that night, I asked her why she had left the restaurant so abruptly. She had no answer. Quite simply, Katarina was not a social person. My wife did not enjoy mindless chatter, and she had even less tolerance for joking around.

"When I'm entertaining clients, you can't just leave me alone in the middle of an evening," I explained. "I need you to be right there beside me. It's very important."

My wife agreed. I, too, saw that I had no right to be angry with her over a personality trait: Katarina was a serious person, and I had to accept her for who she was.

GO WEST

My life, on both a personal and professional level, was continuing along a good path in Graz. Toward the end of 1950, I was feeling deeply satisfied about so many things: I was happily married, my business was thriving, and I was optimistic about the future. Everything was beginning to fall into place, and then the tables turned. In December 1950, my situation in Graz suddenly became extremely precarious.

As I had feared since leaving the country in 1944, Bulgaria's government had not forgotten about me. I had long since reached the age of majority, and the nation was demanding that I do my duty and serve in the military. I began receiving letters from the Bulgarian embassy in Vienna conveying a simple, direct message: return to Bulgaria and enlist right away.

The very thought of it crushed me. I had come so far and was doing so well in Austria. I wanted to continue with the life I was building. I knew in my heart that I was not a soldier, and I had no desire to fight. I was a businessman meant to operate in the market, not on the battlefield.

Naturally, I ignored the first letter, crumpling it into a little ball before tossing it into the trash bin. I tried to put it out of my mind. Having paid so much to get out of Bulgaria, one little note was not enough to make me run back.

A few weeks passed, and I received a second letter. This one scared me a bit, but still I paid it no mind. Into the garbage it went, as I did my best to forget about it entirely. I went along with my life as if I had never received either letter.

But the third letter in January 1951 frightened me. This one instructed me to report to Yambol, Bulgaria, by May 1, 1951, to enlist in the army. Failure to do so would lead to a warrant for my arrest and prosecution before the Bulgarian Military Court. Once convicted, I would be classified as a deserter, considered to be a major criminal offence.

I was in a precarious position and did not know how to proceed. In the past, I would have asked my father or Bai Kolyo for guidance, but now I was alone with my own predicament. The stakes could not have been higher. Any misstep would mean being sent back to Bulgaria to serve in the army, being thrown in jail, or being tossed away to work in the uranium mines.

After years of building myself up in Austria, the future was suddenly dark and uncertain. I had no idea what to do, but one truth was becoming clear: I was going to have to leave Austria, and do it soon.

Graz was fast becoming a dangerous and hostile place for Bulgarians. The Bulgarian secret police were grabbing people off the street. They would pull up in a car, apprehend an unsuspecting Bulgarian, and drive off without a word. Often they would do this in broad daylight and were even known to go into people's houses to snatch them up. Peter Petroff, a friend of mine from Bulgaria, was abducted while casually strolling through Graz shortly around the time I received my third letter from the Bulgarian embassy in Vienna, sending me into a further panic.

A well-known organizer for the Agrarian Party, Mr. Petroff had anti-establishment political beliefs that made him an easy target. He was popular in his village of Krivina and respected as a public speaker — not unlike my father. This made him an obvious antagonist to the communist government, which had been in control of the country since 1944 and was still keen to reinforce its power.

Mr. Petroff was taken to Sofia. Once there, he was put on Sofia Radio against his will and forced to deliver the government's propaganda message, urging Bulgarians living elsewhere in Europe to return home at once. This went on for several weeks, after which Mr. Petroff presumably outlived his usefulness. He was taken off the radio, never to be heard from again.

As a Bulgarian living in Austria, I suddenly felt the need to look over my shoulder at every turn. I began to live in a state of high anxiety. The secret police could come for me at any moment.

Luckily, I knew one man who might be able to help me get out of Austria. During my time in Graz, I befriended a man named Mr. Frank, to whom I regularly delivered fruit and vegetables. Mr. Frank was a purchasing agent in the British Army, and I knew him as a well-connected person who was always enthusiastic to tell me about the latest happenings throughout Europe. He was a very intelligent man, and I quickly came to trust his opinions about the world.

With nowhere else to turn for advice, I decided to show Mr. Frank the most recent letter from the Bulgarian embassy. I also told him about Peter Petroff. He studied the document, grumbling quietly to himself the entire time. Then he gazed at me with genuine sympathy in his eyes, reached into his pocket, and passed me his business card.

"Here's my contact information," he said. "If anybody comes to apprehend you, call me immediately."

I could only laugh. I was thankful for this offer, but I scoffed at the notion that it would somehow help me.

"Mr. Frank," I said, "once I've been apprehended, there's no way I'll be able to make a phone call to you or anyone else."

Mr. Frank considered my remarks and agreed that I was correct. If abducted, I would be far beyond the reach of anything he or anyone else could do to help me. I would most likely vanish without a trace.

He then presented a more practical suggestion. "Natzl, you should go overseas. Australia, New Zealand, the United States, and Canada are all accepting new immigrants right now."

At this point I was willing to consider any option that did not in-volve the army, jail, or the uranium mines. I listened carefully as Mr. Frank described each country in detail. His opinion was particularly valid because he had been stationed in each place at various times. Mr. Frank was a man of the world, and he offered his unique perspective on the advantages and disadvantages of living in Australia, New Zealand, the United States, and Canada.

From the start of our conversation, however, it was clear that Mr. Frank favoured Canada above the other countries. Having spent sever-al months there while training Canadian soldiers in 1939, Mr. Frank explained that Canada was the ideal place for an ambitious young man like me.

I could not go back to Bulgaria, nor could I remain in Austria. Based on Mr. Frank's advice, Canada appeared to be my most appealing option. Every day I stayed in Austria, it became ever more likely that something terrible might happen to me; there was no time to waste.

With that, the decision was made — I was going to Canada. One of my main reasons for choosing it over the other countries was Mr. Frank's claim that a large segment of the Canadian population — 27 percent at the time, so he told me — spoke German. I felt that being able to com-municate would ease my transition to a new country. Of course, later on I discovered that almost nobody in Canada spoke German. In fact, speak-ing the language could actually get you kicked out of the country back then, but I could only go by what Mr. Frank was telling me at the time.

In the days that followed, the situation in Austria went from bad to worse. Without warning, a distinguished and outspoken Austrian profes-sor was snatched from the streets and sent off to Russia. After his abduc-tion, the professor's wife — a nice lady who bought her produce from me — went to the British military and asked about her husband. She was told that the Russians had taken him, and that if she wished to further inquire about his whereabouts, she would need to speak to the Russian commissar.

By the time she was allowed to speak to the commissar at the Russian consulate, her husband seemed to have vanished from the face of the earth. The commissar offered no help whatsoever. He simply stated that if something were amiss with her husband, he would have surely contacted her by now — an absurdity, because her husband was almost certainly being held against his will. This poor lady never saw her husband again. Abductions and disappearances were happening ever more frequently in Austria, and I could feel the walls beginning to close in around me.

We didn't hesitate. Katarina and I went to the Canadian consulate in Salzburg to work out the logistics of our immigration. A Canadian official interviewed us, asking me, in particular, what I planned to do in Canada for employment.

"I intend to work in construction," I answered.

I told him that I wanted to draw upon the skills I had acquired while rebuilding homes in Wels during and after the war. Without knowing how to speak English, I told him that I believed that construction offered me the best chance to make a living in Canada right away. The interviewer agreed.

Satisfied with my answers, the official approved us for immigration to Canada. He asked me if I would be able to pay for our travel costs, and I assured him that I could. Hopeful immigrants lacking the required funds to cover their travel expenses sometimes had to wait up to five years to leave the country, but financial reasons would not delay us. The official told us that as soon as we could produce X-rays and medical records confirming our good health — along with tickets for passage aboard a ship to Canada — he would permit us to make the move to our new country.

As I left the office, the Canadian official made a remark that filled me with confidence that I was making the right decision: "Canada needs young men like you."

Unfortunately, getting approval from a Canadian official was only one small part of what would prove to be a terribly complicated immigration process. There was also the matter of exchanging my money into Canadian funds, as well as buying the tickets, all of which turned out to be more difficult than I might have imagined.

In those days, Austrian schillings were not considered "hard currency": they were not fully convertible into other currencies. Therefore, I was unable to simply withdraw my Austrian money from the bank to carry with me into Canada in a bag along with the rest of my luggage. If only it had been so easy to draw on my hard-earned funds!

The first sign of trouble appeared when I tried to exchange my schillings for Canadian dollars at a bank in Graz. My request was promptly denied. At the time, Austrian banks were only willing to exchange money if the funds were going to be used for buying seeds or agricultural equipment from America. My request for a straight currency exchange for the purpose of travel was rejected.

Seeking answers, I turned to Mr. Frank again. I explained that I could not exchange my money to get out of the country and asked him to do the transaction on my behalf, telling him I could only buy tickets to board a ship to Canada using American, British, or Swiss currency, none of which I could acquire.

For a variety of reasons, Mr. Frank could not do the exchange, either. First, he was still a member of the British military and therefore obliged to show his support for the occupation of Austria. Second, he lacked access to non-local currency. Wherever he travelled, Mr. Frank had to use strictly local cash for the duration of his stay in Austria.

"Natzl, I haven't seen a British pound in twenty years," he told me.

But Mr. Frank understood that I was at an important crossroads in my life. I was either going to be apprehended by the Bulgarian secret police or I would escape to Canada. He came through for me in another way. He knew a man who could help me, an American purchasing agent stationed in Salzburg who was allowed to exchange money into virtually any country's currency.

"Wonderful," I said.

Mr. Frank called his friend on my behalf, and I hopped into my truck to make the three-hour drive to Salzburg from Graz. I was determined to get to Canada before the secret police nabbed me, and I was hopeful that Mr. Frank's friend could help me do so.

When I got to Salzburg, I made my way to a villa on the outskirts of town, rang the bell at the gate, and was let inside to be met by a guard immediately. I passed him the letter of introduction written for me by Mr. Frank, and he examined it carefully before telling me to wait as he drove off in a jeep.

A few minutes later the guard returned with another man, the person I had come to see. He was an American Southerner whose German, to me, was more difficult to understand than that of an American Northerner. Still, we communicated rather easily. Mr. Frank's letter explained my situation well enough for us to understand each other. The American agreed to help me.

The Southerner told me to hop into the jeep, and together we drove to the American Express building, which was nothing more than a cigarette booth–sized structure in the middle of Salzburg, right across the street from the Canadian consulate. We pulled up to the building, and I handed him an envelope containing 100,000 schillings to exchange into $3,000 Canadian.

At this point my entire future rested in the hands of a virtual stranger. I could only hope that Mr. Frank had sent me to an honest man. There was nothing stopping him from disappearing through the American Express building's back door with all of my money, never to be seen again.

Thankfully, Mr. Frank's friend turned out to be an honest gentleman, just as he had been described. He returned a few moments later with my freshly exchanged money. I counted it up, with the sum being the agreed-upon $3,000. I thanked the man from the bottom of my heart, as both he and I knew that he could have easily taken advantage of the situation. Once again I felt as if someone was looking out for me when I needed it most. Once again I was lucky.

The American also did me the favour of purchasing two second-class tickets aboard a ship to Canada on my behalf, which bought Katarina and I the privilege of occupying a private room on a vessel carrying more than twenty-three hundred passengers. Some rooms might be crammed with as many as fifteen people, putting comfort and privacy at a premium. Compared to most of the other passengers, my wife and I would be travelling to Canada in style.

I thanked Mr. Frank's American friend once more and went straight back to the Canadian consulate, tickets in hand. Along with our medical records and X-rays, I showed the Canadian official our travel documents. He looked them over before approving my request with his rubber stamp.

"You're free to go to Canada now," he said. "Good luck to you."

I breathed in a deep sigh of relief. It was official: in eleven days we would set sail for Canada, leaving behind Austria, the country I had called home for the better part of a decade. I was excited about going to Canada and relieved to be evading the secret police, but a part of me knew I was going to miss Austria. I had built a life there, after all. Now, once again, I would have to start over.

The only thing left to do was liquidate the rest of my assets. At the time the law stipulated that unless I sold my house to a native German or Austrian, I would not be permitted to take that money with me outside the country. Because of this stipulation, I could not get a fair deal; a forced sale almost always meant a steep discount on the price. That being the case, I ended up selling my house to the Bulgarian anti-communist government-in-exile for much less than its true value. Even worse, I did not receive the money upon the completion of this transaction. I was instructed to call the organization's headquarters in Washington, D.C., when I arrived in Canada to collect the money owed for my house and other assets, which totalled about $6,000 in Canadian currency, the equivalent of almost $60,000 in 2018.

This $6,000 would provide me with a much-needed financial cushion while acclimatizing myself to a new country in which I did not speak the language or possess any obvious means of support. Katarina and I could easily survive for quite a while if I was unable to find a job.

Everything was happening so fast, but I felt prepared to make the biggest move of my life. I was ready to go to Canada.

SETTING SAIL

After paying for our travel expenses out of the $3,000 I had received by exchanging the schillings with the American Southerner, Katarina and I had a fair amount of cash left over. We were simple farming people, the salt of the earth, but this time we decided to live the high life before leaving Europe. We toured the continent, vacationing in Switzerland and visiting Paris, spending lavishly all the while.

For the first time, my wife and I were experiencing some of the finer things in life. My business in Austria had been an undeniable success, and I saw this as a time for celebration. We bought meals and poured drinks for all the friends we made throughout our travels, burning through most of our money before we even left Europe.

I was down to my last $5 by the time we set sail for Canada from the busy port in Le Havre, France. It mattered not, however, because all of our food, drinks, and accommodations while sailing were included in the price of our tickets. And, after all, I enjoyed peace of mind in knowing that $6,000 was waiting for me upon arrival in Canada.

The date of our departure finally arrived, and we boarded our ship enthusiastically. As we left port and headed into the Atlantic Ocean, I reflected upon my journey in life thus far. Drifting ever farther away from land, I felt a rush of excitement and nervousness, believing now more than ever that I had a real opportunity to become a somebody in Canada.

As it had been described, Canada was the land of opportunity for a young man like me. Europe would soon become a part of my past; I could only hope and pray that opportunity awaited me on the other side of the ocean.

With the land fading in the distance, so were, I believed, the worst of my struggles. Throughout my life to this point, I had survived everything from personal tragedy to ever-present violence. I had left home as a boy and grown to become an independent man and a business owner. What I did not realize was that the worst of my struggles were yet to come.

8

Arriving

It all felt like a dream, as if I were floating through the air. We were crossing the ocean, en route to Canada, and my life seemed surreal. I was thrilled, elated, excited, and nervous all at once. In my mind, I still saw myself as the little farm boy from a tiny Bulgarian village; it was difficult — if not impossible — to fully comprehend how far I had come, and where I was yet to go.

Together with my wife I was sailing second-class to Canada along with more than two thousand other passengers. It was an overwhelming experience, and even now, so many years later, I can hardly believe I had the nerve to go through with it. But we were young and bold. In those days, I lacked the patience to overanalyze my decisions. I was forced to trust my instincts.

Katarina and I spent seven days sailing across the choppy waters of the Atlantic. For some passengers, this voyage to Canada proved to be among the seven worst days of their lives, since the stormy April weather brought on seasickness for many. Unfortunately, Katarina belonged to this group; she spent much of our week at sea suffering from nausea.

Of all the passengers aboard the cruise liner, only five managed to avoid illness altogether, and I was one of the fortunate few, along with three gentlemen and one lady from Scotland.

Although it provided a small consolation to my poor wife, she and I shared a private room on this voyage, allowing her a small amount of comfort. The majority of the poor souls with whom we travelled slept like pigs stuffed into pens along with far too many others. My wife might have been sick, but at least she was able to suffer in relative comfort and privacy.

On the other hand, I happily enjoyed myself aboard the ship. With so many passengers unable to keep anything in their stomachs, those of us left standing feasted on what seemed to be an unlimited supply of food. I stuffed my belly at every meal and never once reached into my pocket, since everything had been paid for in the price of our tickets.

There was a secret to sailing without coming down with seasickness — an old natural remedy. Like the others who did not fall ill during this voyage, I had been eating cloves of garlic before setting sail. I offered some garlic to my wife, of course, but she refused it. I offered it to her again after she got sick, but at that point Katarina had no interest in putting anything into her stomach, whether garlic or anything else.

My new friends and I passed the time at sea by eating, drinking, and playing cards. Personally, I never drank alcohol before 1958, but if I had wanted to I could have drunk myself into oblivion during this voyage. My shipmates sipped wine and beer as we played hand after hand of blackjack, making small, friendly wagers all the while just to keep things interesting.

Avoiding illness was not my only lucky event at sea. I had the good fortune to meet a man of Croatian descent who would provide me with one of the most important pieces of information I would ever receive.

My new Croatian friend had already spent twenty years living in Canada. In 1945, he had purchased a shoe factory in Trieste in northeastern Italy, around the same time that Yugoslavia was liberated. Josip Broz Tito, the Yugoslav partisan leader and later dictator, had taken over this part of Italy before giving it back in 1947. When this Croatian fellow arrived at the port to release his factory's shoe inventory, the Yugoslav police arrested him. They confiscated his passport, took away his business, and threw him in jail, where the poor man languished until 1951.

I was able to communicate with my new friend in Croatian — I had learned the language years earlier and often spoke Croatian to my wife — and we quickly formed a bond. During one of our conversations, we talked about where I was planning to settle in Canada. I let him know that Katarina and I were headed to Fort William, Ontario. I knew very little about Canada, but from what I had been told, Fort William, which would become the city of Thunder Bay in 1970 when it amalgamated with Port Arthur and two townships, looked like as good a place to live as any.

"Fort William?" said the Croatian. "What are you planning to do there?"

I told my friend that I intended to work in construction. It was an industry in which someone like me — a man lacking education and language — could learn a trade from scratch.

But, truth be told, I had only chosen Fort William for a weak reason. I happened to know a fellow from Austria currently living there; I thought he might be able to help me get a job. I knew almost nothing about the place itself.

My Croatian friend shook his head in disapproval. As far as he was concerned, Fort William was no place for a young man looking to work in construction.

"Fort William has nothing but forests and granaries," he said. "You can work in forestry or in a silo. If you happen to like bears, go to Fort William. But if you want to build houses, then Toronto's the place for you."

It was an amazing coincidence that I ran into this man. His advice completely altered my future in Canada. Had I never met my Croatian friend on the ship, I might be living in Thunder Bay even now.

Finally, we approached the conclusion of our journey. After seven long days and nights at sea, our liner sailed up the Saint Lawrence until we could see the Château Frontenac of Quebec City rising high above our ship's bow. It was an amazing sight. As we drew closer to land, my heart began to swell with happiness and pride.

Our ship docked, and we disembarked to step into our new lives. On my Croatian friend's recommendation, I decided Toronto would indeed be our destination. Katarina and I hopped aboard a train that took us through Montreal and on to Toronto. We rode the rails on the beautiful spring day of April 18, 1951. At the end of an eight-hour trip, we found ourselves in Toronto.

At long last I had arrived.

DR. BORIS MITEV

Before leaving the train station in Quebec City, I sent a telex message — using a communication network that predated the Internet or fax machine — to Dr. Boris Mitev. He was a Bulgarian who had attended university in Austria during my time in the country, earning his degree in chemistry. As fellow Bulgarians living in Graz, it seemed quite natural that he and I had become acquainted. I always sought out other Bulgarians wherever I lived or visited.

Even back then I valued education. Once I started making good money with my market gardening business, I wanted to help other Bulgarians pay for their schooling. I never had the opportunity to receive a proper education myself, but I understood its importance in building an intelligent, informed, and well-read society. Therefore, when the future doctor, Boris Mitev, asked me to help pay his tuition, I was happy to do so.

Before 1947, Bulgarians were permitted to send money to Austria to help support their own people. After 1947, however, the Bulgarian government removed this privilege. Boris was already a husband and father in Austria, and he desperately wanted to complete his degree. Once again I tried to follow my father's advice to help others whenever possible. I gave Boris money every month and helped support his young family while he received his education.

During those days in Graz, I worked in the market every day. Since the university was right next door, I saw Boris often. He frequently dropped by my stall to buy produce, and I would inquire about his studies. Boris was a highly intelligent man, and I always looked forward to his thoughtful answers to all of my questions. He and I became good friends.

Of course, Boris was not the only Bulgarian I helped with money in those days. With my successful business in Graz, I was able to assist a number of Bulgarians in paying their way through school. It filled me with pride to know that I helped these young people receive their education. I was not able to give everybody as much as I gave Boris, but I provided as much as I could to those who needed it and asked for my help. All told, I helped Boris pay his way through school for two years, after which he would come to be known as Dr. Mitev. That was how I addressed him in the years to come.

After graduating from university, Dr. Mitev moved to Canada. He was a member of the Bulgarian anti-communist government-in-exile, and it made sense for him to flee communism as soon as possible. Before his departure from Austria, my friend and I had one last conversation.

"Gatyu," he said, "I don't know how I'll do it, but someday I'm going to pay you back."

I assured my friend that helping a fellow Bulgarian was its own reward, but he insisted he would somehow repay me. Dr. Mitev gave me his word, and I believed his word to be good.

"Gatyu," he said once again, "I will pay you back."

That being the case, I knew I had one friend in Toronto, which gave me the confidence I needed to go there. After sending word of my impending arrival from Quebec City, I had no doubt Dr. Mitev would welcome me into his home and do all he could to help ease my transition to a new country. Looking back, it seemed strange that I ever considered living in Fort William at all, since Dr. Mitev was in Toronto all along. It was a hasty decision made in the rush to leave Austria.

In addition to Dr. Mitev's loyal friendship, I had one other thing going for me in Toronto: the $6,000 owed to me by the Bulgarian anti-communist government-in-exile. Back then $6,000 was a fortune for a new immigrant in Canada. With it, I could buy six houses if I so chose. It was more than enough money with which to start my new life.

I was a young man arriving in a new country with money in tow. I might not have been able to speak the language, nor did I possess a marketable skill, but I was ready to use my owed money — along with my work ethic and determination — to build a successful life and career in this new country. I was primed and ready to become a somebody in Canada.

DEVASTATION

After spending lavishly on a short European tour prior to our departure — not to mention the expenses incurred while attempting to leave Austria — I arrived in Toronto with exactly $5 in my pocket. Unfortunately, I was immediately relieved of this cash by a dishonest cab driver. After stepping off the train we had ridden from Quebec City, my wife and I decided to take a taxi to Dr. Mitev's apartment because he was unable to meet us at the station due to work commitments. I was wearing lederhosen because I had checked a map, saw that Toronto was a little south of Graz and Quebec City latitude-wise, and assumed my new home's climate would be quite warm. I was wrong; it was snowing!

I hailed a taxi, and we stepped into the vehicle. Unable to speak English, I simply showed the driver a telex I had received from Dr. Mitev and pointed to the address. It read 327 Queen Street East, and I could only hope the driver knew how to get us there.

This man, aware that his passengers did not speak English, took my wife and me on a roundabout tour of the city. Unfamiliar with Toronto, I had absolutely no idea where he was going. I just sat in my seat as mute as a fish. At the end of our long trip through strange streets, I handed the driver my $5. Instead of presenting me with change, he hurried us out of the cab empty-handed. Without any English language skills, I was unable to argue the charge, and suddenly found myself in the streets of a new city without even a dollar in my pocket. Later I found out that the distance from the train station to Dr. Mitev's apartment was about a half-mile, and the fare should have cost us a fraction of the $5 I paid the driver. In more ways than one, I had been taken for a ride.

Katarina and I made our way up the stairs to Dr. Mitev's apartment, which was above a restaurant. After saying our excited hellos, we put down our luggage and collapsed from exhaustion. To my surprise, Dr. Mitev insisted that my wife and I take his bed while he and Mrs. Mitev slept on a mattress he pulled out of the closet. Dr. Mitev's apartment was simple, but my friend did everything he could to make us comfortable. I could tell that he wanted to make good on his promise to repay me for the financial support I had given him in Austria. I was most grateful for his hospitality.

The morning following our arrival Dr. Mitev took me to an office that was equipped with a telex machine so that I could contact a man named Dr. Dimitroff. This man was my primary contact at the Bulgarian anti-communist government-in-exile, which was headquartered in Washington, D.C. I was surprised to receive word that he would arrive in Toronto the very next day, and we made arrangements to meet. I might have lacked cash in my pocket, but soon I would receive all the money for which I had worked so hard in Austria, and not a moment too soon.

The next day Dr. Dimitroff arrived on the doorstep of Dr. Mitev's Queen Street apartment and wasted little time with pleasantries. He delivered the most devastating news of my life. "I don't know how to tell you this, but we don't have your money."

I chuckled at first, assuming he was joking.

"We had your money," he explained, "but we don't have it anymore."

I came to the realization that he was serious, and my entire world began to come crashing down around me. Dr. Dimitroff proceeded to tell me how the United States had begun negotiations with China and the Soviet Union while the two sides were still fighting the Korean War. One of the conditions of these negotiations was for the United States to withdraw its support of anti-communist governments-in-exile. This sudden loss of American support took the organization by surprise: the Bulgarian anti-communist government-in-exile was left without any money. The $6,000 I was to be repaid was not available.

I took in the information as best I could. Dr. Dimitroff kept speaking, but his voice was reduced to a dull buzz in the background as my mind raced like a bullet. I could only think about the fact that I was going to be left without even a dollar to my name in a foreign country with no way of getting home. Three words kept reappearing in my mind, as if they were playing on a skipping record: *You're ruined*, I said to myself again and again. *You're ruined.*

Dr. Dimitroff tried to apologize, but there was nothing he could say to ease my pain. I had made the biggest move of my life with the thought that I would come to Canada a well-off man. But now that I had arrived in the country, I was starting over with nothing, back to zero once again. If I had even a little money, I could have returned to Austria, since now I would be eligible for citizenship there. Instead, everything I had worked toward for ten years was wiped out, as if I had never done it at all.

From the time I had begun working at the farmers' co op as a young boy in Gorno Ablanovo, I had progressed steadily along my path to becoming a somebody. It was an ambition that drove me, and it remained my primary objective in life. In Austria, I was able to make enough money to help people. I was able to make a name for myself. I might have only been known as the little Bulgarian who sold fruit and vegetables, but I knew I did it as well as anybody else.

Now I found myself broke in Canada, with no trace of the benefits of my labour. I was left a penniless immigrant. At that moment I could only conclude that leaving Europe was the worst mistake of my life. Once again I thought to myself, *You're ruined.*

I had come to Canada to become a somebody, but right from the beginning I started my new life as a nobody, forced to rebuild my life and reputation from ground zero. I was blindsided and devastated, and there was no plan in place on which I could rely to reverse my fortunes.

STARTING OVER

My friendship with Dr. Mitev saved me during those first few weeks in Canada. I was an immigrant without even a dollar to my name, but thanks to my Bulgarian friend I had the comfort of knowing there would be a roof over my head and food in my belly no matter what. Things were bad, but I always understood that they could have been much worse.

My father had always told me to do what I could to help others, since the day might come when I would be the one needing help. Once again I saw that my father was right. I had helped Dr. Mitev in Austria, and now he was aiding me in my darkest hour. He proved himself to be a true friend, as well as a man of his word.

My friend was incredibly generous, especially considering that he did not have much to give. Life had not been easy for Dr. Mitev in Canada. In Europe, he was a cultured and respected man. He was a doctor. In Toronto, he was nothing more than a servant. Dr. Mitev, like so many other immigrants, had signed a document upon his arrival in Canada, agreeing to be assigned to work by the government. Despite his status back home, my friend was made to choose between working in a restaurant, on a farm, down a mineshaft, or in the forest. Boris Mitev, doctor no more, chose to work in a restaurant, sealing his fate for the next three years.

Dr. Mitev was assigned to work as a dishwasher. Every night, seven days a week, he worked underground in the basement of a prominent Toronto eatery, scrubbing one filthy dish after another. He slept all day and worked all night, existing in a near-perpetual state of darkness. This was not work befitting a doctor, but back then it was a common scenario for new immigrants. Even today there are doctors from other countries doing manual labour in the forests and oil sands of Canada; many educated immigrants drive taxis in Toronto.

Upon completion of his three-year commitment, Dr. Mitev was able to find a much better job working for Irving Oil at a refinery in Quebec, but he never forgot those first years in Canada. Yet, even as he struggled, Dr. Mitev came through in my time of need.

With my basic needs provided by Dr. Mitev, I was able to focus my attention on finding work, but first I had to officially register our arrival in Toronto. So I found myself on a streetcar with three other Bulgarian newcomers to the city on our way to the pertinent government office. On our way back from that task, my new friends and I spoke Bulgarian, of course, but our conversation was rudely interrupted when the streetcar driver yelled out, "No one speaks a foreign language in my car!" Then he threw all four of us off the streetcar.

Thankfully, community spirit prevailed among recent Bulgarian immigrants in those days, and my fellow countrymen quickly came to my aid and helped me land a paying job. Mere hours after being devastated by Dr. Dimitroff's news, I left the house to go wash cars. I spent the entire night working, at the end of which I took home $11. I used that money to buy forks and knives, a proper set of cutlery. To me, it was a start. These were the first items I was able to purchase in Canada.

Working with my Bulgarian brothers lifted my spirits, if only somewhat. All was not lost.

On one occasion, a Bulgarian fellow introduced me to a Serbian bricklayer, and I agreed to work for him if he taught me his trade.

"Sure," he said. "I can do that, but now I need a labourer. So today do the labour and tomorrow I'll start teaching you bricklaying."

The next day and the one after that I was still working as a labourer. At noon on the third day, I quit because it was obvious the man was never going to show me how to lay bricks.

During those first days in Toronto, I managed to earn a few dollars here and there doing any work I could find. At least two or three times each week, I went around cleaning restaurants with a few other Bulgarians. Sometimes we cleaned offices. I accepted any work available. Even though I was a stranger in a strange land, I still believed I could demonstrate my value through the international currency of hard work.

Soon I felt my luck beginning to turn. I was a young man with grit and a hard work ethic, determined to be successful. Even in an altogether foreign place like Canada, I knew that counted for something.

TURN OF FORTUNE

All told, as I tried my best to gain a foothold in Canada, Katarina and I ended up staying with the Mitevs for three weeks while I worked any odd job I could get, including washing cars to earn extra cash to buy household necessities such as pots and pans. In fact, it was only Dr. Mitev's kindness — along with the unified community of recent Bulgarian immigrants in Toronto — that kept me afloat during the worst of it. I was, however briefly, completely broke in an unfamiliar country, but I never felt fully alone, nor was I ever reduced to being truly hopeless.

As we left their Queen Street apartment, Katarina and I thanked Dr. and Mrs. Mitev before proceeding to move out on our own. Unlike today, finding a place to live in Toronto did not require a tremendous amount of money. We were able to find affordable accommodations at a rooming house on Sherbourne Street almost right away.

When I rented our rooms, I was under the impression that the bathroom next to our door was meant for our private use. The landlord may have explained his terms and conditions, but evidently I misunderstood him. Therefore, it came as quite a shock when I realized we were sharing the facilities with the residents of ten other rooms on our floor. It was far from an ideal situation, but of course, I had endured more spartan conditions in the past.

We moved into our new apartment on Friday, spent the night there, and then left the next morning to visit friends. My wife was godmother to a family of recent Croatian immigrants whom she knew from Austria. They had settled in a nearby area called Toronto Township, or as it would come to be known years later, Mississauga. Our friends lived close to the intersection of Alexandra Avenue and Lakeshore Road East, near Cawthra Park. Conveniently, there was a streetcar that took us nearly the entire way.

As we stepped off the trolley, I spotted a store on the northeast corner of the intersection. With the few dollars I had in my pocket, I decided to buy flowers and oranges for our Croatian hosts.

When I brought my items up to the cash register, the store owner — who was about to head out on a delivery — asked me where I was going. I had figured out that until my English was better I would have to carry a piece of paper with any address I needed to get to. So I showed him the paper on which I had written the address of our destination.

As I would come to learn, this store owner was an uncommonly kind man with political ambitions. In the late 1950s, he became a councillor, then a deputy reeve and reeve for Toronto Township, and in 1968, the first and only elected mayor of the newly christened Town of Mississauga prior to its incorporation as a city in 1974. His name was Robert Speck, but he liked his friends to call him Bob.

Mr. Speck was re-elected mayor in 1970 but sadly passed away in 1972 just before turning fifty-seven. Today a short road leading into Square One in Mississauga is named Robert Speck Parkway in his honour. When I met the future politician, however, he was still just a man who happened to run a shop that sold flowers and groceries.

Mr. Speck offered to drive Katarina and me to the house of our Croatian friends, and we quickly accepted, since he was delivering groceries in that area. I soon got to know Mr. Speck as a friend and as an employer when he hired me part-time as an evening delivery man for his market. He even helped me get my Canadian driver's licence, personally taking me to the Ministry of Transportation in Cooksville during my first day on the job. I was astonished at the simplicity in acquiring a licence in

Canada compared to the various hoops through which I had to jump in Austria. Moreover, the depth of kindness Mr. Speck showed to an immigrant he barely knew amazed me.

At the home of our Croatian hosts, I immediately became friendly with the family patriarch, Stanislav Zita. Although we just dropped by to pay my wife's friends a social visit, this would soon become a pivotal point in shaping my professional future. As it turned out, Stanislav was a carpenter employed by the Shipp Corporation, a big construction company in the area owned and operated by a man named Gordon Shipp.

Stanislav knew I was looking for a steady full-time job, so he told me I should go down to the construction site. He said the Shipp Corporation was always looking for good people and that there was a chance Mr. Shipp would have a job for me, particularly if I went with Stanislav's ringing endorsement. I arrived in Canada planning to work in construction, and now it looked as if I might actually get the chance to do so.

Incredibly, my luck had only just begun to turn, as Stanislav proceeded to tell me about his Ukrainian neighbour living down the street. This older lady, he told me, had a spare room in her house that she was looking to rent out to a tenant of her liking.

Stanislav took me to see his neighbour, Mrs. Bartula. I inquired about the room's availability, but much to my dismay, she told me it would not become available for another four months.

"Right now there's a lady living in the room," said Mrs. Bartula, dashing my hopes. "But I could let you and your wife live in my garage until she moves out."

Like most people, I had no desire to live in someone's garage. However, because Mrs. Bartula offered me the place for a monthly fee of $5, I was left with little choice but to take it. Even for those days the rent was outrageously low, which was especially important for someone in my position. I knew the Canadian winters would be far too cold for sleeping in a garage, but it was already late May and I did not need to worry about freezing.

Therefore, after just one night in the Sherbourne Street rooming house, Katarina and I moved our meagre possessions into Mrs. Bartula's garage. It may have been a humble start, but this was a place to live, and it was ours.

Mrs. Bartula's garage was clean and had electricity. Katarina and I even plugged in a little hot plate, enabling us to brew tea and cook small meals. Of course, there was no plumbing in the garage, but we were able to get water from Mrs. Bartula's kitchen whenever we needed it and there was an outhouse in the yard. Growing up in Bulgaria, I was no stranger to the most basic amenities, so living in Mrs. Bartula's garage caused me no particular hardship.

I had only been living in Canada for a few weeks, but already I felt my luck was changing. I might not have had much money, but in a short time I was able to find a place to live and even got a job delivering groceries for Mr. Speck. Additionally, I had seemingly made a connection to work in construction; I was starting to feel as though I was getting my bearings in Canada.

When Katarina and I moved into our new home, we became residents of what was then Toronto Township. Slipping our few suitcases from the Toronto rooming house beneath the foam mattress and metal bed frame provided for us by Mrs. Bartula, we knew we were fortunate to have run into such a nice lady. She treated Katarina and me as if we were her own children.

Of course, other than Mrs. Bartula's old bed, Katarina and I had no furniture to speak of. We had come to Canada with few possessions, expecting to arrive here with a fortune. So I had sent a train car full of furniture and everything else we owned to Katarina's brother, George. After all, we had planned to buy everything we needed brand-new upon our arrival. It would have cost almost nothing to ship all our furniture to Canada, but I figured we would not need it.

Oddly enough, we never did make the move to the room in Mrs. Bartula's house from the garage. Before its occupant moved out, I met a Polish gentleman named Mr. Brock — years later I built him a house — who lived with a lady named Mrs. Zuck in a house she owned. Katarina and I ended up living in that house during another transitional period.

After our move into Mrs. Zuck's house, I met with Stanislav and his daughter, Anne. Together we went to Gordon Shipp's construction site. Anne was there to interpret so that I could communicate with Mr. Shipp's superintendent in applying for a job. It was a brief interview in

which I was asked about my experience in construction. The superintendent seemed to be looking for men willing to work hard, and I fitted the
bill. He told me I had the job and could start work the following day.

My job could be defined most simply as "general labourer."
Sometimes I swept up sawdust, other times I carried lumber from one
area to another. It made no difference to me. I was constantly in motion,
doing what I was told. If I had nothing in particular to do, I occupied my
time tidying up the job site. I never stood still, only hoping to do a good
job so the boss might notice me.

I was elated to be working for Mr. Shipp and was getting paid good
money to do so. At first my pay was $1.10 per hour, which was a gener-
ous wage in those days. Two weeks later I got a raise to $1.20 an hour.
Just a few weeks after that, by August 1, I was promoted to carpenter,
even though I was not trained for the job. Luckily, I was able to learn fast.

While I was still a labourer, I did everything I could to help the
carpenters so that I could be around them to learn on the job while
also doing the work for which I was hired. When Mr. Shipp gave me
the opportunity to become a carpenter myself, I jumped at the chance.
Although I still had a lot to learn, I knew I was more prepared for the job
than most newcomers.

A few months into my job with Mr. Shipp, I was told by Dr. Dimitroff
that a subcommittee of the anti-communist government-in-exile had arranged for Bulgarians in Toronto sympathetic to its cause to donate $1
per month to repay my lost $6,000. I was touched by the fact that recent
immigrants — men earning a mere 40 or 50 cents per hour — were
repaying me because they felt it was the right thing to do. I remembered
my father's words about helping others, and it became clear to me that
these Bulgarian Canadians subscribed to the same philosophy.

Soon after, I received the first $300 payment. By this time, I was
working steadily and making good money. No longer was I living hand
to mouth, as I had been while staying with Dr. Mitev. I was already in a
better financial position than many of the men contributing part of their
wages to me. So, although I accepted the first payment, I never took another dollar from this generous group of men. The next month I refused
to accept their money because I knew I did not need it anymore.

I had only been in Canada for a few short months, but I was already moving up the ranks at the Shipp Corporation. At the time of my second promotion, I was making $1.75 per hour, which was big money to me back then. To put that number into perspective, a worker with that salary could buy a new house for his family in about five years without borrowing any money, if he saved up for it carefully.

My boss, Gordon Shipp, was an incredibly influential figure to me during the start of my career in construction. I remember vividly how he often drove past the construction site in his Cadillac, always slowing down to get a good look at the project from afar.

The first few times I met Mr. Shipp, our interactions were brief and instructional. "Iggy, you should shut off that band saw," he would say from his car. "Electricity costs money."

Another time Mr. Shipp was driving past the site as usual and called me over to his car window. He pointed to one of the buildings. "Iggy, the eavestrough on that house is uneven."

Mr. Shipp was at least twenty yards from the house, but he was still able to spot a nearly undetectable mistake that several others had missed completely. I called over a few of the other employees, and we checked the eavestrough with a level. It turned out that Mr. Shipp was right. He was always right.

Gordon Shipp was a very intelligent man who paid attention to the smallest of details. Working for him, I began paying attention to those details, too. I could see that Mr. Shipp's success was no accident. At six foot four, my boss was a towering figure, even in his mid-sixties. He was very distinguished-looking and radiated success. Mr. Shipp was always dressed impeccably with neatly combed grey hair. I never saw him wearing anything other than a finely tailored suit — a habit I later adopted for myself. I love wearing a suit and tie. Mr. Shipp commanded respect at all times.

I liked my boss for many reasons, but I respected him especially for the fact that he was a self-made man who had built himself up from nothing. After years of hard work, he was now the owner of a major construction company. More than anything, however, I liked the confidence he inspired me to have in myself. As I watched him sell houses as if they were sausages, I knew in my heart I could do the same.

My boss was building his first subdivision in Toronto Township on Applewood Road near what would someday become the site of Dixie Mall. He was building forty-five houses all at once, which was considered a big subdivision in those days. As I watched him operate, I thought, *This is a business I'd like to be in.*

In addition to my boss, I met two other people at the Shipp Corporation who wound up having an impact on my professional life. One was a German Canadian named Beltz; the other was Jozef Glista, a Polish Canadian. Mr. Beltz was one of my bosses at the Shipp Corporation, and he taught me how to cut roofs using a square. These two men started building their own houses during off-hours and often brought me along to help. Evenings, Saturdays, Sundays, and holidays, we were out working on one of their houses. The things I learned while working with Mr. Beltz and Mr. Glista — along with the education I received from Mr. Shipp — helped me create the plan I would use in time to build my own house. Besides teaching me carpentry and many other things, Mr. Glista also introduced me to his son, Ted, who would become an important part of my later life.

Work on the Applewood subdivision was nearing completion, and soon Mr. Shipp would lay off all his workers until he could start up another project. This was standard procedure for the construction industry.

While I was working for Mr. Shipp, I always went home at the end of the day, cleaned myself up, and had something to eat before returning to the job site to tidy up. I never put in for the extra hours I worked, but I knew this was one of the ways I might be able to catch my boss's eye. I wanted Gordon Shipp to know my name. Just as I had gone the extra mile to differentiate myself while selling produce in Austria, I tried my best to stand out from the other guys on Mr. Shipp's payroll.

I believed that Mr. Shipp appreciated my extra effort in making the job site look neat and tidy. He had lots of customers coming by to visit throughout the construction process and understood that a clean job site helped put their minds at ease. No one wanted to see their future home as a disorganized mess.

On December 15, 1951, as I stood in Mr. Shipp's office in Toronto's Bloor West Village, unsure of where I would work now that the

Applewood project was finished, suddenly, from across the room, I heard a familiar booming voice. "Iggy, come here!" Mr. Shipp called out.

I went over to his desk at once. Looking around the office and out the window, I realized what it meant to be one of about two hundred men about to face joblessness.

"Do you have another job lined up now that this one's over?" Mr. Shipp asked me.

Using the little English I knew, I told him that I did not.

He then picked up the telephone and called one of his friends, Rex Heslop, over at another construction site. Mr. Heslop was a major land and residential real estate developer. He would become famous for developing the area of northern Etobicoke that came to be known as Rexdale in 1955. In the meantime, Mr. Heslop was developing farmland in other parts of Etobicoke.

"I'm sending over a young man who's been working for me," Mr. Shipp said to Mr. Heslop. "He's a very hard-working guy."

After a bit more conversation, Mr. Shipp replaced the receiver in its cradle and told me I should report for work the next morning, handing me a note and instructing me to present it to the foreman. Once again I could not believe my luck. Gordon Shipp — one of the best-known businessmen in the region — was looking out for me.

Why did my boss choose me from a group of two hundred workers? I was not the only one who needed a job, and I was not the only one who worked hard. I believed it was because Mr. Shipp always saw me running around and putting in extra hours. I had done everything I could to be noticed by Mr. Shipp, and my efforts had paid off. Going beyond my job description, more than anything else, had led to this "lucky" break.

The next day I went to a new construction site to see about the job with Mr. Heslop's company. As I arrived on the scene, I spotted one major problem: three hundred other men were gathered around the office, all of them looking for a job just like me.

Mr. Heslop's foreman kept us all waiting for most of the morning. Finally, around eleven o'clock, he spoke. Addressing a large group of soon-to-be-disappointed men, he said, "We're not hiring anyone until the end of January at the earliest."

I was discouraged and more than a little bit confused, given that Mr. Shipp had sent me to this place. Before shuffling away along with the 299 other disheartened souls, I reached into my pocket, pulled out my note from Mr. Shipp, and handed it to the foreman, who quickly read it.

"Have you got your tools with you?" he asked me.

I assured him that I did.

"Go and see Mr. McCourt right now."

Many others had been turned away, but thanks to Mr. Shipp's endorsement, I was able to get a job with Mr. Heslop's company at a time when I really needed it. I was hired as a carpenter.

At the time I was one of the worst carpenters around. However, given the opportunity to hone my craft every day, I worked hard and learned quickly. I was only hired because of Mr. Shipp's recommendation, but I did everything possible to earn my keep. In addition to making steady money, I learned a great deal about carpentry during this time.

Unfortunately, there was one major problem with my new job: I had to walk about four hours to get to the construction site every morning, and another four to get home after work. My days consisted of eight hours of working and eight hours of walking. And, since it was the beginning of the Canadian winter, I did not have the luxury of riding a bicycle to cut down on my travel time. Even worse, there was no public transportation to help me make my trip. I had no choice but to walk; it was the only way I could get to work. I hated that walk. But the way I saw it, I was lucky enough just to have a job. I needed to eat, so I had to work, which in this case meant I had to walk.

My days were long and exhausting. Mercifully, on the Friday of my first week on the job, I caught another break. On my way to work, I was about five minutes from the job site when Mr. Heslop pulled up beside me in his black Cadillac.

He rolled down his window and called out to me, "Young man, where are you going?"

He knew I was going to work. The fact that I was carrying my lunch pail provided confirmation enough of that. He told me to get into the car, looked at his watch, and reminded me I was late for work.

I explained to him, as much as I could with my limited English-language skills, that I had been making the long walk to Etobicoke all the way from Dixie Mall.

That was all I needed to say. By the end of my shift, Mr. Heslop had arranged for me to carpool into work with one of the superintendents. Right away my life improved by leaps and bounds. Mr. Heslop had no obligation to help me get to work, but he saved me eight hours of walking every day with his simple act of kindness.

More significantly, I was starting to pick up the all-important English language. I was now able to communicate effectively most of the time, which eased a great burden I had been carrying since my departure from Austria. Even today my grammar is far from perfect — and everyone who knows me has heard me pronounce certain English words like German ones — but I can proudly say that I was conversing in English within a short time of my arrival in Canada.

To survive, I had to learn English. In a way, I think that learning languages has always come naturally to me. Just as I had picked up German and Croatian, I learned English out of pure necessity. Looking back on my early life, perhaps it is more accurate to say that I do not know for sure whether I have a knack for learning languages or if I simply possess a strong instinct for survival.

By this time, I had my eye on a lot in the community of Lakeview near the intersection of Cawthra Road and Lakeshore Road East. Conveniently, the $300 I had received from the anti-communists covered almost the entire expense. The land was priced at $300, the building permit cost me $2, and I paid another $8 in legal fees. By the time my birthday came around on October 6, 1951, the deal closed and I owned the land I needed.

Starting in the new year, I worked during the evenings, weekends, and holidays — with the help of many Bulgarian friends — to build a simple wooden house on this plot of land. It would become the first Kaneff-built home in Canada, a structure that remains standing to this day, and would prove to be the first of many.

rough

its to build my home at 947 Tenth
Street in Lakeview, I was able to start construction at the beginning
of January 1952, toiling away on the project during the weekends while
continuing to work for Mr. Heslop during the week.

I happily worked for Mr. Heslop during the next months until Mr.
Shipp started another job on the north side of the Queen Elizabeth Way
in April 1952 and I went back to work for him. Mr. Shipp was paying me
$1.75 per hour when we finished the last job and offered to raise that by a
quarter. Mr. Heslop was only paying me $1.25, so it was an easy decision.

By now, I had acquired many of the important skills of a good builder, but I did not yet have the confidence to build an entire house without
relying on the expertise and help of others. For those first critical weekends of building, I leaned heavily on my friend, Stefan Vasilev.

Stefan was a Bulgarian from the village of Dve Mogili — located
twenty miles south of Ruse — who was currently living in Buffalo. We
knew each other from our time spent together in Austria. He used to

send me carloads of vegetables from Vienna to sell while I was in Graz, and we became good friends in the process.

Around the same time I moved to Canada, Stefan immigrated to the United States. We managed to stay in contact through letter writing. When the time came to build my first house, Stefan, an outstanding handyman, was only too pleased to drive up from Buffalo to lend an able hand.

The guidance and help Stefan offered me when he came into town was invaluable. He drove in from Buffalo on Saturday mornings, worked all day Saturday and Sunday, and then returned home on Sunday night. It was an hour-and-a-half trip each way, and Stefan made it without ever complaining. He worked tirelessly on my house.

Along with Stefan, Veliko Todorov also helped me build that first house. He was another Bulgarian from a village near my own, and a skilled builder in his own right. Although I had learned a great deal about construction while working for Mr. Shipp and Mr. Heslop, my experience with Stefan and Veliko took my skills to another level.

Putting up that first house played a huge role in shaping my future as a builder, even though the structure itself was quite small. My house was just seven hundred and twenty square feet, stationed precisely twenty-one feet from the front of the property line and twenty-five feet from the back, as per the building code of the day.

There was nothing complicated about the construction process. It was a simple frame house that I built without a plan or blueprints. I found another house I liked, took some measurements, and drew a little sketch based on that model. Then I took the piece of paper to the building inspector, and he issued a permit to build. That was all it took in those days.

After pricing it out, I knew I could build this house for about $2,000 — cheap, even in those days — but I still needed to acquire materials, and with approximately $800 in savings, I did not want to go into debt to do so.

Ready to build at last, I made a trip to the lumberyard. I knew the owner, having bought lumber from him on many occasions while working on some weekend building projects in the area. I told the man I needed lumber for a little house I was building. He gave me the wood without asking me for any money in advance, assuming he could send me an invoice at any time, even though we did not negotiate a price.

The next time I saw the lumberyard owner, he asked me how I intended to pay for the lumber.

"Listen," I said to him, "I'd like to pay for the lumber as I go along."

Like most people, lumberyard owners generally prefer to be paid up front, and this man was no different. He wanted to collect his money as soon as possible and even offered to set me up with a financing company if I was unable to pay him right away.

This lumberyard owner suggested I obtain financing from the bank, but I refused. The problem was not that I would be unable to get a loan. At that point I was making $60 a week while also earning some money on the weekends at various side jobs; I easily qualified for a loan. However, it was paying the interest to which I objected. I had learned my lesson the hard way when I borrowed money earlier that year to buy a truck. The bank expected me to start repaying the money immediately, even deducting the first payment from the amount I was being loaned. Borrowing money was a prohibitive expense to me in those days.

Having worked on so many projects in the area, I had been coming to this same lumberyard to buy lumber regularly. When the owner realized I could easily take my business elsewhere, he relented, allowing me to pay off my purchase little by little and at more favourable rates than those at which the local banks were lending.

In the end, it worked out well for both of us. I had the opportunity to build my house without relying on any financing or going into debt, and since I was already making good money, the lumberyard owner was paid in full by the end of 1952. He and I even became good friends. Thanks to his flexibility, I was able to build my first house in Canada without borrowing a cent.

With the help of Stefan and Veliko, I was able to complete the construction of that first house in just over a month. I ended up only needing Stefan's help for two weekends while we were framing the house and putting on the roof. Veliko assisted me throughout, helping with the heavy lifting and acting as an adviser. As it turned out, building a frame house was easy.

Katarina and I finally moved in on March 30, 1952, proud Canadian homeowners at last. It was a humble dwelling, but I was proud of the work my friends and I had done, and even prouder to have my very own little piece of Canada. It might have been small, but I knew that my first house was well built. I promised myself to give every future construction project the very same care and attention to detail that I gave to the first.

SECOND HOUSE

Before I even finished the first house, my mind turned to thoughts of a second. I was ambitious and wanted to advance my place in my new life. Fred Fuller was a real estate agent in the area looking for listings, and after driving past my little construction project a few times, he approached me with a proposition. Mr. Fuller asked me if I was looking to sell. This would not be the last time a Kaneff-built house was in demand.

"I need this house to live in," I explained to him. "But I'd be happy to build another one if you could help me find some money to do so."

Mr. Fuller was a seventy-year-old man, well known and well connected in the community. If anyone could find the money to help a hard-working new immigrant find financing, he was the man who could do it.

"I'll do what I can," he said.

He was true to his word; it did not take him long to find me financing.

After I got to know Mr. Fuller, I regularly visited his house on Saturdays to help clean his yard. I picked up all the fallen apples and pears, mowed the lawn, and tidied up the property. While I was there one day, Mr. Fuller introduced me to his neighbour, an elderly lady named Margaret Burke.

Nearly ninety years old at the time, Mrs. Burke attended the same church as Mr. Fuller, where she also played the organ. In the following weeks, I began helping Mrs. Burke with her yard, as well.

Eventually, Mr. Fuller talked to Mrs. Burke about lending me the money to build a second house. She agreed to assist me. Although this was undoubtedly an act of kindness on her part, Mrs. Burke did not lend me the money as a charitable donation; she did it as an investment. Mrs. Burke loaned me $4,000 at a 4 percent rate of interest. The loan was to be repaid after three years or when I sold the house, whichever came first.

After receiving the money, I continued to tidy Mrs. Burke's property. Every weekend I spent about an hour working on her lawn, after which I did the same for Mr. Fuller. They had both done so much for me, and I wanted to repay their kindness with my own. In the years that followed, I continued to help Mr. Fuller and Mrs. Burke, often bringing along my brother-in-law as another helping hand.

When I finished building that second house, Mr. Fuller sold it quickly. I went back to Mrs. Burke to repay the loan — with interest. As it turned out, Mrs. Burke was more generous than I had even imagined.

"Sonny, you don't have to pay me the interest," she said.

I asked her why, explaining that I was only too happy to pay her the entire agreed-upon amount.

"No, Iggy," she said, "I don't want you to pay me the interest. You've been so good to me, and you're always helping me cut the grass for nothing. I want you to keep that money."

Mrs. Burke was financially comfortable, but she was not a wealthy woman. She lived in a twelve-hundred-square-foot bungalow. It was a nice home, but hardly a palace. Mrs. Burke simply wanted to give me a boost in my early days as a builder, a gesture I have not forgotten to this day.

Years later, in 1964, I built Mrs. Burke a new house of her own around the time of her one hundredth birthday. She was living with her wheelchair-bound eighty-year-old daughter at the time. It would be the first time I had seen — let alone built — a house with ramps for wheelchair access.

I have great fondness in my heart for my unexpected benefactor. Margaret Burke was a tremendous help to me long before I ever became a somebody. Her $4,000 was the seed money that allowed my company to grow from a sprout and flourish into the flower it later became. Without her help and belief in me, my business might never have had the chance to get going.

PARTNERSHIP

My first business partner in Canada was Veliko Todorov, the same man who helped me build my first house. Veliko was an excellent handyman and builder, but more than anything, he was a fine gentleman.

He grew up in the small Bulgarian village of Obretenik, located four miles southeast of my hometown. Veliko was an apprentice with a window company back in Bulgaria. When my father built our family's new house in 1936, Veliko installed the windows, although I do not remember meeting him at that time.

More impressively, Veliko had been a high-ranking soldier in the King's Guard at the palace in Sofia. He was the same age as my oldest brother, Kanu, who had also earned a prestigious place in the military. They were both very smart individuals, so it came as no surprise that Veliko and my brother prospered in their country's service.

Years later I became acquainted with Veliko while we were both living in Austria. He moved there in 1947 after the communists took control of Bulgaria. As I did, he distributed fruit and vegetables in Graz. His boss had a stand in the market like mine, so we saw each other frequently.

Later still, Veliko and I moved to Canada at around the same time. The secret police were bearing down on him just as they had with me. However, unlike me, Veliko was unable to pay for his own transportation to Canada. As a result, like many other immigrants at the time, he was sent to an Alberta farm on a three-year work term to repay the debt he owed the government.

Also, like many new immigrants in those days, Veliko did not fulfill his end of the bargain. During my first days of working for Mr. Shipp, it quickly became evident that my boss could use a skilled tradesman like Veliko. I wrote my friend immediately, and he left Alberta within days of arriving. There were no repercussions; the authorities did not come after Veliko.

After all, it was in Canada's best interest to have Veliko working as a craftsman. He was a highly skilled worker, the sort of man who could really help build the country. Maybe the Royal Canadian Mounted Police did go looking for Veliko when he left Alberta, but I imagine they most likely did not. Many of the immigrants who abandoned their jobs slipped through the cracks and were able to go on to contribute to their new country in other ways for many years. Veliko was one such immigrant.

Of course, many new Canadians did fulfill their obligations to the government. Boris Mitev was one of these immigrants. Dr. Mitev was simply the sort of man who always paid his debts and honoured his com-mitments, no matter what the cost. It was one of the qualities I most respected in him.

On Veliko's first day in town, I brought him to Mr. Shipp's office, where he was hired immediately. Thanks to his status as a master carpen-ter, Veliko started working at a rate of $1.75 per hour. I was happy for him, of course, even though I was only making a comparatively measly $1.10 at the time. For a brief time, Veliko and I even became housemates.

While Katarina and I were living in Mrs. Bartula's garage, on my way to work I regularly walked past the house belonging to Mrs. Zuck mentioned earlier. She lived with a gentleman named Mr. Brock. After a few days, I finally saw Mr. Brock outside and decided to ask him if he had a room to rent.

"Yes, I do," he said.

Within days Katarina and I moved out of that garage and into a much nicer room with a shared kitchen. After arriving in Ontario a short time later, Veliko moved into the house, too. Incredibly, my friend did not even have to pay rent — Mr. Brock let him live rent-free in exchange for Veliko's services renovating the basement.

We lived together, we both worked for Mr. Shipp, and even our wives found employment together for 50 cents per hour at the Admiral Corporation, a local television-manufacturing plant. When I finished my first house, Veliko decided to build a residence for himself and his wife, and I helped him, as he had done with me. So by the time construction was com-pleted on his house, it seemed natural to continue working together on proj-ects during the weekends. We could both see there was money to be made.

After I moved into my house, people in the area saw what I had built and began asking me to help them build houses of their own, which Veliko and I did, working weekends and evenings. Veliko, my Croatian friend, Stanislav Zira, and I would build the frame, lay down the floors, and put on the roof. After that our clients had to attach sheathing to the frame and provide the finishing touches. It was a great little business, and the three of us started making quite a bit of money on the side.

Soon after we began, Stanislav — who was an older gentleman — withdrew from our weekend operation, leaving only Veliko and me to carry on. In those days, I would earn about $75 net working for the Shipp Corporation from Monday to Friday and then another $300 on the weekend, which I split evenly with Veliko. It was a lot of money to us back then.

Even though I had not particularly enjoyed the partnership arrangement I had in Graz, Veliko and I respected each other and worked well together. While we had no agreement in writing, there was an understanding that we would split all of our profits down the middle.

Although I was more experienced in business, Veliko had much to teach me about many aspects of construction. My associate possessed tremendous expertise, and I learned new things from him every day. He knew how to do things like make kitchen cabinets and install windows from his days as an apprentice in Bulgaria. These were essential skills for any builder.

For a time, my association with Veliko was both fruitful and harmonious. I did a good job of finding business and then laboured alongside my skilled friend to do good work. It was a mutually beneficial situation.

Early on I knew a formal partnership with Veliko could not work for me in the long term. But, for the time being, I was happy to work with Veliko, learn from him, and make good money. Hard to say now how long our arrangement might have lasted, but back then there was no need to speculate much because Veliko's wife, Rosa, forced it into a perhaps premature end.

Unfortunately for Veliko, he told Rosa how much we were making. She quickly decided that her husband — being the skilled craftsman he was — deserved a bigger slice of the pie. Rosa believed that because he brought superior carpentry and construction skills to our partnership, he deserved a full partnership interest. I disagreed. I wanted to have Veliko as my valued full-time employee. It was I who was finding the clients and making the decisions, and I wanted this to be my own business.

"Veliko is the maestro of this operation," she said. "Why are you dividing the money in half? My husband should be taking home much more than 50 percent of the profits!"

"Is that so?" I asked indignantly.

Given that Veliko and I had started our little business together, I could not agree with his wife's suggestion that my partner deserved a bigger cut of our earnings. I was working every bit as hard as Veliko in terms of the labour while also attracting new clients. As my friend and his wife would come to learn, without clients there is no business. Besides, as the controller of the business venture, albeit informally, I could have opted to pay Veliko less than 50 percent.

"Rosa, you can keep your husband home and find him a new job," I told her. "Nobody can deny that Veliko is a maestro, but I can find an employee and go into business for myself, if that's how you feel."

Although it was clear Veliko was a superior craftsman to me technically, I knew I could hire a skilled worker to replace him. I enjoyed being the leader of my own company, and I thrived on making important decisions every day.

So I chose to end my unwritten partnership with Veliko and go out on my own. I immediately hired my first employee, a Bulgarian man named Nick Doncheff.

Throughout my many years as a business owner, I have always hired Bulgarians whenever possible. All things being equal, I prefer to give opportunities to men and women from my home country. That is not to say I only hire people from my home country, but Bulgarians have done a great deal for me throughout my life, and it is my sincere hope to help the Bulgarians striving to make a life for themselves in Canada.

During my business's early phase, my only employee worked parttime, mostly on weekends, whenever he could spare a few hours. But that was all I needed. He bridged the gap for a few months, after which I hired three men of Japanese descent who had come to Toronto Township from British Columbia. For several years — before their return to Japan — these men provided me with tremendously skilled labour at a fraction of the cost I would have had to pay Veliko.

Looking back, I see that the business could have grown even more quickly had Veliko and I not parted ways. He truly was a skilled tradesman on the job site, and having him at the helm of our projects would have allowed me more freedom to go out and make good deals. We had already proven that we worked well together.

Veliko's wife realized the error of her ways six months later. She begged me to take back her husband as my partner, but by then it was too late. I was already entrenched as the leader of my own company and had no intention or reason to share control with anyone else. I now recognize that the end of our partnership was necessary for me to continue along my path to success.

Still, I appreciate good workmanship and don't bear grudges. Veliko ended up working for me part-time on and off for years to come. He was a smart man and knew his trade.

There was one big difference between Veliko and me: I was always a risk-taker, ready and willing to bet on myself at any time. To me, there was no better wager than on myself. Veliko was the opposite. Sadly, his wife would not let him take similar risks. For example, as I mentioned earlier, after I finished my first house, Veliko wanted to build his own, so I helped him by signing my property over to the bank to allow him to obtain financing. But, if the shoe had been on the other foot, his wife would have never permitted him do the same for me. She did not want him to gamble on building his business. As I came to learn, making it big sometimes required taking big chances. Nevertheless, no risk I ever took was unplanned or uncalculated.

If at first I questioned the decision to go out on my own, I was reassured when Mr. Brock decided to build himself a second house. Veliko and I both bid on the job. My former partner held the advantage of having already done excellent work in renovating Mr. Brock's basement. But in the end, Mr. Brock awarded the work to me. Despite being a talent with his toolkit, Veliko was not skilled at other aspects of construction work such as the all-important pricing of trades and providing accurate cost estimates. I possessed these skills.

Over the years, I have often wondered about, and have been asked about, the key to my success. What separated me from my competitors — men like Veliko — was that I knew how to sell myself. That was the difference. I understood how to talk to people and was aware of the subtleties involved in making a deal.

With this turn of events, I learned once again that I did not want, nor did I need, a partner in business. That would only hold me back.

LONG WINTERS

I built Mr. Brock's house during the weekends of 1952 while still employed at the Shipp Corporation. By the end of 1953, I decided to leave Mr. Shipp's company to try my hand at running my own enterprise full-time. I started off by building a few houses, including one that was located on Caldwell Avenue in Lorne Park, today part of Mississauga.

It was wintertime, and even if I had not decided to go out on my own, Mr. Shipp would have laid me off until the following spring. Unlike today, when there are heaters on job sites to keep builders warm, we did not work in the construction industry during the winters.

I had begun building the Caldwell house on speculation, believing I would be able to sell it right away. I was wrong. After putting on the roof, I was forced to close the house for the winter because I lacked the funds to finish it.

Unfortunately, this left me without a source of income for that winter. Until I found a buyer, I could not finish the house. I had to be resourceful.

Luckily for me, the Ford Motor Company was opening a big plant in Oakville at that time. I preferred working for myself, but now I needed a job to support myself. I applied for a position and was stunned to see three hundred other men lined up outside the building. Every one of them was looking for work.

Fortunate yet again, I was able to land a job at Ford because I happened to know how to spot-weld from my days of rebuilding houses in Germany during the war. I was a twenty-six-year-old man with a skill that happened to be in demand at Ford, so I got a job that many others coveted.

Not only did I win the job but it also paid a generous $1.54 per hour. This was nearly the same wage I was earning at the Shipp Corporation and was far more than I could earn elsewhere at the time. As far as I knew, nobody paid as well as Shipp, but the Ford Motor Company came close.

Oddly enough, I only worked at Ford for two and a half days. I went in on the first day, they showed me the equipment and told me what to do, and I got to work right away. I spent the next two days welding before I received a call that would alter my fortunes yet again.

When I closed the house in Lorne Park, I left a sign on the lawn, hoping an interested buyer would contact me. After two days at Ford, I got a call from an American man and went to meet him at the house.

With the little bit of English I spoke at the time, this larger-than-life American and I managed to strike a deal, and I agreed to finish building the house for him. The next day I went back to Ford, worked for half of the day, and then asked to see my boss in his office to tell him I was quitting.

"Are you crazy?" he asked incredulously, then led me to his window and pointed down at the street. There was a lineup of people curling around the corner. "Any one of those people outside would kill for the job you're giving up right now."

I knew my boss was speaking the truth, but I also understood that my future at an unfinished house in Lorne Park awaited me. I was a builder, and as of now, I was back in business.

Just as soon as I sold the house, I bought another lot. I was also building an addition onto another man's house in Port Credit, and soon I was working on yet another house. Everything was moving forward for me as a builder.

JACKPOT

I was moving along steadily with my business, acquiring new building projects regularly and making good money. All things considered, I was doing even better than I could have reasonably expected. I was enthusiastic to continue growing my company and optimistic about my future in Canada. When I first came to the country, I would have given anything for the chance to go back home. Now that I was experiencing success, I had absolutely no desire to leave.

On November 11, 1955, another twist of fate altered the course of my future. Instead of progressing slowly toward success, my path was accelerated.

I recall the exact date because it was so important to my professional development, but even more so because it was Remembrance Day in Canada. I was observing a moment of silence for the fallen soldiers while visiting the office of Dell Holdings, a local real estate company owned and operated by Mariano Elia, a man who would later become an influential figure in my life. At this time Mr. Elia's office at the corner of Dundas Street and Credit Woodlands Road was where I went when in search of new building lots.

That day, shortly after the Remembrance Day ceremonies concluded, a real estate agent for A.E. LePage (now Royal LePage) named Sheff Kassan approached me. I already knew Mr. Kassan well from the local realty scene; he was trying to sell one of the houses I had recently built.

After a few moments of chatter, Mr. Kassan revealed he was fundraising for a hospital the community wanted to build at the corner of the Queensway and Hurontario Street.

"Iggy, would you be able to donate some money to help us build the hospital?" he asked.

"Of course," I said. "I'd be happy to help. How much should I give?"

Mr. Kassan thought it over for a moment before telling me to donate whatever I could comfortably afford.

By this time, I was already making very good money as a builder. I had been producing about two houses per year to that point for a total of seven, which put me into a comfortable financial position.

"I'd like to pledge $2,000 for the hospital," I said. "But I'm going to need three years to pay it all off."

Mr. Kassan quickly agreed to my terms.

Truth be told, $2,000 was not unaffordable to me at the time, especially for a cause as worthy as this one. I was building and selling houses one after the other, and by selling my houses privately, I was saving almost $1,500 on every sale, strictly because I did not have to pay commission to a real estate agent.

A few days later I gave Mr. Kassan the first installment of my donation, and that was the last time I thought about it until early in 1956.

During the frigid January days in 1956, my little construction company suddenly became feverishly successful. Without warning I was getting more customers than ever before. One after another they were lining up, paying me to build them houses.

After four or five of these requests, I finally asked one of my clients the question that needed to be answered: "Who sent you?"

The answer was always the same: "Mr. Davis's office sent me," I was told time and again.

Who is Mr. Davis? I wondered.

As I would come to learn, all donations for the hospital Mr. Kassan had approached me about were sent to the office of Davis & Davis, an important law firm in the area. Grenville Davis was the man in charge of this firm, and he was responsible for keeping count of the donations for the hospital. In those early days of January 1956, he was reviewing the list of donors and donations and happened upon my name. Mr. Davis was astounded at the number that jumped off the page.

Later, I was told that Grenville was a highly respected lawyer, the chief Crown attorney of Peel County. In the future, his son, Bill Davis, would go on to become the eighteenth premier of Ontario. What I did not know at the time was that Grenville Davis would become my single most important benefactor, even though I would never actually encounter the man face to face. However, I did meet young Bill later when his father sent him to my house with an election sign for my lawn. My neighbour at the time had a sign for Bill's opponent, which I removed. Today, every time Bill Davis and I meet, he calls me "philosophically misguided," a term he reserves for acquaintances who are not Progressive Conservatives.

As it turned out, my $2,000 was the largest donation made to the hospital in 1956, even compared to the amounts given by the area's wealthy elite. Apparently, our community's upper crust was generally donating $5, $10, or a maximum of $50 toward the hospital. I was later told that the second-largest donation made was $100.

Grenville Davis was stunned to learn that somebody he had never heard of was donating far more than anyone else.

"Who is this Ignat Kaneff?" he asked.

"He's a little Bulgarian immigrant," answered one of his aides. "Kaneff is building houses in the Erindale Woodlands area."

As I was later informed, an astonished Grenville paused to think for a moment and then made a proclamation that would come to change my life: "From now on I want every deal that comes through our office for a house to be referred to this Bulgarian immigrant. Give them all to Kaneff!"

In those days, prospective homeowners would see their lawyer first while preparing to buy a house, not a real estate agent. The solicitor would handle the entire deal, referring the client to a reputable builder while handling all of the paperwork. Obviously, getting referrals from a prominent lawyer like Grenville was a huge boost to my company and my reputation in the community.

I sold twenty-seven houses as a direct result of my $2,000 donation to the hospital. To this day, it remains the best money I have ever spent. For the first time in my career as a builder, clients were coming to me without any solicitation on my part.

I can't believe my luck, I thought as client after client came to me to build their houses.

My decision to donate to the hospital was a tipping point for my business. Before I'd ever heard the name Grenville Davis, my company was building up slowly but surely. Once I made that donation, however, it was as if everything changed overnight.

I knew I could sell houses as well as anybody, and I was confident in my ability to pay off $2,000 over three years. But thanks to Grenville Davis I was able to donate the full amount much sooner than that.

In the coming years, that hospital came to stand as a pillar of what would come to be known as the City of Mississauga. I felt a deep sense of pride knowing that when people entered the dining hall of that fine building, they saw the words DONATED BY IGNAT KANEFF etched on its doors. *Finally*, I thought, *everybody will know my name.*

In November 1955, I was just another builder working hard to sell a house here and there. I was gaining a little traction, but I was still a no-body. By January 1956, when the referrals started rolling in from the law firm of Davis & Davis, I was starting to feel like a somebody.

For the first time, I was getting invited to parties by society's elites, most notably to the gala to celebrate the opening of our hospital.

Attending that party was simply surreal. Everybody wanted to talk to me, congratulate me, and shake my hand. The people of my community were genuinely thankful for what I had done to help build the hospital, and they made me feel very special. That night I felt important, and I beamed with pride as never before since coming to Canada.

Even better, getting invited to this party and others like it helped me find even more clients. For instance, I met a man named Tom Buckley while attending a hospital party at the Credit Valley Golf and Country Club, and he ended up buying not one but two houses from me.

I was beginning to reach a level of success beyond my wildest dreams, but I was far from done. I was only scratching the surface of all that was to come. Iggy Kaneff was just getting started.

10

Putting Down Roots

I spent 1956 to 1964 building houses. During this period, I experienced the rush of success time and time again as I built 307 homes north of Dundas Street in the Erindale Woodlands area of Mississauga. I was selling houses as if it was no more difficult than selling eggs in my village when I was a boy. In my wildest dreams, I could not have hoped for more.

Every day was filled with excitement, and I brought that enthusiasm to my work. I immersed myself in my enterprise, and to my own great delight, I officially registered the Kaneff Construction Company in August 1956. From that point forward I was all about business, so much so that I moved into the Erindale Woodlands development myself. Katarina and I became two of its first residents.

I worked so much in those days, but I never felt as though I wanted to do anything else. Also, interestingly, I do not recall experiencing fatigue from the breakneck pace of my construction schedule. Quite simply, I loved my job. Every morning I arrived on-site by seven o'clock — often six o'clock — with a spring in my step. I always shook every labourer's hand. I wouldn't stop working until the sun set in the evening

— sometimes I even worked through the darkness. It could be seven, eight, nine, or even ten o'clock in the evening before I gave myself a rest, and that schedule often included working on both Saturdays and Sundays. I was putting in long hours every single day but was elated to be doing so.

One of my employees at the time asked me how many hours I worked.

"I'm working about eighty hours a week," I told him before wryly adding, "but that's just the overtime."

We both laughed as he walked away, but I knew my response was probably accurate. Work was my life, and my life was work.

It might seem that I should have gotten tired or burned out working at that pace, but it was just the opposite. I was young and so passionate about my company and my newfound success; I had boundless energy to put into it. Any success I experienced fuelled my desire to work even harder.

For instance, I never took my lunch break while sitting at a table. I always walked around with a sandwich or a piece of fruit that I brought from home, getting things done while I ate — just as I had done as a novice working for Mr. Shipp. I worked through the morning with my employees, and then as they sat down to eat lunch, I hopped into my truck and drove off to get the materials we needed for the afternoon. As I saw it, time spent eating lunch at a table was time that could be spent working. From the very beginning I understood that time was my most valuable commodity.

I recognized that I had been the recipient of a tremendous gift when Grenville Davis started referring clients to me as a result of my charitable donation to South Peel Hospital (later renamed Mississauga Hospital, now a member of Trillium Health Partners), but I also realized I needed to work hard so that I could capitalize on my good luck. After all, they say a man makes his own luck. I did everything possible to meet the needs of my customers, my employees, my family, and myself. I promised myself that even though some aspects of success were out of my control, I would never let myself fail due to lack of effort.

I built seventeen houses in 1956, which was the first big year for my construction company. Better yet, I never had to build a house speculatively. I was always able to wait until a house was sold before I started building it. When everything was pre-sold, I could build without being concerned about overextending my company financially.

If I sold a house, I would start building it right away. If I sold one the next day, I would start building that one, too. At the time subcontractors did most of the work on these houses. I hired licensed plumbers and electricians, while my men and I did all the carpentry. I had a process in place for building quality homes. With practice, my men and I improved at our trade and became more efficient at building houses, a necessity when I became much busier in the immediate future.

MR. ELIA

Other than the referrals I had received from Grenville Davis, the luckiest break of my early years in Canada was meeting Mariano Elia. Like my father and Bai Kolyo before him, Mr. Elia became a tremendous source of guidance, encouragement, and wisdom upon which I could draw. He was a true mentor to me, a father figure in a foreign land.

Mariano Elia and I first crossed paths on the day I went to buy two lots from my realtor friend, Earl Clare. Mr. Clare was a real estate agent, but Mariano Elia owned all the lots, and he had the final say regarding who could or could not purchase them. Builders often buy property from land developers who specialize in rezoning undeveloped land for houses, factories, or any other use. Some builders integrate this important function into their business, but at the time I didn't have the capacity to develop the land as well as build on it. (Over time, I did incorporate this function into our business model.) So, before I could buy, I had to go speak to Mr. Elia in his office. Mr. Clare prepared me by telling me everything he knew about this man. He considered Mr. Elia to be an intimidating figure and urged me to approach him carefully.

At the time of our introduction in 1955, Mr. Elia was in his early fifties. He was a few inches shy of six feet tall but still intimidating with his gruff features and disapproving expression, not to mention his status as a man who could make or break any hopeful builder in the area. Mr. Elia was an immigrant who had come to Canada as an eighteen-year-old boy to avoid being sent to the army in his native Italy. Like me, he had found success in Canada as a young immigrant.

Earl Clare introduced me to Mariano Elia, we shook hands, and then we quickly hit it off, much to even my own surprise. For some reason, Mr. Elia, one of the most prominent land developers in the area, took an immediate liking to me. Mr. Clare had described him as a hard man who was often known to be difficult with builders. When it came to his dealings with me, however, Mr. Elia was incredibly kind and generous from the very beginning.

As best as I could figure at the time, Mr. Elia probably thought I was a nice, harmless young man. However, as the years passed and I came to know him better as a man and a close friend, I realized I probably reminded Mariano of himself as a younger man — a go-getter with endless ambition for work.

Long after the fact, I was told that Mr. Elia already knew who I was, what I was doing, and why I had come to his office. I was still a small-time player among builders in the area, but he was the sort of man who knew about all the players in his circle of influence, big or small. Most likely he had just seen one of the signs I had posted on the front lawn of a house I had completed. When it came to business, Mr. Elia did not like surprises. Clearly, he did not want me to become a surprise competitor.

He owned all the land in Erindale Woodlands, about 450 acres in total, and he was parcelling it out to builders of his choosing. Fortunately for me, Mr. Elia valued quality in building above all else, and he considered my houses to be of the finest quality. He agreed to sell me two lots on that first day and spelled out his conditions. "If you do a good job, I'll sell you all the lots you could ever want to buy," he said. "But if I don't like your work, you won't ever get another piece of land from me."

I took Mr. Elia at his word and thanked him for selling me those first two lots, promising to work as hard as I could to meet his expectations. I knew that if I failed to impress him with these first two houses, I would be all but done as a builder in Erindale Woodlands.

Mr. Elia was involved in the Erindale Woodlands development on every level, from the long-term planning vision right down to the smallest detail. For example, if he disliked the colour of paint a builder chose for a house, the builder had to repaint it right away. Otherwise he could — and often would — stop selling that builder lots. You could not argue with him. Mr. Elia was not an unreasonable man, but he had his own vision for the development of Erindale Woodlands.

Although I was uncertain why Mr. Elia liked me when we first met, I knew why he continued to like me: quite simply, I was selling houses, and more importantly, selling them quickly. Most of my competitors were not able to do that. The other builders in the area saw what I was doing, and many of them assumed they could sell houses, too. They started building houses on the assumption they could sell them later on but couldn't follow through. So many of my early competitors got stuck with properties they could not sell or afford to keep; most of them went bankrupt. I understood that a businessman needs to have a plan. My strategy relied on pre-selling. That was the key to my success.

While my association with Mr. Elia began as a business relationship, it quickly grew into what would become an enduring friendship that spanned decades. I was invited to his house many times and became close to his family. Later on I would become the only outsider he ever brought to golf with him at St. George's Golf and Country Club, a prestigious members-only golf club in Toronto. In business and as a friend, Mr. Elia helped me tremendously.

In many ways, Mr. Elia was an inspiration to me. He was smart and tough, having come to Canada with very little before building an empire. And he did more than just build houses; he funded and erected schools and municipal buildings. Mr. Elia's philanthropy knew no bounds. In 1984, he started the Mariano Antonio Elia Foundation supporting humanitarian, educational, religious, and scientific aims. He was quite literally helping to build his adopted country of Canada, and his success motivated me to do the same.

I was able to keep selling houses thanks to the referrals I received from Grenville Davis, even while my competitors were suffering the consequences of government policy. On February 20, 1959, Prime Minister John Diefenbaker's Progressive Conservative government abruptly cancelled production of the Avro Arrow, a Canadian interceptor aircraft that was being made in nearby Malton, providing so many in the area with good jobs.

More than twelve thousand Avro employees were laid off, placing a tremendous strain on the local economy. My steady stream of referrals kept me afloat while many of my competitors went out of business.

As I showed Mr. Elia my ability to survive among the crowd of builders, my personal and business relationships with my mentor continued to flourish. He made buying lots very easy for me. Whenever I wanted to build a house, all I had to do was send him the plans in advance. Mr. Elia and I made a deal. "You don't have to put down any money when you want a lot," he told me. "Just go out and build the house." Once the house was built, the new homeowner moved in. As soon as that happened, I was paid, allowing me to compensate Mr. Elia for the land then.

The price for a lot was between $3,000 and $5,000 — the equivalent of several hundred thousand in today's market — and doing business this way allowed me to build house after house without financial risk. My deal with Mr. Elia spared me from pre-funding the lot costs, which saved me working capital in the way of borrowing costs, no mean portion of a house's construction budget.

As we developed our relationship further, Mr. Elia began selling lots in Erindale Woodlands only to me. Other than a small parcel of land he sold to his son-in-law to build a few townhouses on, mine was the only construction company working in the area. There were eighteen such businesses building houses in that subdivision in 1956. When the subdivision was finally completed in 1964, I was the only builder remaining. It only happened because Mr. Elia saw a part of himself in me. He believed in me as a builder and as a man.

Coming to know him personally, I realized Mr. Elia was a family man above all else. He had a lovely wife and six beautiful children, two boys and four girls. Despite his many great accomplishments, Mr. Elia took the greatest pride in his family.

In fact, it was just a few months after we came to know each other that Mr. Elia invited me to join his family at the head table for his daughter's wedding. I was honoured by my friend's gesture.

Unlike my own modest marriage ceremony, the wedding of Mr. Elia's daughter, Marlene — a prominent local newscaster — to Elvio DelZotto was a lavish event. It was my first time as a guest of a traditional wedding party — an Italian one, no less — and I was dazzled by its pageantry. The Elia-DelZotto wedding was a spectacular event with no expense spared, far beyond anything I had ever imagined as a boy in Bulgaria. To me, simply being involved in such a special day — let alone sitting at the head table — was an amazing experience. This wedding also marked the first time I ever wore a tuxedo.

As the years passed, Mr. Elia and I remained close friends. His office was just down the road from mine, so we were able to see each other frequently. On the long list of those who helped me on the path to success, this fine gentleman ranks near the top. Mr. Elia was a great mentor, and I am deeply grateful to him for his confidence in me.

Many years later, when Mr. Elia's heart finally stopped beating in 2006, I was asked by his family to deliver the eulogy at his funeral. On the day of his memorial service, it was my great honour to pay tribute to a great man's life. Along with all those who loved him, I bade my good friend a fond farewell.

BUILDING ON

With Mr. Elia giving me the opportunity to build house after house in Erindale Woodlands, I spent countless hours working in the subdivision. So many, in fact, that — as I said earlier — it finally occurred to me that I might as well move into it myself. Katarina and I packed our bags and took up residence in one of the area's nicest homes, which, of course, I had built.

When I first decided to move into the neighbourhood, all of my friends — particularly the men I knew from the construction industry — warned me against my plan. "Iggy, you shouldn't move into the place where you're building houses," they said. "Your customers will be after you all the time for every little thing that goes wrong."

In this case, being around my customers was a privilege. I wanted to be nearby so that if things needed to be fixed I could make the repairs right away. I wanted my customers to be satisfied with their new homes, and living close by helped me make that happen. If a door was hanging improperly, I was right over to fix it. With that satisfaction, my existing clients became an incredible source for my future business. They saw that

I went the extra mile to make sure their homes were perfect, so they made referrals to their friends and relatives, trusting they would enjoy the same positive experience of buying a Kaneff-built home. I became close friends with many of my clients, all of them first-time homeowners.

I was constructing house after house, but the task never became monotonous because, by design, all of the houses were different. I was working with a great architect named Paul Machino, who came to me by way of Mr. Elia's highest recommendation. He designed all of the houses and then I simply built them to plan. Mr. Elia took care of all the roads and infrastructure with the help of his planners. In all, the subdivision consisted of more than 450 houses, enormous by the standards of the time and still impressive today.

In 1957, I was building houses in Erindale Woodlands, but now I thought it was time to go on to bigger things.

When I first applied to start building apartment complexes in what was then known as Toronto Township, the planning commissioner, Max Bacon, strongly advised me against it. I wanted to build two nine-suite complexes near Hurontario Street (Highway 10) on Paisley Boulevard, the first of their kind in what would come to be known as Mississauga. Mr. Bacon thought I would go broke.

"Who's going to want an apartment out in farmland?" he asked me. "Are you going to rent apartments to cows?"

I could only laugh, because from experience I knew he was wrong. During my first months in Canada, I had looked high and low for an apartment complex like the ones I planned to build, but there were none available. This left me living in a string of less-than-desirable places. There was simply nothing of the kind to be found in the area, and I could see clearly that Toronto Township was full of young married couples searching for a place to live.

Canadians were enjoying the prosperous postwar decades. People seemed to be bursting with enthusiasm and wanted to buy homes in a suburban utopia. As soon as I put out the FOR RENT sign before I had even built the complexes, would-be tenants clamoured to rent my suites. I had commitments to rent every unit even before starting the excavation. The apartment buildings on Paisley Boulevard stand to this day.

In 1959, going on to bigger things from that modest project, I built two six-storey buildings nearby on Jaguar Valley Drive, one totalling thirty-five units, the other forty-five. These were my first high-rises, and I was proud to see them go up.

Construction of an apartment complex is actually less difficult than building a house. An individual house requires more detail than a complex. For an apartment building, the builder does everything on one floor — plumbing, electrical, drywall, and so on — and then simply repeats the process again and again, eventually reaching the top floor. At that point the roof is installed and the job is complete. In contrast, building a house requires far more in terms of customized detail.

Still, apartment buildings are overall much bigger projects than houses, and they keep builder-owners busy over a longer period of time.

After completing these first multi-family residential projects, I owned the properties for several years. Eventually, I sold them, which I still regret to this day. Like some of the other apartment buildings I built later, these apartment complexes could still be a part of my company's revenue stream. But what's done is done. If nothing else, these first three apartment buildings provided a valuable learning experience in larger-scale projects.

I discovered that I was able to take on more and more projects without much strain. Having worked for Gordon Shipp, I could see the masterful manner in which he managed a large construction company, and I used many of his methods with my own company. I was filled with confidence that I could run a company just as well as my former boss — if not even better.

Even as I was building up to twelve houses at the same time, I was involved in every aspect of construction, from laying the brickwork, to framing the walls, to even doing some of the plumbing. The only thing I did not attempt myself was the electrical work. I considered that to be a specialty best left to skilled tradesmen.

And yet, even as I did more and more and was putting in increasingly long hours, none of it felt overwhelming. I always thought my career was progressing naturally. I was learning new things all the time and proving once again that I was an apt student. I was taking the time to master different aspects of my profession — gaining skill in a variety of trades —

and this learning always proved to be exciting and rewarding. It all began to feel simple to me.

My little construction company was growing quickly, and I felt as if I could do anything.

TEEING OFF

In 1957, golf came crashing into my life.

I was building a house on Old Carriage Road in Mississauga, across the street from the Credit Valley Golf and Country Club. Golf was still unknown to me. I had never swung a club, held a ball, or even so much as set foot on a golf course. I knew literally nothing about the sport.

Although I was building seventeen houses at the time, I was so involved in my own projects that I was still going to the job site every single day, tending to the smallest of details personally. One day I was cleaning the fireplace area in one of the new homes so that a bricklayer could come in the evening — he was unavailable to work for me during the daytime — to build a proper exhaust vent.

As I crawled on my hands and knees, wiping the floor, I heard a sudden crash and glanced up to see shards of window glass scatter across the floor. I picked up the strange object that had caused the damage — a white, hard, round, dimpled ball. Little did I know that a golfer on the Credit Valley course had badly hooked his tee shot, sending the ball straight through the picture window I had just installed.

A broken window that size would have cost me about $200 to replace back then; the same window is worth at least $2,000 now. I was upset that my property had been destroyed and needed to hold someone accountable, so I stormed outside to find the culprit.

When I got outside, two men were approaching the house, large leather golf bags slung over their shoulders. I was wielding a shovel ready to chase them down just as the farmer had pursued my friends and me when we stole his watermelons in Gorno Ablanovo. I really thought somebody had intentionally damaged my house.

"Calm down, young man," one of the men said when he saw the scowl on my face. "It was an accident. We'll pay to replace your window."

The two men did eventually reimburse me for the cost of the window. Once they shuffled off, returning to their game, I left the scene and called my insurance agent, Mr. Hardwood, to tell him about the damage that had been done to my house.

"Don't worry about the golfers," Mr. Hardwood assured me. "They're good people."

That was a surprise to me.

Mr. Hardwood explained the nature of the game and then invited me to play golf with him on the following Saturday. I graciously accepted his offer. That weekend I found myself swinging a strange club at the same sort of ball that had broken my window.

As I teed off on the first hole of the Peel Village Golf Club in Brampton, my only experience with the game was that of watching Mr. Hardwood hit his first shot a moment earlier. Taking a few practice swings, I copied Mr. Hardwood's motion as best I could, then stepped up to address the ball as it balanced on its tee.

I hit my very first golf shot crisply. The grass was dry that day, allowing the ball to roll favourably. I can honestly state that the first shot I ever hit travelled 264 yards onto the green of a par four on the first hole at the Peel Village Golf Club.

Pleased with the result, I turned to look at Mr. Hardwood, only to see an expression of shock and amazement on his face. "Iggy, I've been playing golf at this club for twenty-five years and I've never made it to the green from the tee on this hole. That was an impressive shot for a beginner, or anyone else for that matter." Without hesitation my friend made another declaration. "You should start playing golf!"

Golf was an expensive game to play on a regular basis — between $15 and $20 for a round of eighteen holes, or an annual membership fee of $100 — but I knew that I had the money to participate in this sport if I wanted to. So I decided right then and there that golf would be my new game. I did not have much spare time, but what little I had would now be spent on the golf course.

With that, golf came into my life just as haphazardly as that ball had come crashing through my picture window. With just one perfectly struck ball, I was hooked on the game for life.

Mr. Hardwood invited me to play at his club many more times. With more experience, my skill and knowledge of the game steadily improved. Once the word got out that I had taken an interest in golf, other people starting asking me to play with them, too. Before long I was playing golf any time I had the chance.

Robert Speck, who would go on to become the first mayor of the Town of Mississauga, taught me a great deal about how to play. It seemed that I possessed some innate ability when it came to golf, but he taught me many important lessons about how to hit the ball consistently. As we played together more and more, Mr. Speck eventually talked me into applying for membership at his course, the Mississaugua Golf and Country Club.

Mr. Speck and Sheff Kassan — my other friend who was also a member of the club — sponsored me for membership. I never had any reason to believe there would be a problem with my application, but after not hearing back from the club for a few weeks, I made my way there to check on its status.

Searching the grounds, I finally located the club's head golf pro and inquired about my application. He asked for my name, and when I told him I was Ignat Kaneff, he began to laugh. "Are you kidding me? We don't take Bulgarians at this club."

The members of the Mississaugua Golf and Country Club were predominantly Anglo-Saxon men, and I had just found out there was no room for a little immigrant like me among their ranks. I left the club, hurt, rejected, and humiliated. I had come to believe that Canada was a land of equality and tolerance, but I was beginning to see that prejudice and exclusion existed here just as they did everywhere else.

A few days later I was invited by three friends to have lunch at the Credit Valley Golf and Country Club. These three were also my customers, as I had built each of them a house. I told them about being rejected by the Mississaugua Golf and Country Club, and they were appalled.

Without delay one of the men offered his support. "Iggy, why don't you join here? Our club will happily accept you."

Credit Valley was a semi-private course at the time, meaning that while only members could play there, the club was owned by one person. At fully private courses, the members themselves owned the club. The owner of

Credit Valley had no apparent prejudice against Bulgarians, and I was approved for membership right away. In those days, joining the Credit Valley Golf and Country Club cost $100, which I happily paid in cash.

Since many of my friends — Dinko Mandarich, Marcello Gasparetto, Ray Dodge, the Fay brothers (Karl, Bill, and Stan), Ted Glista, and Benny Rockett, to name some — were already members, I was soon playing regularly. It was during this time that my love for golf began to blossom. I continued to play at Credit Valley almost exclusively for the next several years, only occasionally venturing off to play elsewhere.

In addition to the athletic challenge that golf provided, I greatly enjoyed the social side of the game. Because I was able to play golf well from the very beginning, I was also able to take pleasure in the game without getting frustrated, which is a trap that befalls many golfers. Golf is at once a game of skill and a game of relaxation. I have always liked golf because even though it is quite impossible to master, I could always enjoy myself, even if I was not playing well. In addition to being a thinking man's game that can be played outdoors, golf provides endless competition against oneself. I loved almost everything about it.

After only one year of playing, I had earned a thirteen handicap, meaning I usually shot approximately thirteen over par, quite the feat for a relative novice. Usually, if I played on a course that was par seventy-two, my score would hover around eighty-five or so. To put it into perspective, a pro like Tiger Woods might shoot sixty-six on a good day, while a novice would likely score at least a hundred, usually a hundred and twenty.

Golf came along at a time in my life when I had a strong desire for recreation and socializing. Before discovering the game, I was starting to feel as though I did nothing but work. Although I continued to work as hard as ever, golf helped prevent me from becoming too one-dimensional, while also connecting me to members of the community who shared my interest in the game.

CANADIAN CITIZENSHIP

I originally applied for my Canadian citizenship in 1955. At the time I was unaware of the rule that a person needed to be in the country for five years before applying for citizenship. I had only lived in Canada for four. Still, I received a notice from the federal government requesting that I appear at the courthouse in Brampton. Once I got there, an old judge told me about the rule.

"Young man, you have to come back in a year," he said. So I did just that.

When I first arrived in Canada, I believed my residence would be temporary. I had come to the country, hoping to avoid the secret police and to sidestep military service, but I knew sooner or later I would be able to return safely to Austria. I would have given anything for the chance to go back. After losing all my money, I desperately wanted to resume my old life. I greatly missed Austria and my network of friends. Austria was also much closer to my family in Bulgaria than Canada was.

What I did not count on, however, was the success and quality of life I would experience in Canada.

In truth, I made the decision to stay in Canada as soon as I began working for Gordon Shipp, just a few months after arriving in the country. The money I made while working for Mr. Shipp — $1.75 as a junior carpenter — was far more than I had ever earned before. The timing worked out well, too, because if I had been making that kind of money right from the start, I would have almost certainly used it to buy a one-way ticket home. But after tasting success in Canada that first winter, it became clear to me this new land would become my home.

In 1956, I went back to file my application to become a citizen of Canada once and for all. In those days, the process of acquiring Canadian citizenship included filling out an application, presenting your passport along with any other personal documentation you might have retained from your country of birth, and then going to the proper location for the swearing-in ceremony. The courthouse in Brampton was the only place in the area where someone could become a citizen at the time. Typically, you were called to the courthouse about three months after filing an application.

On the day I went to become a citizen, there were only about six other people at the courthouse for their citizenship. I needed to pass a brief test, but it was a simple assessment that involved the Crown attorney asking me questions like: "What is the capital city of Canada?" or "Who is the current prime minister?" There was nothing particularly challenging about the questions, and anybody could have passed with even a modicum of preparation.

To me, it was very exciting. Becoming an official Canadian citizen was incredibly meaningful.

After leaving my home the first time as a fourteen-year-old boy, becoming a Canadian citizen was a highly symbolic moment for me. It meant that finally I had a country to call home, a place where I was welcomed and even valued. At last I felt accepted as part of Canada's hopeful social experiment that brought people from around the world to live as citizens of a young country. After five years of being a kind of visitor in Canada, I now felt like a member of the community.

Bulgaria was a beautiful place in which to grow up, but at a certain point it became evident I needed to go elsewhere to grow into a man. Germany and Austria had offered me a taste of success, but sadly, I was forced to leave. In Canada, nobody was chasing me out of the country, nobody was demanding that I risk my life in the military, and nobody was attempting to throw me in jail for arbitrary and unjust reasons. Canada had become my home, and after five years of ever-increasing economic, personal, and social growth, I was proud to be a citizen.

I now had the confidence of knowing I was in Canada to stay. After so many years of moving from place to place, I had put down new roots. At long last I was home.

THE LIONS CLUB

Around the same time I first applied for citizenship in 1955, I decided that if I intended to be part of the surrounding community for the long term, I also wanted to contribute to it in a meaningful way. There is a time, of course, when contributing to society is as simple as writing a cheque. However, back in those days it was equally important for me to volunteer my time as well as to donate money.

It was a friend of mine, Mr. Robinson, who introduced me to the idea of joining the local chapter of the Lions Club International. He was one of the most community-minded men I had met in Canada. As he explained it to me, the Lions Club was an organization that only had the best interests of the community in mind. Founded in 1917, the Lions Club originated in the United States as a secular, non-political organization that aimed to meet the needs of its various communities by organizing services for the less fortunate and promoting the principles of good citizenship. As I deepened my roots in Canada in 1955, it seemed to be just what I was looking for: a way to help me satisfy my need to give something back to a community that had taken me in as one of its own.

Before joining, I sought the opinion of my friend, Peel Police Chief Garnet McGill. Although he was not a member himself, Chief McGill, a man I deeply trusted, had nothing but good things to say about the organization. His ringing endorsement helped convince me to become a member.

I quickly came to learn what the organization stood for: it was all about helping people. Whenever we saw somebody in a bad state, we did our best to help and comfort that individual. Sometimes that meant trying to find him or her a job; sometimes it simply meant giving that person some food. We did what we could to provide whatever was required.

During the holidays, I would do what I could to help families that had something lacking in their homes. As a builder, I had the resources to help those who needed assistance with their houses. For instance, if a family lacked proper cabinetry in their kitchen, I would give them cabinets. If somebody had a roof that was leaking, I would be the one to patch the leak. It filled me with a special sense of pride to be able to help people who truly needed it.

The Lions Club also placed a focus on education, which appealed to me. If there was a bright child in the community who could not afford to attend an institution of higher learning, we collected money to give that child a scholarship. We were unable to help every deserving student, but thanks to the Lions Club quite a few young people were given the chance to enjoy a bright future.

I also delivered food and presents to families in need around Christmas. An amusing story stems from my efforts one year. That winter our local supermarket ran out of turkeys. As a result, I bought a duck and delivered it to a family in the area. I left this duck with the man of the house and drove off, feeling confident I had done a good deed. Later that night, however, the mother of that family called me at home, and she was not pleased.

"Don't you know you're supposed to deliver a turkey at Christmas, not a duck!" she yelled at me over the phone. I explained that the store was sold out of all their turkeys, but she did not care for my excuses. This was a lesson to me that it is not possible to please everybody, even with the best of intentions.

My experience with the Lions Club was overwhelmingly positive, and I remained a part of the organization for many years. In fact, I still consider myself to be a member, even today. Years after I joined the organization, it honoured me as one of its Charter Members, presenting me with a pair of gold cufflinks and a gold tie clip, each of which I treasure to this day.

My father had always stressed the importance of community involvement, and now in Canada I was able to follow his wise advice. I was enjoying newfound success in Canada, but until I was able to give back — and truly give of myself — I knew I would always feel like an outsider. After gaining my citizenship and becoming a member of the Lions Club, I began to feel as Canadian as anyone else. I had always been a proud Bulgarian, but now I was a proud Canadian, too.

I was truly beginning to feel I was becoming a part of something special.

11

Driving Forward

To the non-immigrant reading this book, it might seem as though my rise to success in Canada was a smooth journey, lacking missteps, bad luck, or failure. But that would be the wrong picture. While I benefited from my share of good fortune — some might say more than my share — not everything I undertook was successful. My venture into the automotive industry, in particular, ranks high among my list of professional disappointments.

Things were going very well for me in the late 1950s, and I had no good reason to change anything I was doing. With a focus on construction, my business was rising to new heights. In 1957, in the aftermath of Kaneff Construction's incredible success with homes in Erindale Woodlands, I began building small apartment complexes, which soon led to high-rises and other larger-scale projects. By 1967, I had two twelve-storey buildings called Centennial Towers going up on Argyle Road in Mississauga. I followed these with high-rise apartments of twenty-two, eighteen, twenty, and eighteen floors. Eventually, I put up my first office tower, then several other even taller buildings. And I was also selling houses at the same time. Business could not have been better, my company was thriving, and I was now a success in Canada by anyone's standard.

Although all this happened in just a few years, I almost did not even notice as it developed. In my business, a small success led to a slightly bigger one, then another, and another. Through a series of these smaller steps, I found myself building twenty-storey apartment complexes and tall office towers, and it never felt strange, unnatural, or overwhelming.

It was like planting a young seedling: tend it carefully, give it time, and before long it was a big, strong oak tree standing on its own. As I became more and more successful, my deals were easier to make. More than ever before, prospective clients were coming to me. Thanks to my flourishing reputation as a builder — along with my relationship with Mr. Elia — I could put up as many houses as the market would bear, and even more important, as many as I wanted to build. I was loaded with work, and I was loving it.

During the early days of my company, I always used the basement of my house as an office. Later, when I had multiple projects on the go, I moved my operation into a proper office. I took an apartment unit in one of the Centennial Towers and turned it into my company's first real office. My long-time secretary, Grace Bridges, worked there, as did Eric McKnight, who eventually became my executive vice-president.

Alfred Valentino was my construction partner on Centennial Towers. I was godfather to Alfred's youngest daughter, and he and I became great friends. A hard-working man, Alfred had a terrific family who all worked with him. While we were putting up forms and racing to finish Centennial Towers to deadline, we had to pour concrete at night because the concrete workers were on strike and the material had to be delivered in the evening. To keep my labourers toiling so late, I supplied Kentucky Fried Chicken and beer for dinner.

One night I even treated them to wine with their KFC. However, they enjoyed the change of beverage a little too much and failed to pour the concrete in time for it to dry properly. The next day I had to get my workers to strip the concrete and start over. The lesson I learned on that occasion was never to provide alcohol during working hours.

Back then, as I got busier and busier with my various construction projects, I struck up a friendship with Willy Gnat of Midnorthern

Appliance. Even today, when we get together, we share stories about those early days. Willy always jokes that my left shirt pocket was my accounts receivable and the right one was my accounts payable and that I did a lot of my business out of a small pickup truck I had at the time.

Real estate agents were bringing me offers daily because they knew I was a doer. I was the man to speak to if you wanted to get a good house built at a fair price without any nonsense. I had proven to everybody I could do the job.

Looking back, I sometimes wish I had taken more time to appreciate my life in the 1960s and 1970s. No one who truly knows me thinks I am nothing but *build, build, build.* I have written about the yard work I did for Mr. Fuller and Mrs. Burke when I first moved to Lakeview: that yard work was a labour of love for me, and I still love to pass the time gardening. I read every chance I get — you should see how much I read. My daughters say they have never known anyone who reads as much as I do. I love listening to classical music, too. These are some of life's pleasures — don't people say you should stop and smell the flowers?

Never again would I experience the rush of such rapid professional growth, nor would I relive tasting major success for the first time. These years were magical.

A GM DEALERSHIP

If I had surveyed the landscape of my life in 1963, I would have realized it was undoubtedly in my best interest to continue with construction as my sole focus, just as I had been doing. But a part of me still identified as that little farm boy from Bulgaria trying to make it big in the world, so when the opportunity arose to get my name onto a General Motors Cadillac dealership, I was blinded by the bright lights of the automobile industry. This was an emotional decision for me. I was a victim of my own ego, and my move into cars would prove to be a big mistake.

Although I did not get involved with General Motors in an official way until 1963, I first dipped my toe in the automotive waters in 1958 when my friend, a Colombian named Carlos Lamprea, asked me to build his new Ford dealership.

My mother, Mita, and my father, Hristo.

Here, I am fourteen years old in 1941 (first row, on right) with fellow Bulgarian farm labourers in Wels, Austria (at that time annexed by Germany).

At sixteen years old in 1943, I continued my market gardening work with my father's friend, Bai Kolyo, in Wels.

These are some of the Bulgarians I worked with in the market garden business in Austria. I am seventeen years old here, second row on the far right, crouching.

That is me in the centre, holding up a kohlrabi cutting, celebrating the harvest with Bulgarian market gardeners and their families in 1944, including the Davidoffs, prominent Salzburg vegetable producers.

In 1952, I built my first house on Tenth Street in Lakeview, Toronto Township (later to become part of the City of Mississauga). It still stands, and here I am, much later in front of it.

At the field office for Kaneff Construction, circa 1958, Jaguar Valley Drive, Mississauga.

One of the houses I built in the Erindale Woodlands subdivision in the late 1950s. Later, this became my own house.

In 1958, in an early venture into the car business, I began construction on Woodland Motors, a Ford dealership owned by Carlos Lamprea in Mississauga. Carlos also bought a house from me in Erindale Woodlands.

Heidi and Danny, my children from my first marriage, in the mid-1960s in Mississauga.

In 1963, we broke ground for a state-of-the-art General Motors dealership – Parklane, built, managed, and owned by my company. I am no longer in the car business, but Parklane, now called Gateway, still stands at Queen Street East and Gateway Boulevard in Brampton.

The groundbreaking ceremony in 1967 for La Fontaine Bleue, an apartment high-rise in Mississauga that was completed two years later. I am in the centre with my hand on top of the shovel, while real estate agent and former Mississauga council member Terry Butt (former Conservative MP Brad Butt's father) is in the checkered suit to my left. Alfred Valentino, on my right and also holding the shovel, was my partner on the project and remains one of my best friends today. Most of the others are real estate agents.

Armed with a hard hat, I am In front of one of the many high-rise apartment buildings under construction by Kaneff in the 1970s.

On April 30, 1976, Ontario Premier Bill Davis (left) and Dr. Edward Robinson, principal of the University of Toronto's Erindale College, were among the numerous guests on hand to celebrate my twenty-fifth-year anniversary in Canada. The dinner was held at the Mississaugua Golf and Country Club. At the event, it was announced that two scholarships would be established for students enrolled in urban studies at Erindale.

In 1976, Prime Minister Pierre Elliott Trudeau congratulated me on the twenty-fifth anniversary of my arrival in Canada.

CANADA

PRIME MINISTER · PREMIER MINISTRE

O T T A W A, KIA 0A6
April 30, I976

Dear Mr. Kaneff,

     May I join your friends in congratulating you on the occasion of the 25th Anniversary of your arrival in Canada as an immigrant.

     It is a remarkable achievement that in coming to this country from Bulgaria, not speaking the language, you have been able by dint of initiative and hard work to succeed so brilliantly. We who are native born Canadians can take pride in the fact that Canada can provide the opportunity for a person such as yourself to succeed. We can also be grateful that a person like you selected this country and have made such a contribution to its economic growth.

     No area of Canadian endeavour is more important than that of providing good, economically priced shelter for our citizens. By devoting your energies to the construction of such housing you have served your adopted country well.

     Again, my warmest best wishes to you and your family.

Sincerely,

Mr. Ignat Kaneff
   c/o Mississauga Golf and Country Club
   Mississauga, Ontario

Place Royale, one of the many Kaneff white towers in Mississauga and Brampton, was completed in 1981 near Square One.

Pre-construction marketing for Obelisk 1, 2, and 3 at Square One in Mississauga. The three condo towers were completed at the end of the 1970s and beginning of the 1980s.

In October 1978, I was honoured to join a delegation of Polish Canadians attending the inauguration of Pope John Paul II at the Vatican. I do not recall the name of the man with the moustache but beside him are the Fujarczuk (Fay) brothers: Bill, Karl, and Stan. The fellow directly behind me is my very good friend Ted Glista.

Square One condos built in the late 1970s and early 1980s in Mississauga on and near Kaneff Crescent: Place Royale, Place Avant, and Place IV, along with rental apartment buildings Obelisk 1, 2, and 3. On the right is Hurontario Street (Highway 10) looking south.

Frank Bean, Peel Region chairman, cuts the ribbon with me at the opening ceremony for the apartment buildings at 210 and 220 Steeles West in Brampton in the early 1980s. Directly behind me is my wife, Didi.

Harold Shipp presents me with the 1982 plaque for Businessman of the Year, awarded by the City of Mississauga Board of Trade. Harold was the son of Gordon Shipp, the man who got me started in the construction business and for whom I first started working upon my arrival in Canada on April 18, 1951.

I am being congratulated by Ken Taylor, former Canadian ambassador to Iran and keynote speaker for this event, after accepting the 1982 Businessman of the Year Award from the City of Mississauga Board of Trade. Next to Ken is Ontario Revenue Minister Bud Gregory, while Ken's wife, Patricia, is on the right. Ken and Patricia were instrumental in helping rescue six Americans in 1979 during the Iran hostage crisis.

Ivan Marinoff was a Bulgarian architect who worked with me on numerous building projects over the years, along with his wife, Lucy, also an architect. Ivan joined me at the University of Toronto when I received an honorary doctor of laws from the university in 1994.

I had the pleasure of meeting and playing with many of golf's professional icons. Here I enjoy a round with Lee Trevino during the 1983 Canadian Open at Glen Abbey Golf Club in Oakville. American John Cook won the Canadian Open that year.

A family portrait taken in Mississauga in 1984. Didi and I are standing. Seated left to right are Ana Koleva (Didi's mother), Kristina Maria, Kosta Kolev (Didi's father), Anna-Maria, and Mita (my mother).

My ballerina daughters, Kristina Maria and Anna-Maria, circa mid-1980s in Mississauga.

On the tee in the 1980s at the Credit Valley Golf and Country Club with my golfing buddies of many years, from left to right: Benny Rockett, Marcello Gasparotto, and Ray Dodge.

Two of my very good golf partners — Eddie Del Medico (left) and Joe Messmer (behind me) — at the Credit Valley Golf and Country Club in the 1980s.

Ontario Premier David Peterson (centre) and Erindale College Principal Desmond Morton (near left) give developer Marco Muzzo, Sr. (far left) their undivided attention at the October 12, 1988, Building Fund Campaign kickoff and reception. As Building Fund chairman, I look on at the far right. Didi and I hosted the reception, which was attended by university and government officials plus local businessmen. Marco, as president of the Erin Mills Development Corporation, pledged $100,000 to the campaign.

The official ribbon cutting for the opening of the Kaneff Centre for Management and Social Sciences at Erindale College (now University of Toronto Mississauga) in 1992. From left to right, participants include Member of Parliament Bob Horner, Mississauga Mayor Hazel McCallion, University of Toronto President Rob Prichard, University of Toronto Chancellor Rose Wolfe, myself, and Ontario Lieutenant Governor Hal Jackman.

The Kaneff Centre at Erindale College (now University of Toronto Mississauga) opened its doors in 1992 as the home to business, commerce, and management programs at the school. The centre also features a lecture theatre with room for 350 students and contains the Blackwood Gallery in which students can appreciate different forms of art.

I initiated the annual Kaneff Charity Golf Tournament in 1971. Here Mississauga Mayor Hazel McCallion joins me at one of the tournaments in the 1980s. The event will celebrate its fiftieth anniversary in 2021 and is now under the auspices of the Ignatt Kaneff Charitable Foundation.

My sisters, Kuna (left) and Maria (right), joined me in Niagara Falls with my daughters, Kristina Maria and Anna-Maria, in 1986. Kuna and Maria had come to Canada as a surprise for my sixtieth birthday.

My brothers (left to right), Kanu, Lambi, and Simeon, in front of Toronto's Sts. Cyril & Methody Church celebrating the wedding of my niece, Yolanta (Kanu's granddaughter), in the summer of 1988.

The last time I saw my mother before she passed away, on my visit to Dve Mogili, Bulgaria, in 1988.

My good friend lawyer Mike Weir did much of my company's legal work over three decades from the 1960s through the 1980s.

Brampton Mayor Ken Whillans (foreground) drives the ball at the grand opening of the Lionhead Golf & Country Club in 1991.

Golfing legend Arnold Palmer appeared at the Lionhead Golf & Country Club for a PGA Tour event in May 1991.

Opened in May 1991 in Brampton, Ontario, as the Lionhead Golf & Country Club and now called Lionhead Golf Club & Conference Centre, the thirty-six-hole championship golf course is the the flagship in KaneffGolf's portfolio of courses.

My daughter and son from my first marriage and their children, Christmas 1995: from left to right are Jessica (Heidi's daughter), Heidi, Danny, and Katarina (Danny's daughter, in front of her father).

I have hosted many events at the Lionhead Golf Club & Conference Centre. This one is a Christmas party in the 1990s. Among many at this affair, from left to right, were legendary CHIN Radio founder Johnny Lombardi, former Ontario Premier David Peterson, and Rob Prichard, who at the time was president of the University of Toronto.

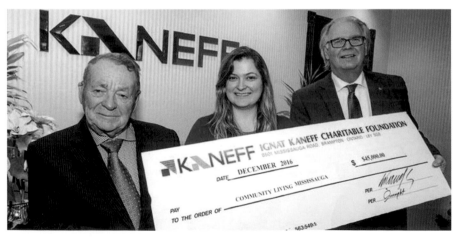

My daughter, Kristina Maria, and I present another year's cheque from the Ignat Kaneff Charitable Foundation to Eugene Nolin, president of the board of directors of Community Living Mississauga. Kristina Maria is the president of our foundation.

Didi and I greet former Soviet President Mikhail Gorbachev at a reception at the University of Toronto following his 1993 appearance at a forum discussion. Gorbachev first visited Canada in 1983 when he was the member of the Soviet Politburo responsible for state agriculture. As president of the Soviet Union, he made a two-day visit to Ottawa in 1990.

In 2010, York University's Osgoode Hall Law School conferred an honorary doctor of laws degree on me. On the left is York University Chancellor Roy McMurtry; on the right is Dr. Mamdouh Shoukri, president of York University.

The official opening of the Ignat Kaneff Building at Osgoode Hall Law School took place in April 2012. Left to right after Didi are architect Jack Diamond, federal Finance Minister Jim Flaherty, myself, York University President Mamdouh Shoukri, and Ontario MPP for Vaughan Greg Sorbara.

I had long thought that York University badly needed an engineering school, so I donated $5 million to help establish one. To recognize my support of the engineering school, York displayed my name prominently on its ten-storey administration building.

Celebrating my eightieth birthday at the Lionhead Golf & Country Club in 2006, with, left to right, Didi, Kristina Maria, Simeon Kanev (my youngest brother), Eric McKnight (friend and our company's former long-time executive vice-president), me, Anna-Maria, and Dave Greenwood (friend and our long-time former company accountant).

As Ontario's lieutenant governor, David Onley awarded me the Order of Ontario at Toronto's Queen's Park on January 25, 2011.

My long-time friend Dr. Konstantin L. Valtchev, M.D., F.R.C.S.(C), F.A.C.O.G., assistant professor, Department of Obstetrics & Gynaecology, University of Toronto, shown here, was a key figure, with me, in the planning and building of St. Dimitar Bulgarian Eastern Orthodox Church in Brampton in the early 2000s. He was also the church's second president, succeeding me. My daughter, Kristina Maria, is the current president.

St. Dimitar Bulgarian Eastern Orthodox Church in Brampton, Ontario, built and donated to the Bulgarian community by the Kaneff family.

Bulgarian President Georgi Parvanov was on hand in the fall of 2002 in Sofia to award me the Order of Stara Planina, First Degree, my native country's highest civilian honour.

The grand opening of the University of Ruse's Kaneff Centre occurred on my eighty-seventh birthday on October 6, 2013. To my immediate right holding the staff, His Holiness Patriarch Neofit, worldwide leader of the Bulgarian Eastern Orthodox faith; to my left, Bulgarian President Rosen Plevneliev, Anna-Maria, Kristina Maria, and Didi.

Wanting to help the University of Ruse in Bulgaria much as I had done with York University and the University of Toronto in Canada, I began to explore what I could do in 2012. By late 2013, in record-breaking time, the Kaneff Centre was completed. The two-storey complex features an eight-hundred-seat auditorium, three lecture halls, and a press conference hall.

Professor Hristo Beloev, Ph.D., D.Sc., D.H.C. (mult.), Core Member of the Bulgarian Academy of Sciences, and rector of the University of Ruse.

Over the decades, my family and I have done as much as we can for higher education institutions. The same applies for hospitals, such as University Hospital in Ruse, Bulgaria. I was honoured when its building was renamed University Multi-Specialty Hospital Kaneff.

For many years, I wanted to do something for my hometown of Gorno Ablanovo in Bulgaria. In the early 1970s, I paid for the building of a kindergarten and renovations of the village church. But I felt I had to do more, and I did when I fully funded this brand-new community centre and library, which opened its doors in 2014.

One of my proudest moments and accomplishments was being awarded the Order of Canada by Governor General David Johnston on May 12, 2017, at Rideau Hall in Ottawa.

In August 2015, Justin Trudeau came to my home for a campaign fundraiser before his successful election as prime minister in October of that year.

March 31, 2016

Dear Friends:

I am pleased to extend my warmest greetings to everyone attending the Community Living Mississauga Foundation's annual tribute dinner.

Tonight's event is special as it recognizes the notable career of Mr. Ignat Kaneff with a Lifetime Achievement Tribute. This is a wonderful occasion for his many admirers to offer thanks for his remarkable business achievements and philanthropic endeavours. As a supporter of Community Living Mississauga, the Credit Valley Hospital Foundation and St. Dimitar Bulgarian Eastern Orthodox Church, Mr. Kaneff has helped to create a more caring community.

Proceeds from this evening's activities will support Community Living Mississauga's summer programs for children and youth. Since 1955, Community Living Mississauga has been an invaluable community asset that helps individuals coping with intellectual disabilities.

On behalf of the Government of Canada, I offer everyone my best wishes for a memorable evening and for every success in reaching your fundraising goal.

Sincerely,

The Rt. Hon. Justin P.J. Trudeau, P.C., M.P.
Prime Minister of Canada

As prime minister, Justin Trudeau sent this letter in 2016 marking Community Living Mississauga's Lifetime Achievement Tribute dinner honouring me.

Tracey McMahon (left) has been with our company since 1976. We hired her straight out of high school in her teens to be our receptionist. For the past five years, she has been executive assistant for both Didi and me. Crystal Frail (right) has worked for us for more than forty years, helping out in reception initially and then in our accounting department. For the past twenty years, she has been in accounts payable. She is my niece from my first marriage.

In the spring of 2018, we broke ground for Lionhead Marketplace, a two-hundred-thousand-square-foot commercial retail plaza project on nineteen acres in Brampton, Ontario. Behind all of us, across the road, is the head office for the Kaneff Group of Companies.

An artist's rendering of Lionhead Marketplace in Brampton, Ontario, currently being completed and leased.

Keystone, my latest condominium project in Mississauga, Ontario, is currently being marketed in the pre-construction stage.

At home with my daughters, Anna-Maria (left) and Kristina Maria.

My daughters, Anna-Maria (left) and Kristina Maria.

My family: to my right, Ignatia (Anna-Maria's firstborn), Michael Walsh (Anna-Maria's husband), and Anna-Maria. To my left, Kristina Maria; Didi; and Emmanuelle (Anna-Maria's second child).

I had already built Mr. Lamprea's house in Erindale Woodlands. He was impressed enough by my work that he requested the services of Kaneff Construction for this much bigger project.

I had recently purchased a parcel of land at the corner of Argyle Road and Dundas Street West in Mississauga and believed it would be a perfect fit for Mr. Lamprea's dealership. In fact, I owned six acres of land there, more than enough to build the car dealership and a few other properties, too. I sold a piece of that acreage, which was then used for a gas station, and another piece to an auto glass company. Even after these sales, I still had space left over to build two high-rise apartment buildings.

Incredibly, I was able to recover my costs on the six acres with just the money I made from the gas station deal. This was a very good piece of land and the only one in the area with sanitary connections. There was also a creek that would be utilized as a storm sewer, making it an ideal location for a wide variety of new businesses that could tap into this service.

Even though I could have made more money with this land by using it to build housing, I liked the idea of having my company's name attached to a more prestigious project. Building a car dealership would be another feather in Kaneff Construction's cap, and it would serve as a testament to our versatility and craftsmanship. Building the dealership was also a form of advertising for me.

The dealership project went according to plan, and I built Mr. Lamprea the best car dealership in town. Having worked together twice, he and I became good friends. I often found myself visiting his dealership, if only to fix something small. Most of the time, however, I just stopped by to chat with Mr. Lamprea and his employees. (I don't just talk to the boss!)

During one of these visits, I found myself in a conversation with the controller at Mr. Lamprea's dealership, a man named Ron Sutherland. Mr. Sutherland saw that I was a successful local businessman, and he also knew I had built the dealership in which we stood. Given those two facts, Mr. Sutherland asked me a very interesting question. "Iggy, why don't you get a car dealership?" He then added, "We can run it for you."

At no point had I ever considered getting into the car business. Yet, for some reason, I found myself nodding in agreement. *I should get a car dealership*, I thought.

Mr. Sutherland gave me the mailing address for the zone manager at General Motors, and I promptly sent him a postcard expressing my interest in purchasing a dealership.

After dropping my note in the post, I simply forgot about it. I did not know if I would hear back from GM in two weeks, two months, two years, or never.

At the time I saw getting into the car business as little more than an investment opportunity. After all, I would have Mr. Sutherland's steady hand to run the operation. I would keep operating my construction business with minimal distraction, confident the dealership was in good hands. I would see my name in bright lights, make some money, and enjoy the spoils of owning a Cadillac dealership without any of the headaches.

Three days after sending out my postcard I was shocked to answer the telephone and find myself speaking to Ron Lorimer, zone manager for General Motors. Over time, Mr. Lorimer and I grew to be good friends, and I would build him four houses. However, when he called me in 1963, I was speaking to a complete stranger.

"Hello," I said.

"Hello," said the man on the other end of the line. "Am I speaking to Iggy Kaneff, the builder?"

"Yes, that's me."

"The guy from Bulgaria?"

"Yes, this is Iggy Kaneff from Bulgaria. What can I do for you?"

As it turned out, Mr. Lorimer and I had done business back in 1954. I was building a house near Lorne Park in my spare time. Mr. Lorimer was a salesman for the Toronto Brick Company. He showed up on my site at eight o'clock in the morning while I was chatting with some of my employees around the coffee truck, discussing the basement block work we were about to start. Then I noticed a man standing off to the side. At six foot four he was difficult to miss. After I finished with my bricklayers, I approached Mr. Lorimer, and within five minutes I had purchased my bricks from him and we toasted our transaction with a cup of coffee from the truck.

Now, on the phone in 1963, Mr. Lorimer explained that he had been impressed that I showed consideration for his time so many years ago.

Unlike some other builders in the area, I did not keep him waiting or prevent him from going off to make another sale. That left an impression on him, and it still resonated nearly a decade later when he read my postcard expressing interest in buying a GM dealership.

I told Mr. Lorimer that I had an experienced man, Ron Sutherland, set to run the business on my behalf. I was confident I could be successful in the car business and told him how excited I was to join General Motors. It is important to remember that in 1963 cars were considered a luxury item. For an immigrant like me to own a car was unlikely. For me to own a car dealership was unheard of. I asked Mr. Lorimer to alert me immediately if a dealership became available to buy.

"Actually," Mr. Lorimer said, "I have one available now. It's in Brampton and you can have it right away."

As Mr. Lorimer explained to me, I would be given the opportunity to purchase Morrison Motors, which had previously been owned by John Morrison, who was set to retire. The dealership was located at the corner of Wellington and Main Streets in Brampton, an intersection that years later in the 1990s would be home to the new Brampton City Hall.

I had no idea Mr. Lorimer had been following my career from afar since he sold me those bricks in 1954. He was eager to make a deal as soon as he recognized my name on the postcard. "I want General Motors to be in business with Iggy Kaneff," he told me.

The following morning Mr. Lorimer and I ate breakfast together. Eleven days later I was the proud owner of a dealership in Brampton where I would sell Cadillacs, GMC trucks, Pontiacs, and a few other car brands. As part of our agreement, I would also build a new facility.

Kaneff Construction broke ground on Parklane, a new General Motors dealership, in 1963. Built on Queen Street East in Brampton — where it remains standing to this day — the facility featured a showroom with pedestals for nine cars, a service garage, a body shop, and a parts department. In all, I had seventy-two employees, none more important than my vice-president, Ron Sutherland.

My dealership facility was the first of its kind in the area. It was also the first truly modern building for General Motors. Because of a new design feature in showcasing elevated pedestals, it took the concept of a car dealership to another level. Needless to say, General Motors was quite impressed with what I had already brought to the table.

Unfortunately, I was not nearly as impressed with the car business as it was with me. From the beginning there were problems with my dealership, the worst of which were related to the man I had hired to run the show. Sadly for me, Ron Sutherland quickly proved himself incapable of making smart business decisions for my dealership.

A few weeks after opening our doors to the public, Mr. Sutherland made a mistake that cost me a lot of money. It also cost him his job.

In those days, I still wrote and signed all my company cheques personally. When I saw a bill that broke the news to me that Ron Sutherland had spent our entire advertising budget in a bowling magazine, I was furious.

"Ron, can you explain this $54,000 expense?" I asked him. I don't like to get angry with people, but this time I could barely hold it back. Six or seven Cadillacs could be bought for $54,000 in those days.

He told me how an advertisement for my GMC Cadillac dealership would appear in a bowling magazine that circulated in alleys throughout our area. At the time I did not know anything about bowling, but the little I did know informed me that the men and women frequenting bowling alleys did not generally possess the disposable income to buy a Cadillac.

Mr. Sutherland took me around and showed me all the local alleys, but all I could see within them were people who would never buy a car from me.

"Ron, how many bowlers are going to buy a Cadillac?" I asked him. Before he could even respond I answered the question for him. "Zero!" I yelled. It was one of the few times I ever lost my temper with an employee.

Right then and there I made a critical decision for my new business. "You know what, Ron?" I said to my soon-to-be-former vice-president. "You're a good worker and a nice guy, but you're not good at making decisions. I need somebody here to make good decisions, and that person isn't you."

I fired him on the spot, offering him a severance of $10,000 to leave my company. Overall — counting the $54,000 of wasted advertising money — I lost $64,000 right off the bat thanks to Ron Sutherland's poor judgment.

My vice-president's bad choice in advertising also cost me some pride. Everybody in the car industry saw that I was running ads in a bowling magazine, and they laughed at me. It was humiliating.

With the dismissal of Ron Sutherland, I suddenly found myself working more hours at the dealership than I had expected. Every day I was clocking in at ten o'clock in the morning and staying until three in the afternoon, if not later. Having already put $300,000 — still a lot of money today, but a fortune back then — into the dealership, I needed to protect my investment. The only way to do that was to spend more time overseeing the operations of the dealership in person.

My management style in the car business was the same as it was in construction. I started showing up every day and being on the ball with every aspect of the business. I got daily reports on what was bought and sold, as well as anything happening in the body shop. The automobile industry moves very quickly, so I had to stay on top of what was passing through my shop.

I tried to hire another VP, but when I caught my new man drinking on the job I had to fire him, as well. It soon became clear that I had to run the business myself. Failure to do so would likely result in a write-off of $300,000 or more. Unfortunately, I was spending time away from my construction projects, and construction was my true passion.

Even before the management problems at my car dealership, the investment was already looking as if it would have an unfavourable outcome. Shortly after buying the dealership, I had the opportunity to purchase a sizable parcel of land along Hurontario Street (Highway 10) from Burnhamthorpe Road all the way to where Highway 403 runs now. This area, now considered the downtown core of Mississauga, is home to the municipality's Civic Centre (its city hall) as well as Square One, one of the largest shopping malls in Canada.

Having sunk so much money into the dealership, however, I could not buy the land. Had I been able to do so, I would have made far more money on that one deal than I could have ever hoped to earn selling automobiles. It seemed like just another bad omen indicating I had no business selling cars. It was also a painful reminder that I should have stuck to doing what I knew. Construction was the industry in which I had proven to be very successful.

Still, I did enjoy selling cars to Toronto Maple Leaf hockey players such as Tim Horton, Bobby Baun, Frank Mahovlich, and Red Kelly. However, when these players were eventually traded or retired, I was so upset that I gave up my four season tickets at Maple Leaf Gardens!

STOPS AND STARTS

Believe it or not, despite all the problems, I found my experience in the automotive industry to be generally positive. I liked working at the dealership because it allowed me to interact with customers each and every day. More than anything else, I enjoyed meeting my clients face to face. It was time spent chatting, joking, and most importantly, selling. I loved it.

What I loved less was the poor luck that followed me. It was completely unlike my construction experience, in which every decision I made seemed to turn out well.

One major problem was that General Motors experienced annual labour stoppages while I owned the dealership. For six straight years, workers at the GM plant on which my dealership relied went on strike — for sixty days up to seven months!

During these far-too-frequent work stoppages, I would not receive any new cars to sell. To say this cut into my overall profit margin would be to put it mildly. All I could do was hope the labour union and management came to an agreement in weeks, not months. These strikes cost car dealers like me a lot of money.

Even when it was business as usual, owning a car dealership was still a poor money-making venture. At the time, the Dealers Association was not properly organized, and I only made an average of $91 gross on the sale of any car that was not a Cadillac. Sometimes, if too many things went wrong with a car during its warrantable period, I even lost money on the deal. Fortunately, the facility provided other sources of income by way of servicing the cars and selling parts in our mechanical shop. And by offering financing to customers, we made back some money by collecting interest on car loans.

I learned all too quickly that the car business required considerably more time, effort, investment, and risk than I had been led to believe.

At any given moment I had between a hundred and a hundred and fifty cars on the lot, amounting to about $500,000 in inventory. But once a car sat on the lot for two weeks, General Motors started charging me interest on it. As a result, if I did not sell a car within fourteen days of receiving it I would lose money until I could sell it. As a dealer, I never really owned the cars and was always vulnerable to a loss.

It was yet another example of what happened when I was not my own boss. I might have owned the dealership building and licence, but GM controlled the terms of trade. I was subject to their rules, and many of those rules did not benefit me. Yet again I learned that I operated most efficiently when I made all the rules for my business.

Despite all the challenges of being a car dealer, there were times when business was brisk and I could turn a handsome profit. I was my own best salesman. Many of my friends and associates from the construction industry had the money to buy a Cadillac, and they only wanted to buy one from me. In those days, I could make a profit of up to $2,500 on a Cadillac, and I could sell almost fifty of them in a year. A Cadillac retailed for between $7,000 and $8,000 back then.

Furthermore, I had contacts in construction that brought in some big deals. For instance, after subcontracting work on the Argyle Road apartments to Armstrong Construction, I was able to sell its owner, Mr. Armstrong, three hundred trucks for his fleet. This was a monstrous sale, and it made an enormous profit for the dealership.

A few months later an Oakville-based construction company purchased seventy-five cement-mixing trucks. These vehicles ranged in price from $75,000 to $80,000 each. Today a similar truck would cost about $500,000. It was a hefty price tag for an important piece of equipment, and many of the builders in my area knew and trusted me enough to know I would treat them well and give them a fair deal.

More than trucks, however, I was able to sell a lot of cars. I was actually selling more Cadillacs than anyone else in the area. In fact, my dealership sold the most Cadillacs in all of Ontario during 1964.

All the big suppliers and their employees — ranging from brick sales-men to lumberyard owners — came to me when they wanted a Cadillac. It was considered to be a status car at that time, and many of the men I knew from construction who were making good money wanted to show it off through their choice of automobile.

I brought in the deals, and when it came time to close the sale, I sent in my best employee. Jimmy Morrison was the grandson of the dealer-ship's previous owner. Because I sent him deals that were all but done, Jimmy was also reaping the benefits of my connections because he col-lected the commission on every sale.

Often I walked into the showroom and immediately called him over. "Jimmy, go see this man right away," I would tell him. "He's going to buy a Cadillac." This arrangement allowed him to outsell my other twelve salesmen combined. Jimmy made more money than anyone without having to ever negotiate a deal from start to finish.

Even though I made it very easy for him, my young salesman de-served every penny of his commissions. I gave these sales to Jimmy be-cause I knew he would never spoil a deal for me. He was a sure thing, and he gave me no reason to use anyone else. Jimmy was a fine, honest young man, deserving of all his success.

Despite the annual work stoppages at GM, I managed to turn a prof-it every year at the dealership. I can attribute a large part of that to the mechanical shop we had on-site — we were able to make money from repairs and parts sales. But even that side of the business did not come without its pitfalls.

Just as things were starting to go smoothly, I discovered that two of my employees were stealing from the dealership. I pieced it together eas-ily while doing an inventory check: the managers of the body shop and parts department were ripping me off. When customers came in to have their cars serviced, these two men would create a false document that would not account for the actual parts that had been sold, keeping the money for themselves. It was a short-sighted scheme.

I called the police and they sent over an undercover officer. He set up his sting in the shop and caught my employees within a couple of days. At the time I could have had them thrown in jail for stealing hundreds if not thousands of dollars of inventory, but I decided against it. I had no desire to see these men suffer; I just wanted to protect my investment. Once they were gone, the stealing stopped.

VAUXHALLS AND VIVAS FOR SALE

Owning a GM dealership was — more than one might think — a local business. Each dealership is given a zone and is prohibited from selling cars to people living outside the assigned territory. For example, I could not sell a Cadillac to anybody with an address that was south of Burnhamthorpe Road. If I did, I was required to pay $1,000 to a man named Ross Hawley, owner of the GM dealership in that zone.

Since selling a Cadillac brought the dealership — and me — an overall profit of between $2,000 and $2,500, it was still worth selling to customers outside my territory. I considered it unfair that I was forced to give away nearly half my profit to Ross Hawley, but those were the rules that governed the car business. My customers were men I knew from the construction industry, and they only wanted to buy a Cadillac from me. Every time that happened, Ross Hawley received $1,000 for doing nothing.

General Motors eventually offered me one alternative to paying Ross Hawley: for every Cadillac I sold I would also be required to sell one of GM's low-performance, highly inferior British-made automobiles, either a Vauxhall or a Viva. GM stipulated that every time I sold one of these lesser cars I would be given a Cadillac to sell to a customer of my choosing, regardless of that person's geographic location. That motivated me to sell the British cars as quickly as possible, often meaning I would price the vehicle at my cost. Sometimes I even took a loss.

Eventually, car dealers would become organized and work these problems out more logically, but in those days I had to sell British lemons or pay Ross Hawley.

The Vauxhall situation epitomized my overall disenchantment with the automotive industry. There always seemed to be unnecessary obstacles and bureaucracy muddying my path to success. With every passing day, I was growing less enchanted with the car business. Soon I would look for a way out.

MRS. GRACE BRIDGES

It was during the years I was spreading myself so thin between running a car dealership and a construction company that I came to realize my business had already acquired its most valuable asset. In 1959, I hired Mrs. Grace Bridges — back then she was Mrs. Grace Stubbs — as my first secretary.

My accountant and I were both looking for secretaries around the same time in 1959. Motivated to find a secretary right away, he placed an advertisement in the classifieds section of our local newspaper, hiring one of the first women he met. My accountant chose wisely, since she stayed with him for many years, but he also interviewed another candidate who stood out from the rest. Knowing I was also in need of a secretary, he sent Mrs. Grace Stubbs to my office. "This lady will suit you," he assured me.

Mrs. Stubbs was about fifty years old at the time of our meeting. To say she suited me was a big understatement. She was perfect for me right from the beginning. Mrs. Stubbs was kind, trustworthy, and an extremely professional woman. She did everything I needed to have done, and she was always on time. She was my secretary, bookkeeper, and more. She answered the phones, typed my letters, and did all of my administrative work. She was instrumental to my continued success for more than twenty-five years.

Sadly, Mrs. Stubbs's husband died of cancer in early 1963, right around the time I went into business with General Motors. It was a terrible time in her life, and she went into a deep state of mourning. She was so sad, in fact, that she told me she would not attend that year's company Christmas party.

Since 1955 my Christmas party had become an annual event that many suppliers, employees, and friends enjoyed. During those first few years, it was held in the basement of my house. But, as the years progressed, I had the party at different, successively bigger houses. As the company continued to grow, I eventually held the party at one of the golf courses where I played, and then, finally, at my own golf course.

For me, it was important that all my employees attended the party if possible. The night was meant to be a celebration of everything we had accomplished together throughout the year. It was a way for me to thank them.

It was not so much that Mrs. Stubbs wanted to miss the event — I got the impression she wanted to be there — but she was worried about going unescorted, not an uncommon concern for ladies of her generation.

I understood her reservations and left it at that. A few days later, however, it occurred to me that my head mechanic, Bob Bridges — a recent widower — might serve as a willing escort to my secretary.

I spoke to Bob Bridges and persuaded him to ask Mrs. Stubbs to accompany him to the party. Mr. Bridges — who had been lonely since his wife passed away — followed through on my request. He asked Mrs. Stubbs to the party, and she agreed.

Incredibly, that was all it took. My secretary and mechanic soon became inseparable. Within a year they were married; Mrs. Grace Stubbs became Mrs. Grace Bridges, and that was how I addressed her for the rest of her life. It was the first time — but not the last time — I would play matchmaker.

Despite our enduring friendship, Mrs. Bridges and I always remained quite formal with each other throughout the years. She never called me Iggy; it was always Mr. Kaneff. And I never called her Grace. I always addressed my friend as Mrs. Bridges.

Mrs. Bridges was my secretary for twenty-seven years, and I could not have asked more of her than what she gave to me and to my business. She was always an important asset to the company, but never more so than when I was dividing my time between construction projects and the car dealership. She often represented me when I could not be present. Without her services, my dalliance in the car industry could have had a far worse result.

SPUTTERING OUT

Getting into the car business was, to me, a professional failure, but in some ways I benefited from my involvement. First, I learned that selling cars required an innate ability. One has to be born with a sense for sales, like a musician has to be born with a song in his heart. I sold cars the same way I sold houses, vegetables, and eggs. It all came naturally to me.

I also learned some important lessons about running a big business. General Motors is a massive corporation and knows how to do business on an immense scale. For instance, all the dealers in our area would go to a hotel in Grimsby for meetings whenever the company rolled out a new product. During these meetings, GM would hire a professor from New York City to teach us how to better understand the mentality of our customers. This man conducted research and taught us more about what our clients wanted. For most of the dealers, it was a subtle lesson that might have a slight effect on business, but I saw it as GM taking extra steps over and above what its competitors were doing to help dealers sell cars.

Even though I was selling more cars than anyone else at the time, I still considered the GM meetings to be a valuable learning experience. I was the owner of an ever-growing construction company, and there was nothing better than learning at the feet of General Motors how to improve my own selling techniques.

I respected the company for its incredible success. In turn, the people at GM treated me with respect, too. The executives at General Motors often asked my opinion on various matters of importance. They could see that I ran a successful dealership while simultaneously operating an even more successful construction company. Their actions demonstrated that they were impressed by my industriousness.

At one point, James Roche, who was then president of General Motors, sent an airplane to pick me up in Malton — now part of Mississauga — just so I could have lunch with him in Detroit. That very evening he flew me right back home. In my mind, I was still an immigrant who had come to Canada aboard a boat not so long ago; whirlwind journeys like that one made me feel like a big shot.

"You're the only Bulgarian in the world who owns his own Cadillac dealership," Mr. Roche often liked to say.

Still, it had also become clear that I was involved with GM for the wrong reasons. I liked the prestige of having my name on a Cadillac dealership, but I did not like dedicating so much of my time to cars when I could have been selling and building homes.

Like anyone else, I enjoyed being recognized for my accomplishments, and owning a car dealership provided a great deal of recognition. When I first arrived in Canada, many of the people I met had never even heard of Bulgaria. To them, my beloved home country did not represent so much as a speck on the map. When I told people I came from Bulgaria, they often looked at me blankly and asked, "Did you mean to say Bolivia?"

Through my achievements, I wanted to make myself — and Bulgaria — more relevant to the people of Canada. I wanted to help put Bulgaria on the map. I was starting from nothing and working hard every day to become a somebody. It was on this basis, in large part, that I became involved in the car business. However, as I came to learn, pride was a bad reason to own a dealership and a dangerous motivator. After six years, I finally decided to get out of business with GM once and for all.

At the time, I had a deal in place to build two residential high-rises of 242 units each on Argyle Road. A project that size would require my full attention. Running the dealership could only distract me, and I would not let that happen. Expecting to be low-balled by GM's settlement offer, I was prepared to tear down the dealership. I planned to build over it and walk away from the automotive industry forever. The land was worth more to me as the site of a future construction project.

Finally, I called up my zone manager at General Motors and told him plainly, "Listen, you can either buy me out of the dealership or you can come take your cars away. I'm quitting GM."

A few days later General Motors sent over an appraiser, and it did not take long for us to agree to terms. GM and I settled for $800,000, which got them the facility I built and the land on which I built it. The zone manager even threw in a $5,000 bonus because he had liked me from the time I had built him a home in Erindale Woodlands several years earlier. After a terrific string of successes unlike any I had ever known, the Parklane dealership stood out as an obvious mistake. Even though the dealership did not end up costing me money, I missed out on a fortune in lost opportunities.

I did get one other valuable asset out of my involvement with the car business. The certified accountant Dave Greenwood had joined the accounting firm Buckley McCarney Swinarton in September 1966 and became one of its partners by May 1967. Before Dave joined Buckley McCarney Swinarton, it was already handling accounting matters for

Parklane, and in 1967 it began doing the same for the Kaneff Group of Companies. In fact, Dave worked on our year-end that year out of the basement of my house before I moved our headquarters into a converted apartment in one of my Centennial Towers buildings on Argyle Road in Mississauga. Eventually, Dave joined the huge accounting firm MNP but is now retired. We are still very good friends.

Building was my specialty, and construction needed to be my focus. Although I would have side businesses again in the future — my brewery comes to mind — never again would I become so sidetracked from my primary vocation.

DRIVING LESSONS

This is as good an opportunity as any to pause and reflect on what these experiences taught me about myself and about other people. When all was said and done, my time as a dealership owner reinforced many of the principles I believed to be true in business. I benefited from spending time on the showroom floor, interacting with customers who were in the process of making one of their biggest purchases. It served as a form of market research. I repeatedly learned the one lesson that would help me make deals again and again: it is important for everybody involved in a deal to feel like a winner. For example, when a client pays his deposit on a house and then tries to get it back, even today, I almost always let him have it, despite being under no obligation to do so.

When a husband came into the dealership to buy a car for his family, he wanted to feel as if he was getting a good deal, if only so he could look like a hero to his wife. In those days, many men saw buying a car as an opportunity to seem macho.

So if I could make a deal and save my customer $50 — which was something like a week's salary for a lot of people back then — I was letting that man be a hero to his wife. He could go back to her and say, "I beat Kaneff for fifty bucks," and feel good about himself.

For my part, I was content to let my customer have it. It might have cost me $50 — not an insignificant sum — but I was always thinking about the next time. I knew that if my customer felt like a hero with his wife today, then he would feel good about me tomorrow. When a client knows he or she got a good deal, or at least a fair deal, that person is more inclined to do business with me again in the future. In my line of work, next time was always around the corner.

There were many times when I could have tried to take advantage of a customer, but I never did, nor was I tempted to do so. I wanted everybody to feel good about doing business with me, and I wanted clients to feel confident and proud about referring me to a friend. In construction, as in the car business, reputation is everything. I went to great lengths to cultivate and protect my good name.

This notion of never trying to step over anybody first crystallized during my time building houses in Erindale Woodlands. Shortly after I began construction at the development, the Diefenbaker government shut down the Avro airplane plant in Malton. Many people lost their jobs, and several were my customers. Four such men were among the scientists and engineers laid off by Avro. They came to me hat in hand and asked me to refund their deposits. They could not comfortably pay for their homes, and they wanted to back out of these deals. More importantly, they needed that $1,000 deposit returned to keep food on their families' tables.

Of course, I paid back their deposits right away. That very afternoon they came to my office and each picked up a cheque for $1,000. It was a total loss of $4,000, but I was comforted by the belief I could sell those four houses to other customers, and eventually I did.

Several months later those same scientists and engineers eventually found work at the Imperial Oil refinery in nearby Clarkson. The men ended up buying houses from me again, and this time they were able to afford them. Better yet, each of those men brought me at least two or three new customers through referrals. They remembered that I repaid their deposits when I was not required to do so, and they were grateful enough to bring me more business. As it happened so many times, I experienced long-term benefits after taking a short-term loss.

In any deal — whether you are selling apples, cars, or condominiums — the most important thing is that both sides come away from the transaction feeling satisfied. I never wanted to give anybody a reason to think or speak poorly of me or my company.

In another such instance, one of my customers ordered a countertop and a kitchen island in different coloured slabs of granite. He came to me and said, "Mr. Kaneff, my wife doesn't like how these colours look together. And, to be honest, I don't like it, either."

To get a different slab of granite cost about $2,000, but I told my men to replace it right away at no expense to the client. That man got to be a hero to his wife, and I was able to make somebody else feel good. More importantly, this man and his wife felt good about Kaneff Construction. In the end, I was able to use their discarded piece of granite in another house, so all it cost me was a little bit of labour. What it brought, however, was a great deal of goodwill.

Even today that man still sends me new customers. This kind of referral is one of the reasons Kaneff Construction kept growing while other companies failed. Everybody who bought from me received a good house for a fair price. My clients were always happy and satisfied. Among them were the parents of Karen Kain, the great ballet dancer.

With everything I learned from General Motors — and I consider my gains to have been substantial — I went back to construction full-time with a renewed focus on my area of expertise. All the pieces were in place to take my business to an even higher level.

12

Reunion

By the time my parents paid a visit to Canada for the first time in 1963, I was already well established. Not only was I widely known in my community as a builder and developer but I had also settled down as a family man.

Shortly after arriving in Canada, Katarina and I had been advised that she would be unable to have children. The reality that we would be unable to have biological children was tough to swallow. Nevertheless, Katarina and I both wanted to start a family. We adopted a son, Danny, followed by a daughter, Heidi. I loved them both with all my heart.

It might not have been quite as we had always pictured it, but Katarina and I had our little family at last. I enjoyed many happy times with Heidi and Danny while they were children.

When my parents visited in 1963, they were startled to see my lifestyle. They were aware I had found success in Canada, but they did not know the extent of it. Compared to what we had during my childhood in Bulgaria, I was living like a king.

Getting them into Canada was no easy task. At the time travelling to Canada was still difficult for Bulgarians. But, after many years of waiting, I had grown impatient. I wanted desperately to see my mother and father, and I was willing to use any and all connections to make it happen.

Fortunately, I was friendly with Paul Martin, Sr., father of the future prime minister. At the time Mr. Martin was Canada's minister of health and welfare. I also knew the parliamentary secretary, John Munro, as well as the minister of trade and commerce, Anthony Abbott. Mr. Abbott was also my riding representative in the federal parliament. I had supported all three of these men in previous elections.

I went directly to Mr. Abbott and explained that I merely wanted to bring my parents to Canada for a visit. I had no intention of trying to move them here permanently. They were forever entrenched in Gorno Ablanovo.

"It's been so many years since I've seen my parents," I pleaded with Mr. Abbott. "I miss them terribly."

He told me he would do all he could to help me.

From there I visited Mr. Martin and told him the same thing. As I learned that day, Paul Martin, Sr., was a man of action. Without hesitation he picked up his telephone and called John Munro.

"Please get in touch with our Bulgarian representative in Canada," Mr. Martin said to Mr. Munro. "Tell him to let Mr. and Mrs. Kaneff come to Canada at once."

Between 1944 and 1967 the Bulgarian government did not have formal diplomatic representation in Canada. Therefore, bringing one's Bulgarian parents for a visit was almost unheard of. Thanks to Paul Martin, Sr., though, it was achieved.

Having not seen my mother and father for so long, reuniting with them was a deeply emotional experience. When we were finally together, I was overwhelmed with happiness and gratitude. My mother and father were in their late sixties: there had been times throughout my travels that I thought the moment might never arrive.

The months during which my parents visited were some of the happiest and most memorable of my adult life. They were able to stay with us for a year. My father accompanied me to work every day, and I benefited from his companionship and wisdom. Above all, I just loved spending time with him again. It was as if I were a boy once more, listening to my father tell stories on our long wagon rides to and from the fields. I still revered my father as much as ever.

As a boy, I would listen for hours as my father told war stories. But now, in 1963, my father listened as much as he spoke. He wanted to hear all about my life since I had left home for the last time in 1944. These were special times for me with my father; I was reunited with my hero at last.

While my father joined me at work, my mother stayed at home with Katarina and the children. Although I never mentioned it to them, my parents could see right away that Danny and Heidi were not my biological kin. My parents loved Danny and Heidi, but they were sad that I did not have biological children. They regretted that I was missing out on one of life's greatest joys.

On November 22, 1963, my father, as he often did during his stay in Canada, accompanied me to my new General Motors dealership. That day we ate a late lunch at a nearby restaurant that had a television. While we were eating, the regular CBC program on the television was suddenly interrupted with a news flash that U.S. President John F. Kennedy had been shot in his convertible limousine in a motorcade driving through Dealey Plaza in Dallas, Texas. Like everyone else in the restaurant, we were riveted to the TV screen as more news about the shooting was announced bit by bit until the American broadcaster Walter Cronkite came on the air to confirm, in a choked voice, that the young president was dead. My father and I burst into tears at that announcement. It was a day those who were alive at the time will never forget.

GOING HOME

In 1967, Canada and Bulgaria established diplomatic relations, and an ambassador from my home country was received in Ottawa. This would pave the way for me to travel to Bulgaria for the first time since I was a boy.

For so many years, I had wanted to visit my family in our village. Unfortunately, I could never get any assurances for my safety. If I had gone to Bulgaria before 1967, I might have been arrested, or even worse, I could have disappeared altogether. I had no interest in spending the rest of my life in jail or down in the uranium mines.

In 1967, however, the Bulgarian government revoked my sentence for avoiding military service, along with the sentences of many others like me. Suddenly, I was free and clear to go home, or so I hoped.

By 1968, I did not need help from Minister Martin or anyone else to travel to Bulgaria. I had already established a relationship with the Bulgarian Trade Commission, helping to get some of their products — mostly wine and preserves — into the Canadian market.

When I decided to visit in 1968, I travelled to Ottawa and asked for my visa personally. Thanks to the assistance I had provided the trade commission, the Bulgarian government granted my request. This was a stroke of good fortune, given that I was not very sympathetic to the communist regime of the time.

I flew out of Toronto International Airport (now called Toronto Pearson International Airport) with Katarina and our kids. The four of us were going to Bulgaria to attend the wedding of my sister Kuna's daughter, Velitchka. The ceremony and reception were to take place in my home village of Gorno Ablanovo. Even more importantly, I would be able to spend time with my family. We had so much catching up to do.

We landed safely in Sofia, arriving late in the afternoon and staying at a hotel overnight. In the morning, the four of us would continue our journey, refreshed.

My brother, Simeon, however, did not want to wait even one more night to see me. He drove the 185 miles from our village to greet me in Sofia, arriving at our hotel in the middle of the night.

It was two o'clock in the morning, and the hotel staff did not want to let him wake us. But Simeon was insistent.

"That's my brother in that hotel room!" he shouted at the clerk. "I haven't seen him in twenty-four years. You need to wake him up right now."

The hotel staff relented. I was awakened from a deep slumber into a joyous reunion that was better than any dream. After twenty-four long years, my youngest brother and I were reunited at last.

The next morning we drove to the village. As I approached Gorno Ablanovo, I started to recognize the landmarks of my youth and was flooded with many fond memories.

As we chatted in the car, I could see that Simeon expected me to somehow be a different person from the brother he had known. Simeon believed I was coming back to the village as some big, fat, cigar-chomping businessman. He envisioned a rich capitalist as depicted in the movies, not his brother. When he realized I was the same person he once knew, Simeon was happy and relieved. He had rushed to see me at two o'clock in the morning out of pure excitement, and now he knew I would have done the same to see him.

When we reached Gorno Ablanovo, I was required to register at the local police station before I was allowed to stay the night in the village. Ever nervous about the communist regime, this was the moment I had been dreading.

The next day my three brothers accompanied me to the police station in the city of Ruse, and the first person I saw upon entering was the front-desk receptionist. I noticed she was giving me a wicked look, then recognized her as a daughter of one of our village's troubled families. Simeon had warned me that she was distrustful of anyone returning to Bulgaria; I could plainly see that she disliked me.

She picked up the telephone and told the person on the other end of the line that Ignat Kaneff had arrived. Before I knew it, a tall, neat looking officer approached me from the hallway. This officer was a strapping young man over six feet tall — towering by Bulgarian standards — dressed immaculately in his police uniform. He approached me with a blank expression. As he got closer, the corners of his lips curled into a smile and he greeted me warmly. I breathed a sigh of relief.

My brothers and I were fearful of what could happen at the police station. They paced in front of the building, unsure if I would re-emerge as a free man.

I had been given assurances in Canada that I could travel safely and freely. But there were no real guarantees when it came to the communist regime in Bulgaria. Many Bulgarians had been sent to the uranium mines of Siberia never to be heard from again.

I was led into a huge room, intimidated and unsure of what the future held. The office belonging to the police chief, a former general in the army, boasted a massive oak desk in its centre. His secretary was a tall blonde with movie star looks. Before I could even sit down, she approached me. "How do you take your coffee, Mr. Kaneff?"

With those eight little words, all my worries melted away. I finally saw that I was going to be treated well in Bulgaria. Evidently, my accomplishments in Canada carried a certain cachet back home.

I smiled with relief, but the feeling was fleeting. I glanced at the police chief's desk, upon which lay a newspaper dating from 1951. The police chief turned the paper to face me and slid it across the desk in my direction.

This newspaper — published in Washington, D.C. — had a photo of me with an accompanying article, and its banner headline referred to Ignat Kaneff and his generous contributions to the Bulgarian anti-communist government-in-exile. Suddenly, I felt all the blood rush from my face. Sitting across from the police chief, I began to sweat.

"What do you have to say about this?" he asked. "You've been supporting anti-Bulgarian elements in Canada."

This was too much for me. I straightened my posture and looked the chief squarely in the eye. "General Penchev," I began, indignation in my voice, "I support every single Bulgarian — man, woman, or child — who comes to my door in Canada."

I paused for a moment, insulted by the implication that I was anti-Bulgarian in any way. "I support every Bulgarian in Canada, and that includes communists and anti-communists alike. For instance, when a Bulgarian Trade Commission representative came to me asking for assistance selling Bulgarian products in Canada, I was happy to help." I then continued to rebut the police chief's accusations, relaying in great detail the many cases in which I had supported Bulgarians in Canada.

For a moment, silence filled the air. Finally, he opened his mouth to speak. I expected to hear an angry retort, but instead what came out was laughter enhanced by a broad smile. "Okay, okay, let's just forget about it."

Obviously, the police chief was having a little bit of fun with me. He knew everything about my life in Canada before I had set foot in his office. This included my support of all Bulgarians in Canada, in addition to helping

Bulgarian companies gain access to the Canadian marketplace. He had probably brought the newspaper to our meeting for his own amusement.

After that initial bump in the road, General Penchev and I became fast friends. Our meeting began at ten o'clock, and we chatted casually until noon before leaving the office together for lunch. Despite the police chief's politics, I was pleased to discover that he and I got along quite nicely. We engaged in a long, interesting conversation about the challenges facing Bulgarian immigrants around the world, and I was impressed by his carefully considered and intelligent opinions.

For his part, General Penchev seemed impressed that I had been able to learn English so quickly after moving to Canada, and for the first time I began to see that my success outside the country carried weight with Bulgarian communist officials.

By the time General Penchev and I wound up our lunch at two o'clock in the afternoon, we felt like old friends. I was very pleased to make his acquaintance, and we would remain friendly for many years. He paid me a visit nearly every time I came to Bulgaria.

After spending much of the morning and early afternoon with the police chief, I was finally able to rejoin my brothers, who had been nervously waiting for four hours for me to emerge from the police station. Knowing General Penchev's reputation, they were relieved to find me alive and well. The next year, when I visited Bulgaria again, I took a silver coffee/tea service for His Holiness, the Bulgarian patriarch, which I had engraved especially for him. For some unknown reason, customs at the airport in Sofia denied me entry. I told them about the gift for His Holiness, and when they saw it, they allowed me to enter the country.

After far too many years away, I was finally able to return to my family home in Gorno Ablanovo. The last time I had set foot within its doors I was seventeen years old, a boy. On this day, I returned as a forty-one-year-old man.

Coming home in itself was an emotional experience, since I was reuniting with my family for the first time in twenty-four years. But instead of being overwhelmed with joy, my heart became filled with sadness. I was shocked and dismayed to see the state of our village. Everything around me appeared poor, dilapidated, and broken down. So much had gone by the wayside since I was seventeen. The local infrastructure was all falling apart, and my beloved village was beautiful no more. My parents had given me no indication they were living in such awful conditions. I had imagined that the village remained as I remembered it. Now, as I looked at it, Gorno Ablanovo seemed as though it had been neglected and then forgotten.

I had come back to revisit my treasured childhood, but the village I had grown up in was gone. During my childhood, every family in the village had owned its own piece of land to farm, but the communists had expropriated — without remuneration — and nationalized each family's plot. Now there was not even a chicken to eat. It was eerily quiet, almost as if the birds and animals had abandoned Gorno Ablanovo, too.

When my parents visited me in Canada in 1963, they gave me no indication of how bad life had become in Bulgaria. I knew they were poor, but I assumed it was the same type of material poverty we had experienced when I was a boy; we did not enjoy modern comforts, such as plumbing and mattresses, but food was abundant and we had everything we needed to live well. We never had a lot of money, but we always had delicious, fresh food because we were proficient farmers. Now the government controlled the population's food source and everything else.

After my mother and father returned to Bulgaria in 1964, I sent them away with only a few hundred dollars to spend during their travels. Had I known the conditions in which they were living, I would have given them much more. I still feel guilty about sending them home with so little.

I perceived my father as the same strong, powerful man who could never need anything from the likes of me, and in a sense he was still that man. But in another sense I was completely wrong. It was only when I visited Gorno Ablanovo that I realized how hard Bulgarian life had become for everybody, including my beloved father and our family.

In Canada, I was living in a five-thousand-square-foot house with five bedrooms and a swimming pool. I had everything, yet my family in

Bulgaria had nothing, not even access to drinking water in their house. I felt ashamed to discover that my loved ones lacked basic necessities like indoor plumbing, while I was living a life of luxury.

Fortunately, I was in a position to help those I loved. Right away I paid to have the house connected to the water supply. When I got back to Canada, I started sending them regular aid packages with maximum quantities of flour, sugar, and anything else I thought they might need. Back then you were allowed to send those kinds of goods overseas without difficulty.

As soon as I felt satisfied that their basic needs had been met, I began lavishing upon my loved ones some of the finer things in life. For instance, I bought my brother, Simeon, a beautiful Mercedes, the only one of its kind in the entire region. All my other siblings got new cars, too.

In 1970, I built my parents a brand-new house in Dve Mogili — about eight miles south of Gorno Ablanovo — that was up to Canadian standards. Dve Mogili's name means "Two Hills" due to the pair of ancient Thracian burial mounds just north of the municipality. Living in a modern home for the first time, my parents were finally able to enjoy some of life's creature comforts. It brought me true joy to help them.

The following year I returned to Bulgaria to visit my brother, Simeon, and my parents, who were now living in the house I had built for them. I decided to invite family and friends to celebrate the new house, only to have the Communist Party organize a mob to throw rotten eggs at our guests. The house came to be known as the White House among the locals.

Over the years, I was able to bring all of my brothers and sisters to Canada at one time or another. Many of them visited me repeatedly for various lengths of time. Many of their children and grandchildren came over, as well.

On the one hand, I felt a sense of pride that I was in a position to help my family. On the other, it saddened me that my help was needed. These were immensely proud people, and it was humbling for them to accept anything from me or anyone else. Fortunately, I was eventually able to convince them to accept my assistance.

But on this first return from Canada, putting aside the dejection I felt about the state of my village, I did what I could to experience the rest of my trip to Bulgaria for what it was: an opportunity to reconnect with my family. We had been apart for far too long, and there was no time to waste.

My vacation in Bulgaria lasted six weeks. We spent the first week in Gorno Ablanovo and attended the grand event that was my niece's wedding. For the first time in a long while, I was able to participate in a joyful family celebration. As I danced and drank with my parents, brothers and sisters, nieces and nephews, aunts, uncles, and cousins, I was overcome by a deep sense of gratitude for the moment.

After that first week spent in the family home, we moved east to vacation on the Black Sea. In advance of our trip, I had reserved every room in a large hotel on the beach to accommodate my family, my extended family, and myself. There were forty-five of us in total.

Shortly after arriving at the hotel, I was visited by a friend from the past. Bai Kolyo, my former boss and mentor, had come to reconnect with his old protégé.

I owed much of my success to Bai Kolyo. Had he not plucked me from my job at the farmers' co-op in Gorno Ablanovo and brought me to work in Austria, I might have never left the village. Bai Kolyo had played a key role in my journey to success.

When I spotted Bai Kolyo walking through the hotel lobby, I was struck by his appearance. Time had not been kind to my old friend. Since turning his back on the communist regime he had at first welcomed, Bai Kolyo no longer experienced the comforts he once had, and it showed.

Bai Kolyo told me his disturbing story. In 1944, while I was still trying to return to Wels to continue working in his market gardening business, he was told by his communist contacts to sneak back into Bulgaria. There, during the last days of the German occupation, he awaited the arrival of the Soviet army.

The German soldiers always had their own regimental cook. As Bai Kolyo found out — given that he was friendly with the Germans — the cook stationed with the military unit in Draganovo was a Russian who had been captured months earlier. He was meant to be their prisoner, but it turned out that he was skilled in the kitchen, so the Germans kept him around as their cook.

Bai Kolyo was always eager to help others. It was in this spirit of generosity that he approached a German officer about liberating this captured Russian. "You're not going to need your cook once you leave," he said, knowing that the Germans would depart from Draganovo in the coming days.

"You're right," replied the officer.

"Why don't you leave the cook with me so that I can return him to the Russians when they arrive in town?"

"That's fine with me."

With that, Bai Kolyo smiled broadly over the thought of reuniting this once-imprisoned man with his fellow Russians. He expected his new communist friends to be impressed and delighted by his quick thinking and deft negotiating skills. Back then Bai Kolyo believed the Soviet army was a humane, liberal organization that would praise him for his efforts and let the cook return home. He was sorely mistaken.

The next day, September 9, 1944, the Red Army arrived in Draganovo. Since he was now the town's mayor and was appointed with their blessing, the communists visited Bai Kolyo at the city hall for their very first stop in town. He welcomed them warmly, and they all sat down for dinner, drinks, and conversation. All the while, Bai Kolyo was waiting for the perfect moment to present his new friends with a great surprise. Finally, once dinner was cleared from the table and cigars were lit, Bai Kolyo swung open a door to the kitchen and unveiled the Russian cook.

The Russians stood stone-faced and silent. Despite this reunion with their long-lost countryman, none of the men even hinted at a smile. After an agonizing moment, one of the Soviet officers broke the silence with a question. "How long were you with the Germans?" he asked the cook.

"Two years."

"And what did you do for them during that time?"

"I was their cook."

As each successive word left the cook's mouth, the Russians looked angrier. Again, there was a moment of heavy silence in the room. It was the calm before the storm.

"So you cooked for the Germans?" the officer pressed, raising his voice. "You were feeding the Germans?" He was now red in the face.

The cook swallowed hard and nodded.

Finally, the officer screamed at the top of his lungs, "You should have killed the Germans! You should have poisoned them!"

All at once the communists grabbed the cook by his shoulders and dragged him outside, where they shot him like a dog in front of Bai Kolyo, changing his life — and his perspective on communism and Russia — forever.

Bai Kolyo was stunned. He denounced the Russians right away and returned his Communist Party membership card. Almost as quickly, he was booted out of the mayor's office.

From there Bai Kolyo's life took a difficult turn. Unwilling to support communism in his hometown, he became outspoken in its opposition. The Russians retaliated by denying him privileges, including use of his telephone. The government burdened his life with difficulties of every kind.

"I didn't fight all my life to support a system like that," he said to me that day at the hotel. "There was no court. There was no justice. The Russians walked into my house, drank vodka, ate dinner, and then killed a man like it was nothing. I was disgusted."

I came away from our conversation with an even greater respect for my former employer. Once again Bai Kolyo proved that he was worthy of my admiration.

This was yet another example of the poor treatment Bulgarians received in their own country, a recurring theme that struck me during that first trip home. In fact, I was often offered special treatment simply because I was seen as a foreigner.

Whether it was at the hotel, in restaurants, or on the street, I could always hear people whispering, "That guy is from Canada."

After I returned to Canada, the indignities continued for my family in Bulgaria. I had intended to stay at the hotel with them until Sunday night, but I had to leave a few days earlier. Katarina, the kids, and I flew out on Friday around lunchtime. I was about to start a construction project and needed a few days to prepare.

Despite my own departure, I intended for my family to stay at the hotel and enjoy its amenities through the weekend. But it was not to be.

Almost as soon as I left the premises, the hotel staff rushed my entire family out of the facility as if they were criminals.

"This hotel isn't for Bulgarians," the manager hissed. "It's only for foreigners. Get out!"

As I was coming to discover, Bulgarian citizens were treated with blatant disrespect in those days, simply for being Bulgarian.

Flying home on Friday afternoon, I reflected on my first trip home. As much as I loved spending time with my family, I was still stunned by the poor state of our village. Sitting on the plane, I peered out the window and thought, *I shouldn't have gone back.*

My cherished childhood memories of Gorno Ablanovo were the most comforting ones I had, and now they were forever tarnished. The village as I had known it no longer existed. My beautiful home had been replaced by one that seemed to be dying.

I could no longer close my eyes and picture the idyllic, beautiful place that formed the memories for my wonderful childhood years. I could only see the diminished place in which my family now struggled daily.

I was determined to do something to improve their lives.

SEPARATION

In the months and years that followed my first trip back to Bulgaria, it became apparent that my marriage to Katarina would not stand the test of time. I have always had nothing but the highest opinion of Katarina; no one has ever heard me speak a word against her. Katarina and I rarely argued. We enjoyed vacationing together, we went out to the movies, which I loved doing, and throughout our marriage we spent time together whenever we could.

But simply finding the time was a problem. In those years, I was still building up my businesses and spending endless hours on the job. You might think Katarina and I could have found time to spend together in socializing with my clients and associates, which was so important to my success. Katarina, though, preferred to stay home.

Also, a feeling continued to trouble me that something was missing, and a conversation with my father during his trip to Canada in 1963 kept coming back to me.

"Son, I have six children, and each of them has at least two children of their own," he explained to me. "Having a child of your flesh and blood is the greatest experience in life, and you deserve that joy, too."

I did not digest his remarks immediately, but over time they began to affect me. After much consideration, I decided that having natural children was an experience I wanted. Sadly, this experience could not be shared with Katarina.

I loved Danny and Heidi with all my heart and could never abandon them, but I desperately wanted to experience the basic human joy my father had spoken about.

After years of deliberation, I told Katarina I was leaving her. I gave her my reasons and explained that I understood this decision was not completely fair to her. I also told her I intended to support her and the children financially and help them as much as possible. This was, as I saw it, the least I could do.

I felt bad about leaving Katarina because I loved her as a person, but I also knew we were no longer in love. We respected each other like the best of friends we were, but I wanted to experience something different.

It would take nearly a decade for Katarina to sign the divorce papers, but for all intents and purposes our marriage ended during the mid-1970s.

When Katarina and I finally parted ways, Heidi and Danny were seventeen and eighteen years old, respectively. At the time Heidi was living in one of my apartment buildings while Danny stayed with his mother in our family house. Leaving Katarina severely strained my relationship with the children, and despite my best efforts, those bonds would never be fully restored.

At first Heidi and Danny refused to communicate with me. When we happened to see one another, we exchanged pleasantries, but they stopped calling me altogether. There was a lot of resentment, and I tried to see things from their perspective.

Although I had done my best to help raise them, I worked very long hours when Danny and Heidi were children. While I was building my company, my time was scarce. I spent as much time with the children as possible, but it may not have been enough. I worked to repair the relationships with my children over the years. However, for the time being their feelings were hurt and there was nothing I could do to soothe them.

In the years to come, Katarina did everything possible to stall divorce proceedings, forever believing I would come back to her. Whenever we were scheduled to meet in court, she showed up with a different lawyer. This delayed the process, since her new attorney needed time to familiarize himself with the case. It went on like that for years.

I offered Katarina money — more than she would ever need — but she repeatedly turned it down. The sum of money did not matter; she simply refused to sign the papers.

"I don't want a divorce," she would tell the judge while pointing at me. "I only want him."

This legal wrangling continued for years, even after I met Dimitrina "Didi" Koleva and we started a family of our own. Katarina would not accept that our relationship had come to an end.

Had Katarina known she would be diagnosed with cancer and die a relatively young woman, I believe she would not have spent so much time fighting for a marriage she knew was over. Hers was a sad fate, and I wanted so much better for her. Katarina and I enjoyed many happy years together, travelling the world. I sincerely wished for her to enjoy a long, happy, and healthy life.

DIDI

I made the terribly difficult decision to split from my long-time wife based first and foremost on wanting children of my own. However, before I could have any children I needed to find the right woman.

When I left home, Katarina believed my intention was to "have some fun" and then come back to her. But I knew that was never going to happen. I knew I was leaving forever, and I explained this to Katarina in no uncertain terms. Sadly, my words fell on deaf ears. Even as I prepared to permanently leave the house we shared, Katarina insisted on packing my suitcase.

I knew it would be a difficult transition for Katarina, but my decision was final. I left the house and began to seek a different kind of happiness and fulfillment.

I had put out the word to some friends and associates that I was looking for a Bulgarian woman with whom I could start a new relationship. I wanted to be with a woman with whom I shared values, customs, beliefs, and heritage.

When the chief architect and engineer of the city of Ruse in Bulgaria came to Canada, he visited me at work to learn what I was doing in my business. I made sure to tell him about my dream.

It just so happened that the chief engineer had a female employee who seemed to fit the bill. Dimitrina "Didi" Koleva was a university student who also worked full-time at Transstroy, a state-owned construction company in Ruse. Didi had expressed an interest in travelling to Canada to visit her maternal grandfather, Dimitar Kaleff — after whom Didi was named — who himself had immigrated to Canada in 1929. In those days, an employee had to ask his or her boss for permission to travel outside Bulgaria for an extended period. With a notion that he might be doing me a favour, the chief engineer allowed Didi to leave for a visit abroad.

Didi's boss gave her my card before she left for Canada. He told her to call me as soon as she arrived in Canada, though he offered no explanation for this demand. She did not know what she was getting into; Didi had no clue she was being sent to me as a prospective partner. As a matter of fact, due to a gap in communication, I did not know it, either.

Prior to her departure, one of my brothers got in touch with Didi and gave her a letter addressed to me, asking her to deliver it. Unfortunately, Bulgarian officials at the airport confiscated his letter. In those days, Bulgarians were not allowed to carry letters or any other personal documents across the border. In fact, they would not even let Didi carry her diploma to Canada. Dr. Danev, a dear childhood friend of Didi's, was with her at the airport to see her off, and she was able to give him her diploma for safekeeping. Defectors were a risk to the communist government, and control over Bulgarians journeying outside the country was very strict. The official told Didi that if my brother needed to send me a note, he could send it through the mail like everybody else. Of course, the government always read everyone's mail.

When Didi arrived in Toronto on April 2, 1977, her grandfather called me almost immediately. He said his granddaughter was in Canada and had a message for me.

Didi got on the phone and said, "I had a letter for you, but I don't have it anymore. The communist officials at the airport took it away from me."

Her grandfather took back the telephone and proceeded to invite me over to his house for a visit. The very next day I arrived on Mr. Kaleff's doorstep on O'Connor Drive in Toronto with my nephew, along with a box of long-stemmed red roses.

Strangely enough, there was a connection between our families dating back many years. When my father and uncle built our new house in Gorno Ablanovo in 1936, I accompanied them on a trip to buy roofing tiles.

As we approached our destination, the village of Gorna Manastiriza, my father put his arm around my shoulder and pointed. "The man who owns that house is in Canada now," he said. More interestingly, as I would come to learn many years later, the man who owned that house was Didi's grandfather, the same man I would come to meet in 1977.

That day, my father told me he was supposed to travel to Canada with Mr. Kaleff in 1929, but my grandfather fell ill and subsequently passed away. My father had to stay in Bulgaria to look after our family and did not make it to Canada until he visited me in 1963. Incredibly, my father had been so close to coming to Canada in 1929 that he actually bought a ticket and pledged a piece of property to the bank as a guarantee of his return.

As it turned out, Didi's grandfather ended up living in Canada permanently. To me, the whole thing seemed like a sign. Didi and I were intertwined from the beginning.

I knew that Didi was supposed to be carrying a letter from my brother. What I did not know was that her boss had allowed her to travel to Canada partly so she could meet me.

When I arrived at Mr. Kaleff's house and saw Didi for the first time, I was grateful I had brought along the roses. However, I was somewhat tongue-tied when I opened my mouth to speak. Clearly, I was already smitten.

Once I regained my composure, I asked Didi and her grandfather to join me the next day at the Canadian National Exhibition grounds. My company was holding an exhibit there to promote our new subdivision. They enthusiastically accepted.

Didi and her grandfather came to the exhibit on Saturday afternoon, after which they joined me for dinner. At the time I had no reason to believe Didi would be interested in me. After all, she was only twenty-seven years old, and I was already fifty-one. We were separated in age by nearly twenty-five years!

Furthermore, Didi was tall and gorgeous, more beautiful than any woman I had ever known. Not that I lacked confidence, but it seemed unlikely that such a lovely and smart woman would ever take an interest in me. However, as the day wore on and evening came, it was becoming evident that Didi might actually like me, after all. I was over the moon! I found out later that her interest in me was kindled when she heard Bach playing on my car radio that day. Didi loves that I have such an appreciation for classical music. More than forty years later, we still attend Toronto Symphony concerts regularly, and now enjoy them with Anna-Maria and Kristina Maria, who also appreciate classical music. And I captured her eye with how well I was dressed. That day I was wearing the latest in men's fashion — an attractive plaid suit. Of course, fashions change and you might not see me in colourful plaids any longer, but I still like to show that I know how to dress well.

Didi's primary purpose in being allowed to visit Canada was to serve as a caretaker for her grandfather's ailing Ukrainian wife. This woman was his second wife; he remarried after Didi's maternal grandmother passed away. Unfortunately, that task turned out to be more than Didi bargained for, and it was not in line with her own ambitions. She had hoped to continue her economics studies in Canada; she was working on her master's degree in Bulgaria and intended to earn a doctorate or a second master's in Toronto.

After only a few months in Canada, Didi's visa expired, forcing her to return to Bulgaria. In addition to being ill-suited and unwilling to interrupt her studies and career goals to care for her grandfather's second wife — a perfect stranger to her — she was also homesick. Didi was an only child and very close to her parents. Now her father was ill, and Didi wanted to go home to be with him. She also wanted to finish her studies.

It is important to note that the University of Toronto, where Didi had wanted to continue her studies, did not recognize any of her Bulgarian educational credits. A university official explained that Didi would need to start her education from scratch if she wished to pursue a post-secondary degree in Canada.

That was too much of a sacrifice for Didi to make. Because her parents never joined the Communist Party and had both been imprisoned for their political beliefs, Didi was prohibited from studying full-time at any university in Bulgaria. Despite her strong academic results and high standing at the end of her secondary school studies, she was allowed only to sit for exams alongside her peers in absentia. As a result, earning her degree took her twice as long as it should have. For years, Didi spent her days working full-time to help support her family, while occupying her nights by copying notes provided by her classmates.

After more than five years of countless sacrifices to earn her degree in Bulgaria, Didi was not prepared to throw it all away and start over again in a foreign country. Therefore, she was going home.

Fortunately for me, I was able to meet Didi for breakfast on two separate occasions before her departure. Both times we ate in the restaurant of the King Edward Hotel in Toronto. These meetings proved to be crucial, since they progressed our budding friendship just enough for us to keep in touch after she returned home. During the second of these breakfasts, I offered to drive Didi to the airport for her flight home, and she accepted. Frankly, I just wanted to spend as much time with her as possible.

Later, on the day of her departure, I felt my heart begin to ache as we approached the airport. Didi's three-month trip to Canada was coming to an end, and I was already starting to miss her. When I dropped her off at the airport, I watched as she started to make her way toward the terminal.

"Bye-bye, Iggy," she said happily before walking away. That was the first time she called me by my first name. Prior to that I had been "Mr. Kaneff."

Without thinking I blurted out the first words that popped into my mind. "I'll call you tomorrow morning."

Those words hung in the air as Didi took a moment to process them. "Good," she said. "I'll be excited to hear from you."

Didi's plane would soon be in the air, but I was the one floating on cloud nine. My heart was overflowing with excitement about a future with this incredible woman. Even then I knew in my heart that I loved her. Didi was the one for me.

The next day I kept my promise to Didi and called her. It was midnight in Toronto when I dialled her number, meaning it was 7:00 a.m. in Bulgaria. Didi and I chatted about her trip home, her father's health, and the rest of her family. It was such a nice talk that we ended up doing it again the next day and the day after that.

Before I knew it I was calling Bulgaria every morning at seven o'clock. That was how we got to know each other. In fact, it can be said that Didi and I fell in love over the phone.

During one of our conversations, Didi and I finally decided we wanted to live together in Canada. Then, after several months of talking, I told her I would be travelling to Bulgaria with three associates in January 1978. I thought this trip would provide the perfect opportunity for me to meet her parents and ask for their blessing.

When I arrived in Bulgaria, Didi greeted me at the airport. She arranged for my travel companions, Eddie Del Medico and Marcello Gasparetto, and me to attend the opera that evening in Sofia. It was a fantastic cultural experience during my first night back in Bulgaria.

The next day I went out to buy marble for one of my new buildings. While this was the official reason for my trip to Bulgaria, the truth had more to do with seeing Didi and her parents. Didi waited patiently as I conducted business, after which she took our group to watch another musical performance.

Two days later Didi and I drove to Gorno Ablanovo. From there we made the short trip to her parents' home in Ruse. We enjoyed homemade cake and coffee, after which Didi excused herself. Her father, mother, and I needed to have a private discussion.

I explained to Didi's parents that I loved their daughter, that I respected her, cherished her, and wanted to spend the rest of my life with her. I also explained to them my marital status; I was open and honest with them about everything.

Her father put a stop to my proclamation of love, interrupting me in mid-sentence. "If Didi wants to be with you, you'll get no objection from me. It's her decision to make."

With that, Didi and I were all set. Her parents' blessing was the final piece of the puzzle. We were free to live the rest of our lives together.

Overcome with happiness, I looked at Didi and expressed the true love in my heart. "I've been looking for you all of my life," I told her.

After fifty-one years of moving all around the world, I finally found my true place, and it was with Didi. I had been everywhere, but, strangely enough, the woman of my dreams hailed from a city in Bulgaria so close to my own village.

As much as we wanted to get married, it would take years for Katarina to sign the divorce papers. But it made no difference. Didi and I would be together in Canada, and that was all that mattered.

Didi moved to Canada soon after. In the early summer of 1978, we got right to work on what I wanted more than anything in the world: a child. She was soon expecting, and on March 11, 1979, we welcomed our first daughter, Anna-Maria, into the world. Anna-Maria was named after Ana, Didi's mother, and Maria, my own mother, known as Mita.

In Canada, doctors and nurses now often expect the husband to be present at the hospital — if not inside the delivery room — while the wife is in labour. This is not the custom in Bulgaria. In my home country, the father is never present during delivery. Bulgarians see this as a private time for the mother-to-be; the man has no business being in the room. Didi and I followed this Bulgarian custom.

Of course, I was not far. Mississauga Hospital (now part of Trillium Health Partners) was just across the street from my office building at

101 Queensway West. Nervously, I sat at my desk and sipped cognac, waiting for the call.

After waiting far too long and drinking more cognac than necessary, I finally heard my telephone ring. I was told that my daughter had been born healthy, and Didi was doing well, too. I ran down the stairs and virtually floated up the street to the hospital. I was elated.

When I arrived in Didi's room, I met my daughter for the first time. As I held her in my arms, our eyes locked, and mine began to moisten with happiness and gratitude. It was the most overwhelming feeling of my life. Before long, Didi and I were both crying tears of joy.

I phoned my family in Bulgaria to share the great news. I could hear everybody celebrating on the other end of the line and let the feeling wash over me, thinking more than once, *This is the happiest day of my life.*

After Anna-Maria was born, life was truly beautiful. We had a baby, a home, and everything else that we needed. Didi's mother and father came to live with us, too. My own mother, Mita, also came for a lengthy stay after Anna-Maria's birth. Yolanta, my nephew's daughter, whom I had previously adopted, was also living with us until she got married. It was a busy household, and these were some of the happiest days of my life.

But our family was not yet complete. Just over two years after Anna-Maria's birth, our second daughter, Kristina Maria, was born on April 18, 1981, the exact same day on which I had arrived in Canada thirty years earlier. Kristina Maria, who we strongly believed was to be a boy based on what the doctor told us, without the benefit of an ultrasound, was named after Kosta, Didi's father, and Hristo, my own father. Didi and I were overjoyed to have our two daughters. At long last all my dreams had come true. I truly felt I now had it all and thanked God many times for these blessings.

By 1981, I had Didi, my two daughters, a thriving business, and my health. It was truly everything I could have ever wanted. Amazingly, this tremendous happiness lasted for so many years and continues to this day. Every time I see my wife and daughters, my heart overflows with love.

Once Didi, Anna-Maria, and Kristina Maria were in my life, every day seemed like a beautiful dream. I remember driving the girls to school in the morning, and we would sing the entire trip, happy just being together. Driving a teenage Kristina Maria to school, there was only one song she wanted to listen to for an entire term — "I Would Do Anything for Love" by Meat Loaf, an artist I came to playfully call Meat Head. It was all so much fun.

After so many years, I finally felt I was in the right place. I knew I had found my true home, and it was with Didi, Anna-Maria, and Kristina Maria.

Then, after many years apart, Katarina accepted I was never coming back to her and at last granted me a divorce, which cleared the way for Didi and me to get married. We exchanged vows in front of eighty guests — two of whom were our daughters — on the top floor of the Sutton Place Hotel in Toronto. It was a beautiful wedding, an elaborate celebration in honour of the family I loved so very much and had looked so long to find.

Unfortunately, my marriage to Didi did little to improve my relationship with Heidi and Danny, despite Didi's best efforts to include them, their spouses, and their children in our new family life. As I saw it, they would always be my children, and I would continue to help them in life as much as I could. But they were now grown and I had a new life of my own; it was with Didi and our daughters. Of course, that did not mean I would ever stop loving them. I still do love them very much.

Although they both worked for me at various times, Danny and Heidi never quite accepted my new family or forgave me for leaving their mother. It was a loyalty that I could respect, but it was my hope that they would someday make their way past the hurt feelings. Eventually, they were able to be friendly with me, but they were often unkind to Didi and the girls. As Danny and Heidi perceived it, they were being replaced; but as I saw it, there was more than enough of me, and everything else, to go around.

Didi always kept trying to have a relationship with Danny and Heidi, but they kept turning her away. When Danny's daughter was born, Didi was at the hospital with gifts in hand, willing and able to help. When Heidi went back to school to further her education after she had become a mother, Didi was the first to offer to babysit. My wife wanted us all to get along as a family, but it never quite worked out as we had hoped it would.

Eventually, the resentment Heidi and Danny had toward Didi and the girls drove a wedge between us. Didi never said anything about it to me, but I saw the conflict with my own eyes.

I wish I could have been closer to Danny and Heidi when they became adults. During the 1980s, however, I was focused on enjoying life with my girls and raising them to be outstanding women. I was also extremely busy with my company and needed to ensure it remained a primary focus, particularly in view of the economic turmoil of the early 1980s.

My personal journey had been a long one, often filled with struggle and danger. Life had not always been easy. But now I found myself part of a beautiful family in an existence of my own creation. When I looked at my daughters, I saw true love staring back at me, and I felt fulfilled.

At long last I had my own family. I was finally home.

13

Growing the Business

When I moved to Toronto Township shortly after arriving in Canada in 1951, the municipality sprawled over a vast territory but only contained about twenty-eight thousand people. Since the end of the Second World War, immigrants, like myself, had been streaming into Canada, and tens of thousands of them settled just west of the City of Toronto. By 1961, the population of Toronto Township had more than doubled and five years after that it nudged past one hundred thousand. The old villages of Port Credit at the mouth of the Credit River on Lake Ontario and Streetsville, farther north on the same river, were separate municipalities then. Their populations also swelled significantly in the 1950s, so much so that they incorporated as towns in the early 1960s.

Dating back to the nineteenth and early twentieth centuries, a number of prosperous industries centred around sawmills, gristmills, and of course, farming, became prevalent in Toronto Township. Larger firms soon developed, as well, in Port Credit and various neighbourhoods of the township, including the St. Lawrence Starch Company and the Cooksville Brick and Tile Company. They were joined later by others in the 1940s and 1950s such as Dominion Small Arms Limited in Lakeview and the St. Lawrence Cement Company and a British-American oil refinery in Clarkson.

In 1937, an airport that eventually expanded dramatically to become Toronto Pearson International was constructed in Malton, which itself was annexed in 1968 by the newly minted Town of Mississauga, providing even more jobs to its residents. Malton was also the home of Avro Canada, the designer and manufacturer of one of the first passenger jets, the Jetliner, and more famously, the Arrow interceptor.

In later years, the demise of Avro Canada and other old-line industries, such as Cooksville Brick and Tile and St. Lawrence Starch, were more than made up for by the emergence of dozens of other companies, ranging from a resurgent aerospace industry represented by Bombardier, Honeywell, and Magellan, to numerous pharmaceutical and high-tech firms. Today, all told, Mississauga is home to the Canadian or international head offices of sixty of the Fortune 500 companies. It is also projected to top a million people by the middle of this century, already has almost eight hundred thousand citizens, and is the sixth-largest city in Canada.

To accommodate all the new companies flocking to Toronto Township, industrial parks in the southern part of the municipality were developed south and north of Dundas Street between Cawthra and Dixie Roads in the 1950s and at the Sheridan Park Research Centre between the Park Royal and Sheridan Homelands subdivisions in the early 1960s. Later, particularly after 1974 when Mississauga incorporated as a city, huge swaths of land in its northern half were specifically slated for industrial and business uses.

In order to serve the swelling population and burgeoning new industries, road and highway improvements were vital. Toronto Township's existing thoroughfares such as the east-west Lakeshore Road, the Queensway, Dundas Street, Burnhamthorpe Road, and Eglinton Avenue, as well as north-south routes such as Dixie Road, Hurontario Street, and Mississauga Road were widened or upgraded. The construction of Highway 401 in the late 1950s and early 1960s, the increase in lanes of the Queen Elizabeth Way (QEW), and much later, the expansion of Highway 427 and creation of Erin Mills Parkway in the 1970s, all contributed to enhance transportation in the township and the later City of Mississauga. So, too, did the inauguration of Ontario's GO Transit commuter service, which debuted in 1967 with three stations in the Town of Mississauga, later expanding to the current nine, connecting the municipality to Toronto and other surrounding communities.

In the 1950s, I was busy constructing houses and later mid-rise and high-rise apartment buildings, but I also had my eye on office towers and commercial retail plazas. I have often been asked how I go about determining where to buy land for development. Certainly, I am not an economist, but it was obvious that Toronto Township was booming. Where new roads were being created or old roads improved, expansion would follow. I spent a great deal of time attending City Hall planning sessions to listen to what urban planners had in store for our municipality and could see that big things lay ahead for anything clustered around or near existing or proposed roads such as Highways 401, 403, 407, 410, and the QEW. However, I got distracted from development and construction by my excursion into the car dealership business, which in many ways I now regret. Had I not done so, today I would likely have an even larger development company, and potentially might have been the largest builder in the Greater Toronto Area. Construction and development have always been chief passions in my life, specifically because through these processes, you can create something, which does not happen when you sell cars and trucks.

I have built numerous office towers in the past few decades, but there are two projects that stand out in my mind: 89 and 101 Queensway West and three buildings on Central Parkway West. Everything I build is of the highest quality, and these five structures are no exception, but they also represent a certain degree of disappointment for me.

89 AND 101 QUEENSWAY WEST

In the mid-1960s, partly with the money I received when I sold my General Motors dealership, I bought a great deal of land in Toronto Township, especially on Argyle Road near Dundas Street West and on Queensway West near Confederation Parkway. Initially, on the land I purchased, I built three apartment high-rises — La Fontaine Bleue

(1969), The Carillon (1970), and The Brookside (1974). Later, toward the end of the 1970s, after the 1973–75 recession, I completed two side-by-side, similarly designed white office buildings on the Queensway: the eight-storey 89 and the seven-storey 101.

Two of the early architects on my apartment buildings were the husband-and-wife team Ivan and Lucy Marinoff. I had known the couple since 1948 when they were both enrolled in the University of Graz's architectural program and I was selling vegetables in the region. Almost every morning they would come by the market garden and pick up a few items. After they graduated, they moved to Venezuela, one country you could emigrate to immediately. In 1967, they relocated to Toronto and called me. We had a long conversation, got reacquainted, and eventually I enlisted their services to help me build La Fontaine Bleue. From that point on, they worked on numerous projects for me. The Marinoffs both lived to be nearly one hundred years old, and I was very proud to call them my friends.

Just as I had responded to a need for houses and apartment buildings in the township and built them, I now saw the increasing demand for office buildings where there was little or no supply. Instinct and my own research had a lot to do with finding the right properties to build on strategically, but I also had a great deal of help from the people I employed. Sometimes too much. Looking back, I realize I should have held on to the two buildings on the Queensway. Instead, I was advised to sell them, and I did so to Desjardins, a Quebec trust company. Had I kept ownership of them, I would have made millions of dollars more in the long run. They have been sold and resold a number of times over the years, each time for far more than it cost me to purchase the land and construct and lease them.

The two Queensway buildings still stand and remain as elegant in design as the day I finished them, though now they are devoted to medical services and are known collectively as the Queensway Professional Centre. They are now managed by NorthWest Healthcare Properties, a publicly traded real estate income trust company listed on the Toronto Stock Exchange. Whenever I pass the buildings, I have to admit feeling somewhat wistful and quite regretful of my decision to sell them.

CENTRAL PARKWAY TRIO

The three buildings — 1270, 1290, and 1300 — on Central Parkway West also have a special place in my heart. To buy the land for them, I used the money I received from selling 89 and 101 Queensway to Desjardins. The sharp and very nasty recession of the early 1980s, with its sky-high interest rates, was over in Ontario and a certain normalcy had returned to the economic situation in the province as a whole and in Mississauga in particular.

By the late 1980s, GO Transit had expanded its operations in Mississauga. More stations had been added, including Erindale station adjacent to my property at Central Parkway West and Burnhamthorpe Road. My land was also very close to the Civic Centre (Mississauga's new city hall whose design was based on a "futuristic farm" celebrating the municipality's agricultural origins), Square One Shopping Centre, and ever more gleaming office towers and high-rise condos. As they say about how to achieve success in the real estate industry, "Location, location, location!"

The three buildings I built on this prime site complement one another perfectly — 1270 and 1300 are six and four storeys, respectively, and are graceful glass, steel, and concrete structures with light brown spandrel panels, while 1290 has eleven floors without the panels. The design of 1290, the tallest, was innovative at the time of construction, since full-length, curtain-wall office buildings were still in their nascency. Nevertheless, all three structures' glass windows harmonize with one another.

Over the years, the Kaneff Group of Companies has had several head offices. In the early days, as I mentioned before, I ran operations out of the basement in my house. Later, in the 1960s, I converted an apartment into an office in one of my Centennial Towers buildings on Argyle Road in Mississauga, and still later, I set up the corporation's headquarters in 1290 Central Parkway. But once again I listened to bad advice, and instead of keeping the three Central Parkway buildings, I sold them to Great-West Life in the 1990s, along with several high-rise apartment buildings. Since then the buildings have been turned over twice for at least $20 million more each time they were sold. Needless to say, I would have made a great deal more money if I had held on to them. Today the three buildings are collectively called Erindale Corporate Centre and are managed by the Redbourne Group.

The stark reality of selling the Queensway and Central Parkway office buildings is that I was never able to replace them for anything close to the same price as I sold them. Relentless inflation, ever-rising real estate and construction costs, and a blistering escalation of the price of land in proportion to overall project costs materially above inflation made that impossible. Twice bitten, but lesson learned.

These days, in Mississauga and elsewhere, we are not building office towers the way we once did, but I am not done with them yet and have plans for a few on the land we are currently developing around our headquarters at 8501 Mississauga Road in Brampton, just north of Highway 407 and Steeles Avenue West.

SETTING UP SHOP IN THE SUBURBS

After the Second World War in Canada, subdivisions were being built across the country to house returning military and their families as well as the hundreds of thousands of immigrants flowing into the country. Toronto Township was no different, particularly when it came to newcomers to the nation who were attracted to the "suburbs," especially as more companies set up shop in the township and plenty of jobs became available for both existing residents and immigrants.

The Shipp Corporation built Applewood Acres, Credit Woodlands, and Riverview Gardens subdivisions, while in the late 1950s I was occupied as a builder in Erindale Woodlands. People in these new subdivisions needed places to buy merchandise and food, so strip malls and shopping plazas began sprouting up everywhere, first with the Lorne Park Shopping Centre in 1953 and culminating in the gargantuan Square One in 1973, once the largest in Canada and still the biggest in Ontario.

In 1976, I established the Commercial Division of the Kaneff Group of Companies to specialize in the design, development, and management of Kaneff-owned office and retail properties across Mississauga and eventually Brampton and Oakville, buying sizable tracts of farmland for future development in these municipalities. But it was in the mid-1980s that

I got into commercial retail properties in a big way when interest rates dropped to more normal levels after the earlier sky-high upper teens and low 20 percent ranges they had reached. My first shopping plaza was Huron Heights Market on Central Parkway East in Mississauga, which I built in 1987 and still own. When it comes to strip malls or shopping centres, I do not sell them after I build them the way I did with the Queensway and Central Parkway office buildings.

Today, in Mississauga, Brampton, Oakville, and Hamilton, the Kaneff Group of Companies owns and manages a wide range of commercial retail and office sites, totalling nearly a million square feet. However, it is in Brampton that I meaningfully extended our company's interest in shopping malls. We have significant land holdings around our current corporate headquarters in that city north of Highway 407 on Mississauga Road, and it is there that I opened the Lionhead Golf Club & Conference Centre in 1991. Our latest commercial retail plaza, Lionhead Marketplace, has now opened across the road from our head office on nineteen acres with almost two hundred thousand square feet of retail space. We also have plans for future office buildings in the vicinity.

By design we have also launched Forest Gate, a new subdivision of detached homes and townhouses across the street from the Lionhead Golf Club & Conference Centre. It is a good strategy, for obvious reasons, to have the full package available for people: housing, diverse shopping, entertainment, and where possible, places of employment. Elsewhere in Brampton we have applied this procedure in Streetsville Glen; Huron Heights and Roseborough in Mississauga; and Sheridan Gardens in Oakville.

Our strategy for these neighbourhood developments has been quite straightforward: identify a well-located property, purchase the land at a reasonable price (the trickiest part!), develop it into a mixed-used site by building low-rise and mid-rise housing units adjacent to a commercial retail or office site, sell only the dwelling units, keep the income-generating commercial site, and repeat where possible.

Brampton, like Mississauga, holds a special place in my heart. As my company has grown, and as I have matured as a man, I have watched Brampton develop from a town of fifty-six hundred people in the 1950s to more than six hundred thousand residents today. By the middle of this century, the city's population is expected to hit nine hundred thousand. It is already the ninth-largest city in Canada.

Often people ask me why I have not developed properties in places farther afield, but occasionally in the past I have. As far back as 1971, I built two subsidized apartment buildings in Toronto's Cabbagetown, and I even found myself involved in projects in London, Brantford, and Guelph, Ontario. However, my father once told me, "Son, if you cannot visit a site you own today, don't have it." I took this to mean that if I could not supervise a development without staying overnight away from home, then I should not become involved. As usual, my father's advice was wise, and I have followed his words to the letter since.

During the late 1980s and early 1990s, I built office towers, a golf course, subdivisions, apartment buildings, and shopping plazas at a furious pace. But just as I had gotten distracted with selling cars in the late 1950s and early 1960s, I ventured into unknown territory once more — this time in the beer business!

BREWING UP A STORM

After years of being dominated by the big three brewers in Canada — Labatt, Molson, and Carling O'Keefe — the beer business in the country experienced an incredible transformation in the 1980s as one micro or craft brewery after another popped up. The big three owned 96 percent of the market, but that was about to change, at least in a small way. First in Canada to arrive on the scene were Brick Brewing in Waterloo, Ontario, and Granville Island Brewing in Vancouver, both founded in 1984. In Ontario, they were quickly followed by Upper Canada in Toronto, Wellington County and a revived Sleeman in Guelph, and Creemore Springs in Creemore. By 1989, there were forty-two new microbreweries in Canada. The demand for them was growing quickly, and supply was just starting to come on stream.

So, in 1988, it seemed like a good idea to get involved in the action. Four former Carling O'Keefe marketing men joined forces with me and my executive vice-president, Eric McKnight, to form the Northern Algonquin Brewing Company, usually just called Algonquin Brewing.

When the Formosa Springs Brewery, founded in 1870 and touted as the oldest still-standing brewery in Canada, came up for sale after largely lying idle for seventeen years, we purchased it and the land it was on, and the planning began.

Formosa, Ontario, is in Bruce County, about 115 miles northwest of Toronto. To assume ownership of the brewery, all we had to do was pay off the debts of the mineral water company that had been operating out of it. However, none of the brewing equipment was usable, so several million dollars had to be spent to get the brewery up and running again.

After many delays and difficulties, we finally produced our inaugural beer in January 1989, and at first, everything appeared to go well. From 1991 to 1993, Algonquin was ranked the number one microbrewery in Ontario, and by 1995 we had captured 1 percent of the provincial market. Always in the background, though, were substantial problems. We tried to compete head-to-head with the big three brewers by introducing trendy beers as they did, something virtually impossible for a small firm like ours; we attempted to enter the U.S. market with disastrous results; and, as was the case with many of our microbrewery colleagues, we saw our profitability eroded by various domestic and international regulatory changes.

Mortally wounded, the company staggered on until we sold the Formosa brewery and our brands to the Brick Brewing Company in 1997 for about $6 million. However, in reality, we gave it away, more or less, and I estimate I lost at least $3 million in the adventure all told, money I could have used for profitable projects, not to mention the opportunity cost of the money invested in the business for nearly nine years.

Why did I get into the beer business? Back in 1988 at the beginning, I told the media that I saw Algonquin "as an aggressive firm with a concept and brands that are on the leading edge of the North American brewing industry," and so it seemed then. In the past few years, of course, the craft brewery business has exploded all across the country. In Ontario alone, there are now more than 270 microbreweries and brewpubs in more than 110 communities.

As such, I was not wrong in my assessment of the fundamentals of the burgeoning, high-growth niche market. I was wrong in that I entered a highly capital-intensive business that I did not understand, and worse, whose operations I did not control. Furthermore, it is extremely difficult to compete in an intensively regulated, oligopolistic market. Finally, Algonquin's location in Formosa was too far from our head office for me to visit and oversee the business regularly. For all these reasons, our attempts to run and grow a profitable microbrewery, notwithstanding the backdrop of a swiftly growing market segment, failed.

Today, the craft brewery business is a very crowded field, and the remaining two big operations — Labatt and Molson — are now foreign-owned. So I am very happy to be out of beer as a commercial enterprise, though I certainly enjoy drinking it!

TED GLISTA

My life in the 1970s and 1980s was not all about business, of course. I have always forged very strong bonds with many of the people I have encountered in my life. One such was Ted Glista, the son of Jozef Glista, the man who taught me carpentry at the Shipp Corporation so long ago.

After Ted finished school, I hired him as my insurance agent, and we became fast friends. When he married Marina, I attended their wedding in Brantford. Later, we even partnered in the insurance business.

Ted was one of Mississauga's greatest volunteers and community leaders. He worked hard to promote multiculturalism in Canada when the direction in the 1960s was biculturalism — French and English. Ted believed that all of Canada's immigrants should be represented and honoured.

A fundamental aspect of his volunteerism and leadership was his lifelong involvement in the Polish-Canadian community. Even though he was born in Canada, Ted had deep respect for his cultural heritage. He was president of the Polish Alliance of Canada for more than ten years and founded the Reymont Foundation to help advance Polish culture in Canada. The foundation was named after Władysław Reymont, the Polish winner of the 1924 Nobel Prize in Literature.

One of my fondest memories of Ted concerns the ecclesiastical inauguration of Pope John Paul II on October 22, 1978. Ted and I, along with Bill, Stan, and Karl Fujarczuk (also known as Fay), had the great honour of being part of a delegation to attend the inauguration at St. Peter's Square in the Vatican City. Like many people I became friends with, I met the Fujarczuk brothers playing golf. As did many of their countrymen in Poland, they had suffered greatly during the Second World War before immigrating to Canada after the war.

The early1980s saw the rise of an independence movement in Poland against the communist regime, the first wave of labour unrest that would sweep through the entire Soviet Bloc in that decade and eventually lead to the toppling of the Berlin Wall and the end of communism in Eastern Europe as well as in the Soviet Union itself.

An outspoken electrician named Lech Wałęsa emerged as an energetic and charismatic leader in the shipyards of Gdańsk where the first workers' strikes were organized — an unheard-of event in a communist-controlled nation. As events unfolded in Poland, Ted immediately mobilized the support of Polish Canadians and people from other Canadian ethnic communities to raise funds for Wałęsa's Solidarity trade union. Prior to leaving for Poland to personally deliver the donated money, Ted called Wałęsa directly to ask about the situation and what was needed most. Wałęsa said, "Money to help us grow this movement, visibility in the world to gain support for this movement, and prayers to keep us safe."

In October 1980, Ted and Marina met with Wałęsa in Poland. The meeting received a great deal of press coverage but was frowned upon by the Polish communist government of the day. Unfortunately, Ted fell ill in Poland due to a rare food poisoning that weakened him terribly. Regrettably, he did not live to see Wałęsa lead Solidarity to become the first labour union in the Soviet Bloc or witness the great Pole become president and win the Nobel Peace Prize. Ted died of a heart attack at the age of forty-seven in January 1981.

After Ted's untimely death, Marina and her son, Greg, continued to work in the insurance business. Happily, today I work with a third generation of the Glista family, hope to be around to see the fourth generation, and perhaps even be invited to their weddings, too!

BATTLING A FINANCIAL CRISIS

In the background of all my business activity in the 1970s and 1980s were certain events affecting Canada's and the world's economic health. The state of the economy, whether municipal, provincial, national, or international has an enormous impact on builders, as it does for everyone. Ever since I started in the construction business, there have been financial downturns, but the recession in the late 1970s and early 1980s in Ontario was particularly destructive, forcing many of my colleagues to declare bankruptcy before the economy had a chance to recover.

It all started in 1978 when interest rates around the world started to spike upward. In the West in the 1970s, baby boomers were entering the labour force in large numbers and began buying houses, paid mostly with debt. Oil crises in the 1970s, as well as high wage demands, pushed inflation upward even more. The Bank of Canada attempted to stop the ever-increasing inflation rate by raising interest rates. Unfortunately, by doing that over a relatively short period of time, the bank almost decimated the housing market. During this time, however, my company experienced its most profitable years. I was building thousands of units every year, renting out most of them in short order. Business was not just good; it was booming.

By August 1981, though, the interest rate being offered by the Bank of Canada had swollen to a whopping 21.5 percent. Prior to 1978, it had generally hovered around 10 percent. Concurrently, the average inflation rate had soared to an alarming 12 percent. Not surprisingly, the world's economy tanked, and Canada was not immune. As part of a global recession, Canada saw even more severe underemployment than the United States. More than 12 percent of our population was classified as unemployed or underemployed.

The inflationary period prompted Canadians to protect themselves through investment in the housing market. These transactions were financed through borrowing and eventually caused national debt levels to rise. For Canadians, it was a perfect storm of underemployment, high interest rates, and increased government spending that led to financial calamity. At the same time, Canadian firms started shifting their focus from innovation and productivity to investing in real estate to survive, while also downsizing their workforces during a time of globalization. By 1979, the United States decided to establish a fluctuating exchange rate system with Canada, devaluing our dollar in America and making Canada's foreign purchases more expensive. In so many ways, our country was facing financial strain.

Before the economic crisis of the early 1980s, the Canadian government had devised a system to help lubricate the construction industry. It wanted us to continue providing housing for wealthy professionals like doctors, lawyers, and accountants. Housing, a basic human need, has always been a priority for Canadians. In fact, nearly 70 percent of families in Canada own their homes, while only 30 percent live in rentals. Generally, Canadians prefer to own their homes if they can afford to do so. To many, owning a house provides security and tenure, and in most cases, is considered to be a good investment.

Since the days of the Great Depression, Canada had experienced rapid growth in average annual units constructed, rising from approximately thirty-nine thousand during the years of the Second World War all the way to just over two hundred and twenty-nine thousand in the 1970s. Unfortunately, the global recession saw that expansion come to a screeching halt. From 1976 to 1981, the national home ownership rate only rose by 0.3 percent, from 61.8 percent to 62.1.

As part of a government directive to keep the housing industry moving during the recession, builders were allowed to deduct "soft costs" from taxable income. Soft costs included items such as the use of rented equipment and office supplies, but during the financial crisis, its most crucial derivative was allowing builders to write off interest paid as a tax deduction. This was never more important than in the early 1980s when it appeared interest rates might reach 25 percent.

The Multi-Unit Residential Building (MURB) program was a popular investment scheme in Canada during the 1970s and early 1980s that capitalized on interest deductibility. It was considered low-risk while providing huge tax write-offs. The federal government wished only to stimulate the housing industry, but inadvertently created a tax shelter for those looking to take advantage of this tax write-off.

In 1981, I had more than two thousand apartment units in various stages of construction. The provision to deduct interest paid was one of the things keeping me — and many of my fellow builders — afloat during the financial crisis. It was factored into the price of housing units and allowed us to keep them at an affordable level for customers.

Then, in November 1981, Liberal Finance Minister Allan MacEachen abruptly cancelled the program, causing all hell to break loose. Soft-cost deductions were completely disallowed except in a few circumstances.

When the program ended, it meant we could no longer deduct the astronomical interest paid from our taxable income, along with several other soft costs. Instead we had to capitalize these costs until construction was complete. Most banks, therefore, terminated the loans being used to pay contractors, and money flowing into projects subsequently ground to a halt.

I had sold unit after unit to customers with the understanding they would be able to deduct the soft costs. I took in the money and paid the debts. The customer deducted the soft costs at closing. The program worked very well to create jobs and housing, but its sudden cancellation was a catastrophe.

While visiting Bulgaria for a nephew's wedding, I received a call about Minister MacEachen's decision from George Berzins, one of my junior staff managers. Mr. Berzins went on to become the vice-president of our Commercial Division for many years, but on November 12, 1981, he was the bearer of bad news.

"Minister MacEachen cancelled the MURB program," he told me. "Also, we used to have a loan with Citibank, and now we don't."

From my end of the line there was only silence.

Initially, I panicked when he told me about the program's demise, knowing what this would mean for my business. At the time, I had loans from Citibank in New York for $92 million to fund my projects. Mortgages were also being called, which led to many of my customers being forced to terminate their purchases. The housing bubble was bursting.

I was out of the country, isolated from my business, and all I could think to do was contact the senior-most banker I knew personally. So I called the manager of the Royal Bank of Canada's International Division and later the bank's chairman and CEO, a man I was fortunate enough to know. As soon as I got him on the telephone, I voiced my concerns. Surprisingly, he was very calm about the entire matter.

"Iggy, just enjoy your vacation. Don't even worry about it. Tell your secretary to send the files over to my office."

He was telling me to relax, but I was still worried. Even when he assured me that everything would be fine, I remained concerned. After all, there was so much at stake for my company.

As soon as my nephew's wedding was done, I rushed back home. Less than two weeks after the finance minister's announcement, I found myself in the office of Mississauga Mayor Hazel McCallion. Prior to this visit, Mayor McCallion was already aware of the situation facing builders in our municipality. Many of them were going bankrupt in her fast-growing city, and Mayor McCallion would not stand for it.

Of course, the banks would not tolerate any delinquency on loans whatever the reason. They merely cancelled the deals and the builders' projects, and in some cases the companies were destroyed. The buildings were repossessed, a fire sale was held, and then it was all over. Many long-standing builders went out of business through no fault of their own.

I had six buildings under construction at the time, with hundreds of people employed to work on them. I could not tell these contractors to stay home, and they had to be paid. Normally, I hired a few key people, and they compensated their own employees. At this time, however, I made a deal with the builders' union to hire all the workers directly. Essentially, Kaneff Construction became its own subcontractor during this period. We became responsible for all payments of labour and materials. Throughout this period, we never stopped working. It was a great deal of additional work for my company, but it was the only way we could survive the crisis. Financially, our reward was being able to stay in business.

While I was still in her office, Hazel McCallion called Finance Minister MacEachen, who was also the deputy prime minister to Pierre Elliott Trudeau. At first Mr. MacEachen's secretary put Mayor McCallion on the phone with the deputy finance minister. Mayor McCallion was unimpressed and became even more incensed about the situation.

"I didn't ask to speak to the deputy minister," she harangued the secretary. "If I wanted to speak to the deputy minister, I would've called him in the first place." By now, the mayor was visibly upset. Her face reddened as her brow furrowed. "Put Mr. MacEachen on the phone right now!"

Within seconds the finance minister was on the telephone with Mayor McCallion, and she started in on him immediately. "Who do you think you are, MacEachen? I'm the elected mayor of Mississauga and represent more people in this city than live in your entire province." Minister MacEachen was a resident of Cape Breton, Nova Scotia.

For more than twenty minutes, the only words that came from Mr. MacEachen's mouth were: "Yes, Madam Mayor" or "I'm sorry, Madam Mayor." Allan MacEachen was no match for a determined Mayor McCallion, known to some as Hurricane Hazel for her feistiness. She asserted her will in the interest of her constituents, and ultimately got her way. Mayor McCallion almost always got her way.

The following afternoon Minister MacEachen announced a change to his previous cancellation of the soft-costs program. All construction projects that were already in the process of being built were allowed to use the old rules under a grandfathered provision. Only newly begun projects would be subject to the recent legislation.

In all, the period during which the legislation affected existing projects was merely two weeks, but that was long enough to do substantial damage. Many businesses went under, and many others came close to failure. In fact, I had to hire a chartered accountant — at my own expense — to verify my assets for the bank. Eventually, I paid the accountant $200,000, equivalent to almost $600,000 today, that I would never recover.

Due to this crisis, I also lost my highly skilled foreman, Nick DeLorenzo, who was forced to declare bankruptcy and move back home to Italy. He worked for many builders, and though I was able to pay him during this time, others were not. Without enough money coming in, he was unable to cover his bills and was forced to shut down his operation.

Although I understood that the foreman was in a tight spot, it did not excuse the fact that he took payment for my project and left the country without holding up his end of the bargain. Two years later I ran into Mr. DeLorenzo at a party.

"Mr. Kaneff!" he said excitedly as he approached with his hand extended.

"Don't you Mr. Kaneff me," I retorted.

Mr. DeLorenzo never even offered an apology for taking off with my money. He could have explained that other builders did not pay him and he was forced to leave, but he did not even offer me an explanation. He saw a problem and ran away from it. In the meantime, he had almost put me out of business.

I had many, many sleepless nights. Everything I had accomplished in thirty years could have been wiped out in one fell swoop — and through no fault of my own. It would have been one thing if the problem had been my own mismanagement of the company, but this was another matter entirely. I was working day and night to become a somebody, yet a government policy decision made during an economic crisis — both of which were completely beyond my control — almost ruined me.

Of course, even if I had to declare bankruptcy on my current project, I still believe I could have rebuilt my business. In fact, I had a deal in place to build eight hundred units in Brampton and would have completed that job one way or another.

As usual, the difference between success and failure came down to luck and timing. I had the good fortune to benefit from the MURB program, and the even better fortune of having Hazel McCallion's support when Minister MacEachen ended it. Had the financial crisis occurred a few years earlier, I would not have had the capital needed to keep cash flowing into the jobs. Once again, everything somehow worked out for me.

BACK TO BUSINESS AS USUAL

By 1982, interest rates had fallen back down to 18.5 percent, and the economy was on the road to recovery. Kaneff Construction, due to our sterling reputation, never stopped selling homes or building apartment units. We completed many of our biggest projects during the 1980s despite the prevailing high-interest-rate environment.

In the years both before and after the economic crisis, my company was highly productive. In fact, I did a lot of work in the Square One area in those days, putting up six buildings for a total of 1,850 units. Before 1981, condos made up only 10 percent of homes built in Canada, but as the 1980s progressed, condo fever began to sweep the nation and has only intensified since, especially as the cost of single-detached and semi-detached homes and townhouses has rocketed upward dramatically. In the country's major cities, escalating real estate prices and scarcer availability of land have made the ever-taller condo the way to go. As had been the case with apartment buildings, office towers, and shopping malls, where there was a new demand, I supplied it, and still do.

In the late 1970s, days before we broke ground on a project near Square One, a member of my team attended a committee meeting to name the streets in this new development. We submitted the Kaneff name as a suggestion, never expecting it would be selected.

Months later, as I was putting down asphalt, I got news that a road in our new development would be named Kaneff Crescent. Nestled into the southwest corner where Burnhamthorpe Road meets Hurontario Street is a crescent that bears my name. It is one of the greatest honours I have ever received, and a feeling of gratitude fills my heart whenever I walk or drive on Kaneff Crescent. I built six buildings on Kaneff Crescent, every one of them white, all still standing to this day. Not far from these half-dozen condos, we will commence building Keystone — two white condos, one twenty storeys, the other twenty-three, in late 2019.

In the late 1980s, I also built the Pinnacle 1, 2, and 3 condos in Brampton, which are near two residential rental buildings on Steeles Avenue West that we still own. I was building major projects one after another, and it went on and on like that for quite some time. The fortunes of my company were steadily improving, particularly once Didi became involved in its operations.

My wife began working in the office during the 1980s when our daughters were in school, and she was a great help to me. More than just about anyone I know, Didi gets things done. Having grown up as a side-lined outsider in communist Bulgaria, she has terrific street smarts, grit, and judgment. She managed to achieve her academic goals while living in a system that did not allow her to enroll at university. Didi is a true force to be reckoned with!

As time went on, my wife took a more hands-on role with our customers. At a certain point in the construction process — once a building was enclosed and the drywall went up — Didi took over the project from a customer-service standpoint. She communicated with the clients, discerned their needs, and put a plan into action until they were satisfied. This is an incredibly time-consuming job requiring a very high level of attention to detail, an understanding of the construction process, and the patience of Job to deal with demanding customers. Didi was intimately involved with rectifying any deficiencies or mistakes in the homes we built. Satisfied customers are what keep our brand strong and our name out of trouble, and my wife was in charge of ensuring that our customers were satisfied. This was a major responsibility that required knowledge of our process, the trades, home building, and the economics of building a house.

I love having Didi involved in my business. Not only is she a very smart woman but she is also very trustworthy. In particular, I trust her to deal with customers and employees. Didi opts to offer fair deals through creative means. Although I will always remain heavily involved with the construction side of my business, having my wife on the job provides me with a little bit more freedom. Perhaps, coincidentally, it was during this time that I decided to become involved in the golf industry.

14

Building a Golf Empire

In 1957, golf came crashing into my life when a strange, dimpled ball careened through the window of a house I was building on Old Carriage Road. I became interested and then fascinated with the game of golf, a passion that continues to this day. Golf became my first, second, and third choices for recreation. Simply put, I loved golf.

From my first swing of a club, I discovered that I possessed a natural inclination for the game. Of course, athleticism will only take you so far in golf, so I spent many hours on the course — and on the driving range — honing my swing. Before long I was able to play the game at a fairly high level.

My relationship with golf remained relatively static for thirty years. I was a long-time member of the Credit Valley Golf and Country Club and played with friends such as Eddie Del Medico, Joe Messmer, Benny Rockett, Dinko Mandarich, Ted Glista, and Dr. Branko Radisic frequently. Even more often, however, I played golf with business associates. I can think of no better place to strike a deal than on the golf course while enjoying nature in — hopefully — nice weather. It is the perfect social setting to relax and get to know the men or women in your foursome. Over the years, I have had numerous pleasant golf lunches with business associates and friends. Although

Joe Zentil did not golf at Credit Valley, I did a lot of work with him in the 1970s and we became dear friends. The Zentils and the Del Medicos and my family enjoyed many weekends at the Zentils' splendid farm in King City.

As time passed and I became a better player, I also developed into a full-fledged golf addict. Sport had always been an important part of my life — ever since I brought bystanders and casual spectators to their feet with my quick manoeuvres on the local soccer pitches in Graz and Salzburg — and golf was now my new favourite sport. When I reached a certain level of success with my construction company, I came up with the idea of building my own course, which eventually evolved into a rough plan to one day own my own golf course.

As I considered the thought, it began to make perfect sense: I could buy a desirable plot of land, use some of it to build a golf course, and then, over time, employ the remaining acreage for housing. Or I could even redevelop the entire area, assuming that other development and city expansion would occur around the course. As they say in real estate jargon, it would be a good way to "carry land" for the ultimate long-term re-development of what was otherwise greenfield acreage. Building my own course, as I saw it, could be a good investment opportunity while also allowing me to get involved with golf and its community on a new level.

By 1987, I was ready to turn my idea for a golf course into reality. For years, I had been eyeing a five-hundred-acre piece of property just beyond the northern boundary limit of Mississauga in Brampton. In those days, it operated as a farm; I bought my fruit and vegetables there on Saturday mornings. I was captivated from the moment I first laid eyes on it, with its strikingly beautiful, rolling landscape and its access to the Credit River.

A farmer, Clarence French, owned the property. One morning at the farm I finally approached Mr. French and asked him if he would like to sell me his land.

"I'll consider it," he said.

When I heard him say those words, I knew the land would soon be mine. It was now just a matter of negotiating a fair price. Across the road, during the summer, Didi and our daughters often picked strawberries on land that one day would be the site of Lionhead Marketplace, the retail shopping complex across from the headquarters of the Kaneff Group of Companies.

LIONHEAD

When it came to building a golf course, acquiring Mr. French's property was merely the first of many steps. After a period of negotiation, I was able to purchase Mr. French's farm, but this land represented only one hundred and seventy-five of the five hundred acres I intended to buy. There was one other owner with as many as one hundred acres, but most of the acquisitions I made were from smaller landowners. I negotiated several small deals to assemble the land I desired. In all, there were half a dozen sellers, each of whom wanted a good deal for their land. And a good deal they got.

Mississauga Road, running through the westernmost part of the property, was already in place. It figured into the land's cost. In the future, Mississauga Road would become a desirable location for homeowners, but at the time it was generally used as a scenic route for motorists on the weekends headed north. People liked driving their cars on Mississauga Road, but few lived on it at the time. However, given its proximity to the middle of Brampton, I considered this to be an excellent piece of land; it was perfect for my golf course, and it would surely be excellent for the future development of homes in Brampton.

Assembling the land was just the first of many tasks required to build a golf course. Once I knew what property I wanted, I had to assemble a team to help me make everything happen. I had a real estate agent, a planner, a consultant, and an architect working for me nearly as soon as I took possession of the land. They were all integral to the materialization of my vision. Most helpful of all was my planner, Glen Schnarr. I had been his first client, and he helped me tie up some of the land.

Right away we submitted plans for a subdivision to the municipality. We also presented a proposal to the Credit Valley Conservation Authority. There were many environmental guidelines attached to building a golf course, especially one that would criss-cross the important Credit River.

From the beginning it was my intention for this course to be immaculately maintained while also ensuring the highest standards of environmentally friendly practices. I have always insisted that every aspect of any one of my operations be done in the best possible way. My unofficial motto among employees is that Kaneff does first-class business in a first-class way, so my golf course had to benefit the community, not burden it. I operated the Kaneff Group of Companies according to high standards of integrity, and I would not veer from them when undertaking new lines of business. I have always followed the rules, paid every penny of taxes owing, and even given back generously to my community. Venturing into the golf business, my approach would remain the same.

Gaining all required approvals to build a golf course can be a very lengthy process full of tedium and red tape. At first Donald Gordon, the Brampton parks and recreation commissioner, was steadfastly against my course being built on that plot of land. He felt that such a large swath of property should be owned and controlled by the municipality. But I had bought the land fair and square; eventually, he would have to relent.

In due time, we obtained all the approvals and permissions necessary from the various government agencies. Certain branches of the municipality were against my golf course while others were for it. But in the end it did not matter. I achieved what I had set out to do, and it only took four years.

Going into this project, I expected my initial investment in building the golf course to be around $20 million, and that proved more or less accurate. Before any actual building took place, I paid $4.4 million for the land. As I found out right from the start with this venture — and it would be proven true time and again — running a golf course is a very expensive business.

Still, I knew the land was a sound investment, no matter what. In fact, I bought it at just the right time, since construction of Highway 407 had just commenced. In the future, this area would hold tremendous potential for development. If anything, $4.4 million for those five hundred acres would end up being economical, if not an outright bargain.

Once I received permission from the municipality, I began building a golf course and clubhouse, and a few years later, my company's new head office. I had no intention of developing the surrounding area for housing at that time, knowing only that I would build on it someday. As it turned out, someday came much sooner than expected.

In the short term, I could have made a lot of money if I had developed the land for housing immediately. A large part of the acreage was in a valley — where I could build the golf course and nothing else — but otherwise I could have built many homes right away if it had been my intention to turn a quick profit. However, I was in it for the long term. I intended to see my golf course vision through to completion.

This land was recreational in nature, but soon I would start building homes around its periphery. After establishing the first golf course on this property — eighteen holes that would come to be called the Legends course — I siphoned off part of our golf course lands, rezoned them as residential, and developed 101 homes, an enclave we called The Estates of Lionhead. As the demand for new housing has continued to grow, we have replicated twice more the exercise of splitting off excess golf course lands to rezone and develop residential enclaves, all associated with Lionhead.

When I set out to construct my first golf course, I was not an expert in the field. I had played extensively but had not been a part of the industry in any other meaningful way. To build a facility to meet my own expectations, I needed someone with expertise to assist me. I found my man in Edwin ("Ted") Baker, a local landscape architect with vast experience designing golf courses, and Alex Temporale, a very talented architect based in Oakville who helped me design the clubhouse. Mr. Temporale's modern design won the *Financial Post* Design Effectiveness Award of Merit and the Brampton Gold Leaf Award.

After I hired Mr. Baker, I gave him carte blanche to design the course using his best judgment while providing just one small instruction: "Build me the best golf course there is." Mr. Baker promised to give me his finest effort, and in the end, I believe he created the best possible course within the confines of the land with which he could work.

I wanted a long, challenging eighteen holes to start. I wanted my course to put world-class players to the test. I wanted it to be the toughest and best-designed course anyone had ever seen. I wanted changes in elevation, lots of sand traps, and big, fast greens. I did not provide Mr.

Baker with much more in terms of direction, but he knew I wanted this golf course to be nothing short of world-class.

As the course was being designed, I met with Mr. Baker on a weekly basis. He showed me his latest plans, and I provided my input. The course was planned hole by hole, and though I was involved throughout, I mostly stepped aside and allowed the architect to do his job. I knew what I liked, but I was not qualified to criticize Mr. Baker's work. Today, after more than twenty-eight years of experience managing golf courses, I would be able to provide far more in terms of input.

Had I possessed the golf course knowledge back then that I attained in the future, I would have probably tinkered with certain aspects of the design. For instance, I would not have included so many sand traps. From an aesthetic standpoint they are appealing, and in terms of game play, the bunkers add a degree of difficulty. Unfortunately, sand traps are prohibitively expensive to build and maintain and are rarely worth their cost.

In the process of building this course, we planted more than forty-five hundred trees. In fact, there is only one tree left standing on the property that was there when I bought the land from Mr. French. Of the forty-five hundred trees we planted, a great many of them died from disease or during a particularly harsh Ontario winter. Today the property is covered in a wide variety of beautiful trees, some of which I even planted myself.

Initially, we designed the course and clubhouse as the facilities for a private golf club. Virtually every golf course in those days was private. It was how business was done in golf at the time, though it never sat right with me. Shortly after breaking ground, I made a big decision to alter the direction of the golf course: my facility would be open to the public.

Still stinging from the humiliation of being rejected by the Mississaugua Golf and Country Club when I first became interested in the game, I decided to strike a blow for all the golfers who also happened to be non-elite men and women. It went wildly against conventional thinking at the time. There were very few public courses in those days, and none could approach the quality of what I was building. But I could see how golf was opening itself up to a broader market. By making my course public, golf would no longer be the strict dominion of the rich and the historically elite. Finally, golfers from different income levels would have the opportunity to play on a first-rate course.

As much as I would like to say I acted with pure benevolence, going public was also a good business decision. Ontario was in recession, which made selling memberships to a private golf course problematic. I checked into our membership sales early in the building process, and the returns were not good. I knew the community still loved golf as much as ever, and a pay-as-you-play model was, overall, much more affordable for golfers. Ultimately, the feeling of rejection I suffered during the 1950s combined with current market decisions and my desire to open up golf to all those who loved it resulted in the construction of the finest public course anyone had ever seen in Ontario, and perhaps even at the time, in all of Canada. In 1991, the Kaneff Group of Companies was a pioneer in offering high-end golf facilities on a first-class course to the general public.

Of course, there was one other key reason I chose to make my facility open to the public. When operating a private golf club, an owner — such as myself — sells shares of the facility to its members. This arrangement means that every member of the club is also a partner, giving him or her a say — albeit a small one — in how the club is operated and maintained. With a private golf course, there is a board of directors, along with an annual election to select that board.

A public course operates in a completely different manner. With a public golf course, the owner calls the shots. In this arrangement, I would be able to make all the decisions, and that suited me fine. There would be no board of directors, just me and my managers. The golfers would not have a say in how things were run, other than to provide their feedback through patronage. They would come to the course, play golf, and then go home. It is, overall, the much simpler arrangement, even though it meant that sole responsibility for the facility and all associated costs would be borne by me alone.

Unfortunately, there is a financial downside to designating a golf course public. Whereas a private course might pay between $50,000 and $60,000 in annual taxes, I pay more than ten times that amount. This is because a public course is considered to be "for profit" and more taxes are deemed payable than is the case if the course were private.

Just before shifting gears and making the facility public, I made another important decision: determining its name. It was derived from the Bulgarian coat of arms, which features two rampant golden lions supporting a red shield emblazoned with a crowned rampant golden lion. When I thought about all that, I made the connection.

"We'll call it Lionhead," I said to no one in particular.

And call it Lionhead we did. I loved the name immediately.

I wanted to create the most lavish and best golf course to enjoy with the community, and I believe we accomplished that with Lionhead. When I decided to construct the course, I wanted everything to be top-notch. I had the money to build the best possible course, so that was what I did. It is the same when buying a car. If you have enough money to buy a Mercedes, you purchase a Mercedes. If you do not have enough money for a Mercedes, you buy a Volkswagen. I was in the fortunate position of being able to afford the Mercedes of golf courses, so that was what I set out to build.

It was my intention to have my golf course be the biggest and the best, which was why I built a thirty-three-thousand-square-foot clubhouse and expanded the original twenty-seven-hole facility, consisting of three nines, into two courses of eighteen holes each, named the Legends and Masters courses. Since its initial construction, we have added to the clubhouse to make it even bigger. It is a world-class facility that has hosted a number of PGA Tour and celebrity charity events.

We launched Lionhead Golf & Country Club (now called Lionhead Golf Club & Conference Centre) to the community in grand fashion with a PGA Tour event on May 15, 1991. The facility had quietly opened its doors to the public a few weeks earlier. General Motors sponsored the tournament, and we attracted many of the game's top players, each of whom wanted to get a good look at my new golf course. We had fantastic promotion for the event on television and radio, with spectators swarming to Lionhead to watch legends of golf play the Skins Game. Big names such as Arnold Palmer, Dave Barr, Fuzzy Zoeller, and Peter Jacobsen made up the field.

From the beginning I intended my course to be PGA-calibre. It was also my goal for Lionhead to be well known — and much discussed — by golfers all around the world. With this event, my vision was coming true.

To host a PGA Tour event, Lionhead had to meet certain criteria. For one thing, it needed to have a proper driving range. Also, it had to have a clubhouse that could accommodate up to four hundred people, as well as offer a sizable dining room to host that same number of people. Of course, it also required a big pro shop. Lionhead had all of that and more. Impressively, we provided six hundred lockers for our players. Everything was built to a first-class standard, and it felt to me as though no expense was spared.

Although I was impressed with the incredible golfing ability of the PGA Tour members, I was not star-struck by any of the players I saw. I had already played in several big pro-am events. In fact, I had even played with the great Lee Trevino on three separate occasions during the 1980s. Two of those times we played at Glen Abbey, and the other was in Palm Springs.

When putting together playing partners for pro-am events, tournament organizers will pull an amateur golfer's name out of a hat, at which point that golfer can choose his partner from a field of pros. The first time I played with Lee Trevino I selected him because he was the best golfer on tour, in my view, and I was an admirer of his game. The second and third times we played together, I picked Mr. Trevino because I found him to be a very nice person the first time we played. Lee Trevino is a common man, just like me. He is one of us. Mr. Trevino does not brag, and he never acts like a big shot. He is a fine gentleman and the consummate professional. When we played in Palm Springs, we were in a foursome with Chi Chi Rodriguez, who was also kind and exceptionally talented.

While I was never as good a golfer as Mr. Trevino or Mr. Rodriguez, I was no slouch. For many years, I was a ten to twelve handicap, meaning I usually shot ten to twelve strokes above par. Overall, I was happy with my game, but I cannot help but imagine that I could have been better. I started playing golf when I was thirty-one years old. Had I started at a younger age, things might have been different.

Regardless, I was happy and proud to own a golf course. In fact, I was so fond of owning a golf course that I went out and bought another one. I purchased Streetsville Glen — an existing lower-end course in Brampton located about two miles away from Lionhead — with an eye toward developing much of the land for housing and commercial real estate. Today there are only fifty acres of golf course left where there were once two hundred and fifty. However, we have built some beautiful homes for the community in place of part of the land occupied by the course.

In the mid-1980s, before I launched Lionhead and bought Streetsville Glen, my drywall contractor, Dinko Mandarich, introduced me to a piece of land in Carlisle, Ontario, near Waterdown. He thought it would make a good site for a golf course. Since he was not able to finance the project or get approvals from the provincial and municipal governments himself, I agreed to back the project and we completed the twenty-seven holes of the Carlisle Golf & Country Club in 1991 just one month after I opened Lionhead. Dinko was a loyal friend and partner who became one of my favourite golf buddies. Unfortunately, he passed away in December 2004. I miss him very much.

From there I also developed Royal Niagara in Niagara-on-the-Lake and redeveloped the existing Century Pines course in Flamborough, Ontario. Finally, I built Royal Ontario on Trafalgar Road in Hornby, not far from Lionhead.

In all, I ended up owning the equivalent of eight golf courses on six distinct properties. After deciding to make Lionhead Golf & Country Club public, I followed suit with the other courses. KaneffGolf courses are open to everybody; no one is turned away.

When I opened Lionhead, I did not expect to buy or build any other courses, but that is how it worked out. Each time the land came to me as an investment opportunity. Each opportunity represented good real estate at a fair price, a sound investment for the long term. Given my experience as a builder and developer, I believed I could spot a good land deal better than most of my competitors.

While operating a Cadillac dealership, I learned that any new business venture would require my full attention. I wanted to be in the know every step of the way. An owner needs to be intimately involved with his or her business — in this case, my golf course — if he or she wants the job to run efficiently and profitably. In certain industries, it might be possible to hire an expert to manage your entire operation, but this has never been the case in my experience. When I own the business, I run the show.

Most importantly, I needed to be involved in the golf business because there are so many people involved in the operation. Many of them are inexperienced because they are seasonal workers or high school and university students. It can be tempting for some employees to have sticky fingers, particularly at the time years ago when golf was predominantly a cash business. When Lionhead opened in 1991, credit and debit cards had not yet become standard payment options; the vast majority of our transactions were made with bills and coins.

I was well aware of some of the problems that began occurring at my golf course, since they were industry-wide issues. It might have been in the kitchen, the halfway house, or the pro shop, but I knew everything that was happening. Every night I received a report on that day's sales through a profit-and-loss statement.

Of course, I was still a novice in the golf industry in 1991, and I knew enough to know that I needed to learn. I was quite aware that I lacked the experience required to properly manage my first golf course. There were so many aspects to the business that required an expertise that I had yet to acquire. For that expertise, I turned to Alan Ogilvie, Lionhead Golf & Country Club's initial operating manager.

I was tremendously fortunate to have Mr. Ogilvie join my team. He was an experienced hand in the business and knew every trick of the trade. Mr. Ogilvie had been running golf courses for more than twenty years by the time I hired him. I knew that he was the right man for the job. Truth be told, I actually poached him from Glen Abbey Golf Club, an iconic golf course in nearby Oakville that had been hosting the Canadian Open for many years. I knew that I wanted Lionhead to be the best, and Mr. Ogilvie was the best manager in the business. He promoted Lionhead well, and later, KaneffGolf, the umbrella name we used to market all six properties, and ended up providing me with outstanding service. In fact, I can still call Alan Ogilvie a friend to this day.

To my delight, Mr. Ogilvie came over from Glen Abbey with four of his own assistants, and they set up my entire operation. They hired the whole staff while we were preparing to open the clubhouse, pro shop, and restaurant for business. While I was experienced in construction, I did not know the first thing about running a restaurant. Mr. Ogilvie did it all, and he did it well. Over time, I was able to learn how to do the job from observing him.

It is important to treat golf like any other serious business. If I had treated the golf course like my personal playground, I would have lost a fortune. In season, Lionhead has a sizable staff of nearly two hundred people, including up to forty in the grounds crew department alone. There is also a ten-person food preparation crew in the kitchen, two or three cleaners, and at least a dozen servers. That is all in addition to twelve employees in the pro shop (who are typically golf pros and also offer lessons to clients) and another half-dozen comprising the administrative staff. We have also had people rent out and maintain the golf carts, and a small crew of young people on the course selling food and drinks.

When selling any product, whether it is a hot dog, shirt, shoes, a house, or golf, I stick to the same simple formula: 25 percent cost, 25 percent delegated to overhead, 25 percent for labour, 25 percent profit. I have maintained this basic blueprint for years, and it has served me well.

In the golf industry, as in any business, the people you hire make or break you. Poor management is the number one pitfall that can befall any company, and picking the wrong team can end any promising business venture.

I was fortunate to have Mr. Ogilvie when I opened Lionhead, but that arrangement only lasted five years before he retired. I paid top dollar for his services, and it was well worth the price because he laid out the groundwork for what would become the KaneffGolf model. Drawing on his wealth of experience, Mr. Ogilvie showed us how to do things right.

Once Mr. Ogilvie retired, my staff and I had to apply the lessons learned to running the operation without him. Through trial and error, I also learned how to hire the right kind of people for my golf business.

To manage one of my courses properly, a successful candidate not only needs to understand the game of golf — which might or might not mean being a good player — but is also required to have a management background. I have learned that such a facility needs a real businessman or businesswoman at the helm. Not only does the manager need to run things behind the scenes, but he or she also needs to be seen in the clubhouse by our clientele. The head golf professional needs to be a charismatic figure; this individual represents my establishment as a salesperson in front of the customers more than anyone else other than me.

A true salesperson is needed because everybody wants to be sold, at a golf course or elsewhere. The last thing I need is someone standing in the corner smoking a cigar, acting as if he or she is too good to chat with the customers. I have had professionals who act as if they are doing the golfers a favour by selling to them; instead, I need an employee who approaches the customer enthusiastically and makes him or her feel valued. People should feel good after spending money at one of my courses.

I have learned a lot about the hiring process over the years, both in golf and construction. For instance, it quickly became apparent that background is very important when assessing a potential employee. Just talking to a candidate is not enough; I needed to look at his or her past. Before I hire anyone, I require a vast understanding of how he or she has performed at prior jobs.

It is also of considerable importance to assess a candidate's ambition. This is just as important as figuring out where he or she has been. If I interview people to scrub golf clubs and determine that they want to scrub clubs for the rest of their lives, then they are of little use to me in the long run. I want to hire a person who wants to grow with my company.

In the golf business, a good employee often stays with me for upward of twenty years. For example, our director of sales, marketing, and customer experience, John Dickie, has been with us for nearly twenty years, as has our executive chef and director of food and beverage, Grant Carson. Other long-time KaneffGolf employees include Joe Allen, Ivaylo Valov, Robert Leach, Stoyan Kirov, Vesselin Gueorguiev, Stoyan Donev, Biser Stavrev, Mila Bulatovic, Sue Saad, and Doug Brown, volunteer extraordinaire.

On the other hand, when it goes badly, an employee might not last longer than a few weeks. In the golf business, a bad employee can do a lot of damage within a short period of time.

I like to establish personal connections with all the people who work for me. I like people, and I try to be good to everybody. At times I might seem strict in business, but I am always fair. I often play golf with my staff and consider them to be my friends

It is no different in construction. I shake hands with everybody on the job. I go around the golf course or to the construction site and ask, "How are you doing?" or "How is your family?" I am quite concerned with my employees as individuals. The way I see it, if you work for me but I do not know anything about you, then I am not doing my job.

The closeness I feel toward my employees is why it hurts so much when one of them double-crosses or steals from me. When I was running the Cadillac dealership, two of my trusted managers stole seven cars. Even worse than the loss of property, their actions hurt my feelings. I thought I knew these men. I believed them to be good people — and I still believe it — but they were lured by the temptation of a quick and easy windfall.

Quite often employees who have stolen from me were in a position to do so only because they were in a managerial role. In my experience, thieves are often the best employees. In one case, we caught a signing officer of my company stealing. Although I have never pressed charges against an employee who has stolen from me, I have fired each of these individuals. Once the trust is lost, there is no chance of repairing the relationship.

Depending on the position, it can take several months to find a suitable replacement when I lose an employee, and even then the new person often lacks certain skills and know-how. Therefore, not only am I losing money as a result of theft but I am also losing a good worker, which I consider to be of far greater value.

When I part ways with an employee, I never look to inflict additional hardship on these people and their families. Despite my hurt feelings, I am not vengeful. I understand that people make mistakes and have their reasons for doing so. But they are still good people.

In one case, a man on one of my construction sites stole enough material to build an entire house.

"Why did you do it?" I asked him. "Why didn't you talk to me if you were in need?"

The man could say nothing in his own defence. He had no excuse.

Of course, even if a thief is not charged with a crime, being fired from my organization hurts a person professionally. Unfortunately, when word gets around the industry — and it always does — it can become difficult for the crook to find a new job.

Bad actions can also haunt a person. I believe this to be true because I have seen it happen. Sadly, an engineer who stole from me had a heart attack out of nowhere after being fired. He was an otherwise healthy man. Another individual suffered a stroke after stealing from me.

I think that the guilt can begin to eat away at these people, but more critically, it becomes difficult to find employment when others in the industry know you were stealing on the job. Feeling guilt is one thing, but being unable to make money creates a different kind of stress, and it often leads to bad health outcomes.

Of course, I have had a far greater number of positive interactions than negative ones with my employees over the years. The good employees far outnumber those with whom I have had difficulties. Every Christmas we have a big celebration for all employees at one of our golf courses. It is an opportunity for my family and I to thank all the people who have helped make our business a success. We always have a great evening together filled with good food and good cheer.

I also derive a great deal of satisfaction helping young people at my golf courses. It is a priority for us to employ students to help them pay for their education.

In one case, this philosophy turned out to have an unexpected benefit. A few years ago I went to see an eye specialist. When I arrived at the doctor's office, I noticed there were at least twenty-five people ahead of me in the queue. I checked in with a nurse behind the reception desk and sat down to wait my turn. About a minute later the nurse called out to the waiting room, "Mr. Kaneff, you're next to see the doctor."

I approached the desk and quietly said to the nurse, "I'm not next. If anything, I'm last."

The nurse led me into a corridor and explained that she had worked at Lionhead for four years during university. The money she made helped put her through the nursing program. This young lady made enough selling food and drinks from a cart on my course to pay for her entire tuition at the University of Guelph. Putting me at the front of the line was her way of saying "Thanks."

I was touched. Appreciative as I was to be put to the front of the line, I was even more delighted to learn that my business had somehow helped a young person make her way in life. This young lady used her opportunity at KaneffGolf to put herself through school, and there is simply no better outcome for me when it comes to employing a student, or anyone else for that matter.

A CHANGING INDUSTRY

When I opened Lionhead in 1991, golf was still considered a rich person's sport. In fact, we were charging twice as much for green fees back then as we do now, adjusting for inflation. However, golf is now a game for everyone; it is far less expensive to play and thus more accessible to all people.

Prior to golf's explosion in popularity, one generally had to join a private golf club to play on a regular basis. This meant paying an initiation fee of up to $50,000, along with $10,000 in annual membership dues. Nowadays golfers are free to pay as they play. A round of eighteen holes usually costs anywhere between $40 and $150. It has become a completely transformed, very different industry because there are so many more courses — the laws of supply and demand are alive and well as applied to the golf business. There is far more competition for market share of a shrinking pool of players.

The worst part of the golf business is that the federal government does not allow green fees to be tax-deductible. Although a company is allowed to take a group of clients or staff to a hockey or baseball game and deduct most of the costs as a business expense, this has not been the case for golf since the early 1970s when the government changed income tax rules vis-à-vis deducting golf expenses. My customers cannot deduct green fees from their taxable income as a business promotional expense. This has not been new to our industry since I have been in the golf business, but it has become especially important in the post–Global Financial Crisis era when both large and small companies have dramatically cut entertainment expenses and spending accounts, and companies are generally much more careful about the image they convey if they are seen to spend corporate dollars on golf entertainment, sometimes still unfortunately perceived as a wealthy person's pastime.

I do, however, expect the golf industry to recover considerably in the coming years. Due to land prices and the associated taxes on land, as well as their proximity to growing population centres, many golf courses will become more valuable as developable land rather than income-generating recreational businesses. People who invested in golf courses many years ago will finally cash in and recover the money they lost to the government's rule changes by selling to developers, as long as the golf course lands have not been deemed protected by the provincial government and therefore undevelopable. When that happens, there will be fewer courses on which people can play. This shrinking supply of courses will ultimately cause a rebalancing of prices, and green fees will eventually increase, despite a lower participation rate in the sport of late.

Changes — not in golf but in society — have also affected KaneffGolf, nowhere more so than at Royal Niagara. When we opened in 2000, the course was very profitable. At the time 65 percent of our golfers were crossing the border from the United States.

Business was strong until the 9/11 attacks. After that the American government imposed far stricter regulations on U.S.-Canada border crossings. All of a sudden, golfers required a passport to come over from the United States to play at Royal Niagara. Many of our customers did not possess a passport, and if they did, it could now take up to three hours to get through customs and the border patrol. Prior to the attacks, it only took fifteen or twenty minutes to enter Canada on a good day.

That 65 percent of our clientele coming from America suddenly shrank to 5 percent, causing business at Royal Niagara to suffer immensely. In general, the Niagara region's economy, mostly tourist-oriented, took a major blow. Even today our golf course is not very profitable.

MANY ROUNDS OF GOLF LEFT TO BE PLAYED ... AND MAYBE EVEN TENNIS

These days, at ninety-three years old, I am almost always the oldest person playing golf no matter where I go. For instance, when I play in

Florida, there is only one other man near my age. But he only plays nine holes, and just once a week at that. This fellow's primary motivation for coming to the course is the fact that there is a two-for-one drink deal in the clubhouse every Friday; that is not my motivation. I still come out to enjoy the game, a little bit of exercise, and some socializing.

Speaking of Florida, in the 1970s, I owned a townhouse in Fort Lauderdale. I was — am — a big fan of tennis. During a visit to the townhouse, I wanted to play tennis with someone at the beach club where I was a member. The pro shop told me the only person to play with was a girl, so I agreed to do that. When we met, she asked, "How well do you play?"

"Like a girl," I replied, smiling.

She did not respond to that, and we walked on to the court.

"Take the first serve," I told her.

She did just that, and I ducked to avoid the hundred-mile-per-hour ball rocketing toward my head.

We stopped and joined each other at the net.

Grinning, she said, "Maybe I should introduce myself." Then she held out her hand. "I'm Jeanne Evert. You might have heard of my sister."

Of course, I had. Jeanne is the younger sister of Chris Evert, who at that time was ranked number one in the world in women's tennis and who went on to win eighteen Grand Slam singles championships. Jeanne, in her own right, was already a pro. In fact, Chris's other three siblings — two brothers and another sister, the youngest — were pretty good tennis players, too.

"I guess I should consider myself lucky to be alive," I told Jeanne.

She smiled. "Being a pro, I'm not supposed to play someone like you, but I wanted to teach you a little lesson. Maybe next time you won't be so quick to say I 'play like a girl.'"

She was right about that. Thankfully, another celebrity was absent from the club that day when I embarrassed myself with Jeanne Evert. Ontario Premier Bill Davis was also a member of the club and often spent his vacations in Fort Lauderdale where I would see him lounging around the pool, pipe in mouth.

As for golf, I still play it every day. I cannot hit the ball as far as I once could, but I can still drive it straight. More importantly, I still enjoy the game. During the warmer months, I go to work every day for

7:00 a.m., work until the early afternoon, and then have lunch and play golf with business associates, colleagues, employees, and friends. It is my daily routine. Even my lunchtime meal at Iggy's Restaurant at Lionhead is a routine — they call it the Chairman's Special — and consists of minestrone soup, wild smoked salmon, "naked" tomatoes with no dressing, feta cheese, and a slice of dry toast.

I am quite pleased at how well I have held up, both physically and mentally. It is my belief that I have remained youthful by continuing to be very active. On Saturdays, Didi drives me to the golf courses where I sit in the passenger seat to review and discuss the golf reports with her. When we arrive at each course, we meet with the manager and go over the operations and reports with him. After finishing at one course, we proceed to the next and go through the same process, repeating this procedure until we have visited all of them. Then we head back to Lionhead, have lunch, and play some golf ourselves. Sundays, on the other hand, are reserved for church and family dinners.

I am busy all the time, and that is how I like it. I feel as though I do not have time to get old.

Other than remaining active, I do very little to maintain my health. One of the few things I do focus on, however, is eating well. I eat good food daily, including fresh blueberries for breakfast, and the Chairman's Special for lunch. Of course, I still love cooking a steak on the grill, and thoroughly enjoy a glass of good red wine or a beer. As a matter of policy, I only eat fresh food, with nothing coming out of a box or can. There is a funny story about red and white wine in Bulgarian tradition. Apparently, there are two songs about red and white wines — the red wine song is about how much it enjoys being a red wine, and the white wine song is about how much it wishes it were also a red wine.

My grandmother lived to be 105 years old, and I hope to live even longer than that. There is much that I still wish to accomplish, and there are many rounds of golf left to be played.

15

Giving Back

I have never considered myself to be a philanthropist. Philanthropy is just the most meaningful side effect of my primary job. I am a businessman and a builder, and I do not help others chiefly for pride or recognition, though there is an element of both in philanthropy. I help others because my parents raised me to do so, and I consider it to be my duty as a responsible citizen. It is also an honour: to me, giving is the greatest joy. While the millions of dollars I have donated to charities over the years represent a large sum of money, giving it away has been my privilege and my pleasure. Charity begins at home.

Throughout my childhood in Gorno Ablanovo, I watched and learned as my mother and father constantly helped others in our community. They were involved in many aspects of what we could call civic life, and their behaviour made an early and lasting impression on me. Knowing that my parents placed the highest importance on doing so, I have always taken pleasure in lending a helping hand or a listening ear. I am a busy man, but I am never too busy to help others.

The most important and cherished of my dreams has always been to become the kind of person who is both willing and able to help those in need. I cannot fully describe the feeling of warmth in my heart when I know I have somehow helped a person improve his or her life. I help others as often as possible, and I only hope that one day a person I have helped is able to assist someone else in need.

People find me easy to ask for help. However, when it comes to donations from my company, we have chosen to focus our resources on a few key areas. The main area to which we contribute is education. I am a staunch believer in the power of education and its positive effect in improving students' lives, and it is my wish to provide others with the opportunities for learning that eluded me. Furthermore, I wish to aid those who are disadvantaged in one way or another and need extra support, such as the beneficiaries of the Community Living programs, individuals who have intellectual disabilities. Finally, I have always placed an emphasis on assisting young people. After all, a bright young mind must be nurtured and developed.

When I was a youngster, I could not so much as poke my head through the gates of a university, let alone attend one. Grade seven was my last year in a structured classroom. Despite this lack of formal schooling, I was somehow able to find success, but not before I lived through years of struggle. Had I received a full and proper education I believe my path to success could have been much smoother.

Through my contributions over the years, I have demonstrated a serious commitment to promoting access to education and improvements in how education is delivered. I have helped set up scholarships for students while also literally helping to build facilities for various universities. I believe that all students benefit from using state-of-the-art lecture halls and modern equipment. Students become even prouder to attend the institution and even more eager to fill their minds with knowledge. And as the students become more educated, so, too, does our society collectively. I firmly believe that education is the key to allowing communities to be smarter, happier, and more productive. I also believe that academics are the foundation of a person's life. As I know personally, those lacking education will forever run to catch up to those who have had the benefit of formal schooling.

The Ignat Kaneff Charitable Foundation earmarks a certain amount of money to give away each year. This money is predominantly used for funding academics and helping children with special needs, with the remainder going to support various other charities. The foundation is now run by our younger daughter, Kristina Maria; it was originally founded in my honour by Didi in 1986 to coincide with my sixtieth birthday celebration. After all, she has told me, what do you give a sixty-year-old who seemingly has everything already? Two of my top people — long-time executive vice-president Eric McKnight and accountant Dave Greenwood — helped Didi immensely to organize both my surprise birthday celebration and the foundation.

Due to advancements in technology, business has become more globalized than ever before. As a result, the level of competition for post-secondary entry-level jobs continues to rise. Today China, India, Japan, and Germany are virtually next door. Everybody is chasing after the same resources to improve their lives. Given the global competition, a strong academic background has gone from being a relative advantage to an absolute necessity.

It is important to emphasize that giving back to the community is not a one-shot deal. It is a practice that needs to be done continuously to be effective. I have found myself in a position where many people need something from me because they are incapable of helping themselves; we all need help sometimes. There are many beleaguered individuals asking, "Who will help me?" I am in the fortunate position of being able to ask, "Who can I help next?"

When you love to give, you find a way to do it. Years ago I made a sizable donation to Mississauga Hospital when I did not have the money, pledging to contribute the funds as I earned them. While it is true you cannot give what you do not have, I always found a way to give back. When I worked at the farmers' co-op in Gorno Ablanovo as a boy, I was able to earn a decent amount of money to contribute to my family. I started earning even more money in Austria, so I continued helping my family while also paying for the university tuition of several Bulgarian students in the area. As I began succeeding beyond my wildest dreams in Canada, I was able to give more money to a greater number of people than I ever imagined possible. There is no arrogance or conceit to my giving. From my early days in Canada, I know all too well what it means to be in need.

GIVING BACK TO BULGARIANS

When my countrymen from Bulgaria ask for assistance, I feel it is, in part, my responsibility to help them find employment in Canada. In addition to finding many people jobs with other companies, I also end up employing many of these Bulgarians myself. There are about a dozen Bulgarians working for my company at any given time.

When I send somebody to another company on my word, I expect that person to be respectful, hard-working, and above all, to behave as a faithful employee. Often, in order to help my fellow Bulgarians find work, I guarantee their first month's salary to the hiring company. If the employer does not like the new worker, I pledge to pay for that person's first thirty days — no questions asked. I have made this offer on behalf of hundreds of Bulgarians, but no employer has ever tried to collect the money. That in itself is a testament to the work ethic of the Bulgarian men and women I have helped in this way.

I am very proud of my Bulgarian heritage, and I am equally proud of our Bulgarian community here in Canada. While Bulgarians have been immigrating to Canada since the turn of the twentieth century, they began coming to Canada in large numbers in 1989. At first our community was quite poor. Even fifteen years ago, Bulgarians were still financially strapped by Canadian standards, having arrived in Canada with very few resources after the fall of the Bulgarian communist government. Today, however, many Bulgarians in Canada are highly respected professionals with good jobs and respectable salaries.

Owing in part to the fact that I help Bulgarians so willingly, I have become quite well known in Bulgaria itself. My name is familiar there to those involved in universities, and I am often referred to as a leader among other philanthropists. In fact, the Bulgarian media consider me to be an informal ambassador of the country as well as a great supporter of Bulgarians everywhere. Formally, I serve in a voluntary position with the Bulgarian government as honorary consul of the Republic of Bulgaria. When Bulgarians arrive in Ontario for the first time, they are often told to come see me.

Once, not long ago, a man arrived in Canada from Bulgaria and asked to meet me. He came to my office one morning for a meeting.

"How can I help you?" I asked the man. "What can I do for you?"

"Mr. Kaneff, I don't want anything from you. I just wanted to meet you and shake your hand."

This man told me he was proud to have me as a fellow Bulgarian and thanked me for all that I do to help my countrymen. He never asked me for a thing, and for that reason I will never forget encountering him.

In addition to helping Bulgarians in Canada, I have also tried to help make life better for those living in Bulgaria, including members of my own family. During my first visit home in 1968, I was stunned to see the poor state of Gorno Ablanovo, my beloved childhood home. The village looked and felt deserted, as many of the houses, churches, and schools seemed to be falling apart from neglect. Mothers were being forced to work alongside their husbands, taking long bus trips into the city to get to their jobs, leaving the children behind. This was not the social construct I recalled while growing up.

At the time, in 1968, there was an old church in the village that I wanted to renovate. It had been ruined from years of poor upkeep. Incredibly, the government would not allow me to fix up the church unless there was something else in it for the community. So I came up with an idea.

"Why don't we build a kindergarten here?" I asked a member of the town council.

That was all it took to get the ball rolling. From there we sent money to the Bulgarian patriarch. As head of the church's governing council, the patriarch was notionally in charge of administering the funds we donated to the church for repairs. At the same time we also sent Gorno Ablanovo money to build the best kindergarten in the region. The cost might have been more than I had initially bargained for, but I was more than happy to pay for a new kindergarten in addition to renovating the church.

Our money was put to good use. The kindergarten turned out to be an outstanding facility, with room for ninety-five children. Amazingly, it was built to even better standards than those offered by such schools in Canada then. Here, the children slept on a little mat in the class-room. In our Bulgarian kindergarten, there was a bed for every child. There was also a full kitchen with staff employed to prepare the meals. For the first time, children in Gorno Ablanovo were able to enjoy a top-of-the-line kindergarten facility.

I covered the initial building costs for the kindergarten and then the citizens of Gorno Ablanovo took over its operations. They have done an excellent job of operating and maintaining the facility. As a matter of fact, from the time the kindergarten was built in 1979, it has not needed major repairs.

When the kindergarten was completed, I returned to Bulgaria for its grand opening. I was honoured to see my portrait hanging in its main cor-ridor. I was less enthusiastic, however, when I learned that my photograph was replaced by that of the then-current leader of the Communist Party as soon as I left town. Years later, when I donated a great deal of money to a Bulgarian university, I made a point of insisting they embed my portrait in granite as part of the building. I joked that if the government wanted to get rid of me this time, they would have to tear down the entire wall.

In 2019, my niece, Velitchka, called from Bulgaria to tell me about the celebration of the fortieth anniversary of the kindergarten. Her de-scription of the event in Gorno Ablanovo brought tears to my eyes.

Although building the kindergarten and renovating the church were the first steps toward revitalizing Gorno Ablanovo, we were far from done. Over the years, we helped the village in many other ways, both big and small. Our next major project to improve the village came in 2014 when we built a new library and community centre.

Bulgarians are known to be educated people. While it has fallen in recent years, the national literacy rate was once among the highest in the world. Growing up, I remember that almost everybody in the village knew how to read and write. Therefore, in 2014, when I was able to choose the recipient organization, I decided again to donate to Gorno Ablanovo, this time with a community centre and library. It stood to reason that a surefire way to help my hometown would be to build a new library where people could re-engage with books and renew a common bond through literacy. Just as important, the new library would serve as an important meeting place and community centre in which the towns-people could come together to enjoy civic life.

When I was first approached to help Gorno Ablanovo build a new library, the meeting actually took place in the old library. They wanted to show me first-hand how much the facility needed to be upgraded.

I was welcomed with a traditional performance of Bulgarian dances and folk songs.

I knew just what was about to be proposed to me, so as soon as I began to speak, I said to the assembled crowd, "I think we need to build something here."

Everybody cheered with approval, and with that, we were on our way. As I saw it, Gorno Ablanovo required a new civic centre on the site of its current library in order to start rebuilding what had once been a vibrant community. In addition to renovating the library itself, we also built a fully equipped, modern community centre that featured a restaurant and an auditorium where students and senior citizens alike could gather to enjoy food and drink while discussing literature, politics, or any other topic of interest.

No longer would the townspeople be forced to take public transportation into the city whenever they wished to enjoy a good meal at a decent restaurant. Finally, they could relish an evening out in their own village. At last there was a building and open space where they could gather, and it would be free and open to everyone.

I paid for the entire project and was exceedingly happy and proud to do so.

Now the village had a new building upon which it could look to with pride. People from other parts of the region even started to come into our village to book the new facility for weddings, christenings, and anniversary parties. Even better, our townspeople had a welcoming and respectable place to hold their own events. It was a boon not only for our village, helping to reinvigorate the entire community, but also for neighbouring communities whose residents were invited to share in the use of this centre. Today it appears that Gorno Ablanovo is once again becoming a vibrant community, as it was in the days of my youth. I am extremely proud to have been helpful with this burgeoning renewal.

With some projects, I searched farther afield than my own village. In 2012, I asked Atanas "Nasko" Kolev, my wife's cousin and our close friend, to put out feelers to his colleagues in leadership positions. I wanted to know what was needed at the University of Ruse, one of Bulgaria's leading academic institutions. For many years, Nasko had worked for the city's engineering department and was also acquainted with the university chancellor, its president, and the regional council. As a trusted family friend, he was well qualified to advise us on any donations. My wife's family was closely tied to Nasko's, since their parents were godparents to each other's families and were also cousins. Nasko was immensely helpful in guiding our decisions to assist the University of Ruse, counselling us to do something for the institution overall, then contribute to improvements to its affiliated hospital.

When I arrived in Bulgaria a few months later, I was invited with Nasko to the university for a formal presentation. As they unveiled a scale model, school officials presented their vision for the Kaneff Centre at the University of Ruse. In almost no time at all, school administrators and an architect had put together a fantastic plan. I was most impressed.

I told the school officials that I felt good about the project and would submit it for my family's approval upon my return home. Didi, Anna-Maria, and Kristina Maria were in unanimous agreement that we should proceed. I phoned Bulgaria on November 13, 2012 — I remember the date because it was also the university's anniversary — and gave the school the go-ahead to start working.

As I spoke on the phone with Dr. Hristo Beloev, a member of the prestigious Bulgarian Academy of Sciences and the chairman of the General Assembly at the University of Ruse, I could hear a crowd celebrating in the background. Dr. Beloev was gathered with colleagues and students for the school anniversary party. When I told them we were going ahead, professors, deans, students, and administrators all toasted the news with champagne.

The architect completed his plan, administrators applied for the building permits, and incredibly, the project was set to begin by March 13, 2013 — less than six months from the time of the project's launch. This is unheard of in the modern North American construction industry, where projects are routinely held up through bureaucratic red tape. The university and government knew I was willing to fund the project right away, so they did whatever was necessary to expedite the process.

Dr. Beloev, builder Diyan Vassilev, architect Tsveti Roussinov, and many others all worked incredibly hard to complete the project on time and on budget. Universities hold a prominent place in Bulgarian society, and this was particularly true in Ruse, where the school is widely known throughout the rest of the country for its strong agrarian and industrial programs. Completing the Kaneff Centre was a top priority for municipal and university officials. Even the mayor of Ruse got involved.

On the evening of October 5, 2013, I arrived in Ruse with my family. Before visiting the new Kaneff Centre, we met up with the rest of our family at my nephew's restaurant in the city. I had bought the restaurant for my nephew years earlier, and now it was being managed by his son. It is a beautiful place, and we all enjoyed a sumptuous late supper.

Around midnight Didi, Anna-Maria, Kristina Maria, and I went to the university for our first look at the completed Kaneff Centre. So many people were still working tirelessly into the night, making sure the place was perfect for the next day's grand opening. Cleaners were vacuuming the floors and polishing all the fixtures. Outside there were trees that had just been delivered, waiting to be planted in the morning.

There was a huge celebration when we opened the Kaneff Centre at the University of Ruse on October 6, 2013, my eighty-seventh birthday. I was delighted by the job they had done. The two-storey complex is equipped with three lecture halls and a multi-functional hall with seating for almost eight hundred people. There is also a press conference hall, along with service offices. The lecture halls are equipped with instant translation devices, similar to the ones used by the United Nations in New York. It is truly a state-of-the-art facility.

Aesthetically, the Kaneff Centre is breathtaking. The exterior of the building is adorned with glass, while the roof is covered with a stunning metal dome. At the unveiling ceremony thousands of people were in attendance, including the minister of education, the mayor, the patriarch of Bulgaria, and the sitting and former presidents of Bulgaria, President Rosen Plevneliev and President Georgi Parvanov, respectively. It was one of the biggest celebrations in recent Bulgarian academic history, with media representatives coming in from all parts of the country.

Presiding over the unveiling of the Kaneff Centre at the University of Ruse will always be one of my fondest memories. Happily, I was able to combine my love of education and my love of Bulgaria with my commitment to philanthropy and giving back to the community, all in one successful project.

We have never stopped helping Bulgaria and Bulgarians. Over the years, we have established a scholarship benefiting four students at the University of Ruse, and we recently upgraded the computers at the community centre in Gorno Ablanovo. My love for the country and its people runs deep. As I said, philanthropy begins at home.

COMMUNITY LIVING MISSISSAUGA

In 1971, I was introduced to the organization that would come to be known as Community Living Mississauga. Very quickly, the charity — known at the time as the South Peel Association for the Mentally Retarded, later changed to its more respectful current name — became dear to me. I have remained committed to it ever since.

I became involved with the organization simply because I wanted to help the children. Its stated mission is to provide "support to individuals who have an intellectual disability to ensure their quality of life in the community has been meaningfully improved." This struck a chord with me, as I cannot bear the thought of children suffering.

Today, Community Living Mississauga provides support for more than seventeen hundred children, youth, and adults with intellectual disabilities, while also helping their families. I am thankful to have the opportunity to be involved with an organization with such an important purpose.

Over the years, I have hosted an annual golf tournament to benefit the cause, and I have also donated a sizable sum of money. In fact, helping Community Living Mississauga has become a passion project. It all started when my friend Buck Franceschini picked me up in 1971 to play a round of golf.

On our way to the golf course that day, Mr. Franceschini asked me if I minded making a quick stop at a Cooksville church.

"I don't mind at all," I told him.

"Great! My son is there."

We arrived at the church and went down to the basement. I was shocked by what I saw. There were seventy-five children with intellectual disabilities lying on little patches of carpet that barely covered a concrete floor.

"My God," I said to Mr. Franceschini, "we've got to help these children."

"Iggy, the government doesn't provide us with enough money to help them."

I could not understand why Mr. Franceschini had allowed his son to be cared for in these conditions. It saddened me when I discovered that parents often tried to hide children with disabilities away from the rest of society. I was determined to help his son and other children like him. Fundraising for the organization seemed like a good place to start; I decided to spearhead this initiative by hosting a golf tournament. Since this was before I owned any of my own courses, I approached the Credit Valley Golf and Country Club and explained that I wanted to host a tournament to benefit a local organization that helped children with intellectual disabilities.

Credit Valley was a private course that did not allow public tournaments at the time, but it offered a workaround solution because it recognized the good we were trying to do for the community.

"Iggy," the club manager said to me, "the only way you can do this under our bylaws is to have one club member in every foursome."

That idea sounded good to me. I went around the club looking for members willing to play. Not only did I find thirty-six men eager to participate in the tournament, they even paid their own way. When they saw I was trying to help the community, these men — most of them quite successful — were regretful about their own lack of initiative; supporting me in this tournament was an easy choice for them.

I decided to charge $500 per person for the tournament. This was more than forty years ago; $500 was a lot of money back then. In today's dollars, it would have been enough to pay for nearly two months of rent for a one-bedroom condo in Toronto. I told the chef to prepare the best of everything; we had berries, shrimp, oysters, and lots of drinks. At the end of the day we raised $54,000 for the children. The board of directors at the club even waived the fees we owed them. I was proud that we were able to raise so much money for the children and was eager to continue helping.

Golf has proven to be a tremendous fundraising tool that has allowed our company to help Community Living Mississauga reach some of its goals. We held tournaments not only at Credit Valley but also at Wyldewood Golf & Country Club in Hornby.

Community Living Mississauga holds fundraisers throughout the year, but one of its largest sources of private funds is our biggest annual philanthropic contribution — a charitable tournament we host that benefits Community Living Mississauga. Every dollar of profit the golf course takes in on that day goes to support children and adults with intellectual disabilities. It has been a tremendously successful event, and many of my friends, colleagues, suppliers, and consultants have contributed their time and money over the years. In 2016, we concurrently celebrated my ninetieth birthday and also forty-five years of the Ignat Kaneff Charitable Foundation's golf tournament in support of Community Living Mississauga.

We also participate in golf events held by others to benefit Community Living Mississauga, along with many other charitable causes. KaneffGolf provides sponsorship for many such events. Part of our company's mission is to support organizations that are dedicated to helping disabled and underprivileged children, as well as to select other people in need of help in our communities.

On March 31, 2016, I was honoured by Community Living Mississauga with a Lifetime Achievement Award. It was an amazing event, and we managed to collect a record amount that night. Bill Davis, the former premier of Ontario, and Hazel McCallion, the former mayor of Mississauga — both long-time friends — gave insightful and humorous speeches in my honour. I could not have been more touched. At the end of the night I personally donated $70,000 to make the event's take an even $300,000. In total, I have donated, personally and through my foundation, nearly $2 million to Community Living Mississauga in almost fifty years. If anything, over the years, I only wish I could have given more money and more of myself to benefit the children the non-profit supports.

We also have an annual charity tournament to help fundraise for our church, St. Dimitar Bulgarian Eastern Orthodox Church. Once I owned my own courses, I was able to help the community even more.

ERINDALE COLLEGE (UNIVERSITY OF TORONTO MISSISSAUGA)

I became indirectly involved with the University of Toronto long before there was an Erindale College in Mississauga. Many years ago I tried to buy the land that would eventually become the university's Mississauga home. However, the provincial government blocked my transaction and bought the land itself.

Although I had already worked out a purchase price with the land-owner on a very nice piece of property just off Mississauga Road between Highway 5 and Burnhamthorpe Road, the government had quietly put a lien on the land. Neither I nor the owner could know that the province wanted to buy that parcel of land to build a Mississauga campus for the University of Toronto. But in 1967 the university opened Erindale College in Mississauga, now its second-largest campus with a student body of nearly fifteen thousand.

Although I could practically see the campus from my house — its smokestacks rose over the horizon — I did not get involved with the University of Toronto more intimately until 1976. A surprise dinner was held in my honour at the Mississaugua Golf and Country Club on April 30 of that year to mark the twenty-fifth anniversary of my arrival in Canada. I say "surprise" because I had thought I was attending an intimate dinner with close friends, lawyer Mike Weir and Ontario Mississauga MPPs Bud Gregory and Doug Kennedy. Instead, more than a hundred people were on hand, including Ontario Premier Bill Davis, who acted as master of ceremonies; Dr. Edward Robinson, principal of Erindale College; Gordon Shipp, my old boss from my early days in Canada; and Mississauga MP Tony Abbott, who read a congratulatory letter from Prime Minister Pierre Elliott Trudeau. It was a magical evening!

Money was collected from all those in attendance to fund scholarships for Erindale students enrolled in urban studies. The money continued to compound and pay out an annuity so that today the Ignat Kaneff Awards, as they are called, will remain in place in perpetuity. The scholarships now apply to both geography and urban studies students.

Although the event was held in the spirit of celebration, its organizers had one other agenda: they wanted to get me involved with the university as a benefactor. The big evening was meant to impress me, and it worked. Given my regard for education, I was easily sold on their plan. I wanted to help.

Once I saw how our scholarships were assisting students of such great promise, I eventually visited Erindale College to get a sense of what else I could do to help. There I saw enthusiastic and ambitious young people buzzing around in all directions, eager to learn. I was impressed with what I saw, to say the least.

I visited Erindale several more times over the next few months. On one such occasion, I noticed the professors had to carry books from their cars straight into the classroom. Erindale College was relatively new, and there was much that still needed to be added, upgraded, or improved. When I discovered that the professors had to do all their administrative and scholarly work from home, I knew what Erindale needed.

I told Desmond Morton, the college's principal at the time, that I wanted to help fund a building in which the professors could sit down to do their work. It seemed only logical that they should have proper offices to use for reading, researching, and grading papers.

During my involvement with new buildings on Erindale's campus, I also worked closely with Robert Prichard, the president of the University of Toronto at the time. Rob was one of the great leaders of academic institutions in Canada. Together, he, Hazel McCallion, and I helped make Erindale College become University of Toronto Mississauga, vastly improving its facilities and resources. Canadian universities need more people like Rob! Today, he is chairman of the Bank of Montreal's board, serves as the non-executive chairman of the law firm Torys, and is a director on the boards of several public companies.

My family's relationship with Rob, his wife, Ann Wilson, and their three sons is a long-standing one that has strengthened more and more since we first met them. Ann and Rob have raised three very accomplished sons, each of whom flourishes in his chosen profession. Rob and I used to gather annually for a "chairman's game" at Lionhead, but more recently, we have continued to meet over lunch. I feel very lucky to have met Rob — he is an extraordinary academic, businessman, and community leader, as well as a first-class person. With confidence, I can say that my circle of friends and colleagues has been enriched as a result of becoming friends with Rob, a relationship that has lasted for more than twenty-five years. For all their accomplishments, Rob and Ann's greatest achievement is their sons. Will, Kenny, and Jay are wonderful young men who are hard-working, humble, and very accomplished in what they do. I feel very fortunate that Rob and I crossed paths, and lucky to count him as a good friend.

The Ontario government pledged its support to this project, donating the lion's share of the money. I was in for $3 million, a fortune at the time and still a lot of money now. To put this sum into perspective, I could have used the cash to buy up several hundred acres of land on Hurontario Street (Highway 10) from Burnhamthorpe Road to Highway 403, right along the Credit River. These days the land is worth at least $1 million per acre and the return on the properties I could have built would have been many tens of millions, but I still do not regret my decision. There were many other developers working in Mississauga at the time, but I was one of the few who put so much effort and money back into his community.

I was happy to contribute to the construction of a much-needed building for the university. I also solicited contributions from many of the prominent builders I knew in Mississauga. Marco Muzzo, Sr., Freddy De Gasperis, and several others donated quite generously. Some of my friends even hand-delivered cheques for $100,000 each.

The Kaneff Centre at the University of Toronto's Erindale College opened in 1992, and I was very pleased with the result of everyone's hard work. In addition to offices, it became home to the business, commerce, and management programs at the school. It also features a beautiful lecture theatre with room for 350 students and contains the Blackwood Gallery in which students can appreciate different forms of art. The Kaneff Centre became more than even I envisioned, and I am so proud that it bears my name.

There was another concern at Erindale College, now called University of Toronto Mississauga, that I felt needed to be addressed. As I became better acquainted with the grounds, I discovered that the school lacked a place for students to socialize. There was nowhere for them to enjoy coffee, a beer, or a bite to eat with their classmates. The campus had only a tiny house that had been converted into a café.

I looked at that little coffee shop and saw the potential for something greater. I envisioned a building to accommodate the needs of the Mississauga campus's entire student body.

By this time, Robert McNutt had replaced Desmond Morton as principal of University of Toronto Mississauga, so I contacted him and explained what I wanted to do. We met at the site of the little café, where I made my pitch. "Why don't we create a student centre here?" I asked.

Principal McNutt had no objection.

After much conversation, followed by the usual pre-construction protocol, we ended up building around the old coffee shop. As I saw it, University of Toronto Mississauga was still quite a young institution, and we needed to preserve what little history it possessed. It was not quite a heritage building, but that café held special meaning for many students, both past and present.

That being the case, we designed a building to go over another building. The university hired a talented architect to design a two-storey construct on top of the old coffee shop. The student centre, with its Ignat and Didi Kaneff Great Hall, turned out to be a beautiful and unique space. For this project, our family donated $2.5 million.

We ended up with two Kaneff buildings at University of Toronto Mississauga, and they resolved two unique problems for the institution. Now that students had a place of their own, they could safely go out during the evening to enjoy a bottle of beer with their classmates without leaving the campus. It was impractical and unsafe for students to drive to a local bar or restaurant and drive back after a few drinks. With the new student centre, they could enjoy a drink or two and then safely walk back to their dormitory. I believe the student centre improved the atmosphere on campus, since it finally provided the students with a great place to socialize. University student centres enhance the quality of life for students in numerous other, more meaningful ways: they provide a place to meet and talk about classes, to go over homework, to tutor one another, to convene for group projects, and to plan non-profit and civic organizations.

For many years, I continued to participate in endeavours to improve facilities at University of Toronto Mississauga, donating generously to the William G. Davis Building and Hazel McCallion Academic Learning Centre, among others. In all, I contributed $100,000 to four other buildings on the campus, while concurrently serving on the fundraising board of directors for Osgoode Hall Law School in Toronto. Contributing to education has been a driving force in my life, and I remain deeply committed to this cause even now.

Many brilliant minds continue to pass through University of Toronto Mississauga, and I hope I have contributed to improving their educational experiences in some way, be it big or small.

YORK UNIVERSITY

I had lived in Canada since 1951, but had no awareness of York University's law school until the 1960s. In fact, I only came to know about it because a Toronto Township councillor — who was a lawyer as well as my neighbour — served on the board of directors for the institution's law society.

My late friend, Hyliard Chappell, alerted me to the fact that York University was moving its Osgoode Hall law school from downtown Toronto to a brand-new campus on the city's outskirts. Obviously, such a move would require funding, and that was when I came into the picture.

The councillor invited me to attend a fundraiser for the law school, and that was how I first got involved with York University. I had no particular connection to the school — other than my relationship with Mr. Chappell — but that had never stopped me from contributing to education in the past. As always, I wanted to help if I could. Mr. Chappell told me that Osgoode Hall Law School was the oldest such institution in Canada, having moved into its current historic building on Queen Street West in 1832. Named after the first chief justice of Upper Canada (now Ontario), the school had recently become affiliated with York University.

In 1968, I attended a fundraiser to help finance the law school's move to York University's Keele Campus in North York. It was a lavish event, and I ultimately made a sizable donation to the cause. I did not know it at the time, but this contribution to Osgoode Hall Law School at York University would not be my last. The law school and the university would both figure prominently in my future.

The fundraiser I attended with Mr. Chappell was my sole experience with York University until my daughter, Kristina Maria, was accepted to study at Osgoode Hall in 2004. Didi and I were tremendously proud and very excited that she would be attending one of Canada's best law schools — if not the best — so close to home. We missed her terribly while she was studying first in the United States, then in England, later working in France, then back in England. We were delighted to have her back in Canada near us.

I firmly believed York University's law school was top-of-the-line in every way, based on the fundraiser I attended with Mr. Chappell and the school's sterling reputation. However, when Didi and I visited the Keele Campus during Kristina Maria's first term in 2005, we were sorely disappointed by what we saw.

The campus was drab, unattractive, and uninspiring. I did not like many of the buildings, most of which featured terrazzo flooring, an unsightly and outdated composite material embedded with chips of marble, quartz, or glass. Additionally, there was only one building on the entire campus that students used for studying. There they were crammed into a windowless basement. To be fair, my initial impressions of York's Keele Campus and Osgoode Hall might have been coloured by the fact that we had just returned from a tour of Harvard Business School with Anna-Maria, where she had started her M.B.A. studies. There, many of the beautiful buildings were finished in marble or granite. Either way, I felt that certain facilities at York University were in need of an upgrade.

So I spoke to Dean Patrick Monahan about the state of the campus. "How is it possible that we tolerate such a poor university campus in a rich city like Toronto?"

"Iggy, we don't have the money. It's not like we can pluck cash from the sky. It has to be donated."

I told the dean I would help raise the funds myself.

It became my goal to update the law school's main building. We hired the world-famous Canadian architect Jack Diamond to create the design. The university's governing council was then approached to help support the building campaign. To our dismay, we were told that it did not have the resources. The province, too, declined to help. Finally, two years later, in 2008, the federal and provincial governments introduced a stimulus program to help the weakened Canadian economy, and we received more than $54 million toward the building we wished to improve. We were ready to go and were able to use the money almost immediately. The entire project cost $62 million, of which we helped raise $12 million. I personally donated $3 million.

Incredibly, we raised most of that $12 million in just one night. We organized a fundraiser and gathered all those we thought might be willing to contribute to the cause at the old Osgoode Hall on Queen Street West. Then we held a roaring cocktail party attended by many lawyers who had previously studied at York. When it became known that I was personally donating $3 million — the single largest donation — others were inspired to write cheques of their own. Everybody needed to reach into his or her pocket to get the project done.

After it was all said and done, we transformed Osgoode Hall into a beautiful, modern building that was both aesthetically pleasing and highly functional for the students. To celebrate the building's grand opening, we held a huge gala. That night the facility was renamed the Ignat Kaneff Building and I was also bestowed with an honorary law degree by York University. There were many students, alumni, and dignitaries in attendance for what turned out to be an incredible ceremony; even the federal minister of finance, the late Jim Flaherty, was present for the unveiling. I was humbled and honoured.

Although I never attended school past grade seven, I now have four honorary degrees. The University of Ruse, the University of Toronto, York University, and Sheridan College have all honoured me in this manner. It is hard for me to believe that I have gone from collecting eggs in Gorno Ablanovo's chicken coops to receiving three honorary doctorates and one master of applied sciences diploma. Life is full of surprises.

After our contributions to Osgoode Hall, the next thing we did to help York University was assist in developing its engineering program. The idea was presented to me by Dr. Mamdouh Shoukri, who at the time was president of York University. He is one of the smartest scholars in Canada. As dean of the engineering department at McMaster University in Hamilton, he performed miracles. After moving over to York University, he eventually founded its engineering department — which is where I came in — and lifted the institution's standards so high that today it is one of the most renowned post-secondary facilities in the world. Dr. Shoukri and his wife, Susan, are very good friends to this day, and I often play golf with the former York president.

It was Dr. Shoukri who brought to my attention that his university lacked an engineering department. Despite a student body of more than fifty thousand, the university would require an engineering program before it could truly be considered a world-class institution. Therefore, after consultation with my family, we decided to donate $5 million to that end.

We broke ground for the Lassonde School of Engineering's new home in June 2013. The school was named after Pierre Lassonde, who donated $25 million to its founding. As a major donor, my name appears prominently on the inside of the finished building, which is called the Bergeron Centre for Engineering Excellence to honour Doug and Sandra Bergeron's financial contributions to and ongoing support of the school. The gleaming centre with its undulating facade officially opened in spring 2016.

York University decided to recognize my second large contribution by having my name displayed prominently atop the ten-storey campus administration building. Therefore, upon arriving at York from all directions, students, administrators, professors, and visitors alike can all see Kaneff Tower, the tallest structure on campus.

More than anything, being recognized on a university building memorializes that I have been one of the contributors to the welfare of Canada's future by helping our students, who will soon become our leaders. Someday I will be gone, but the buildings bearing my name will continue to stand, commemorating that I was one of the people who helped build the university, along with this great country.

It is important for me to be remembered because I am — and always have been — an immensely proud individual, as well as a man who feels forever indebted to Canada. I want the citizens of Mississauga, Ontario, and Canada to know I was a part of this community and did everything I could to help it while I was here.

STS. CYRIL & METHODY

When I came to Canada, I inquired about Eastern Orthodox churches in Toronto and was introduced to St. George Macedono-Bulgarian Eastern Orthodox and later to Sts. Cyril & Methody Macedono-Bulgarian

Eastern Orthodox, both in Regent Park. I was told that the majority of Bulgarian immigrants were attending Sts. Cyril & Methody, so I joined it to meet people like myself.

I was very interested in the life of the church and wanted not only to join but also to support it. A little later I also served as president of the Canadian Bulgarian Society, which was closely associated with Sts. Cyril & Methody. Over the years, more and more Bulgarian immigrants came to Toronto and joined us at Sts. Cyril & Methody.

Through my involvement with Sts. Cyril & Methody, where I served as vice-president for a while in the 1970s, I met many Bulgarian families that I became close to, including the Isaeviches, Uvakovs, Rouskovs, and Tsokovs. Concerning the first family, I came to know Helen Isaevich well. She and her family were friends with Tsar Boris III's descendants in Toronto: Maria Louisa, the tsar's daughter; her husband, Prince Karl of Leiningen; and their two sons, Hermann and Boris.

Sophie Uvakov's son, Boris, worked for me as a manager at my Lionhead golf course, and Didi and I are godparents to Boris's four children. My relationship with the Rouskov and Tsokov families, though, is a lot more complicated but shows how interconnections between immigrants who are already in Canada can help would-be immigrants who want to come here.

Two brothers, the heads of the Rouskov and Tsokov families, were living and working abroad, desperately trying to improve their families' futures. Although Western Europe provided a temporary haven, immigration to Canada was their ultimate goal. In the mid-1970s, the elder brother, George, had the address of a woman named Parashkeva living in Toronto, who he had learned through the Bulgarian grapevine might be helpful. The younger brother, Petko, was chosen to travel to Canada from France and arrived in a snowy Toronto. He immediately visited Parashkeva and asked her for help to find jobs so the brothers could enter Canada as economic immigrants.

Parashkeva took the unusual step of pretending the two families were relatives of hers and contacted me. Although I knew nothing about Petko and his other family members, I was intrigued by his story, agreed to meet with the younger brother, and learned a great deal more about the two families' backgrounds. I offered financial assistance, but Petko graciously declined it. Instead, he requested help to secure jobs so that he and George could apply for immigration. I did so without delay, first finding a position in my company for George, who was a civil engineer, and then later for Petko, who was a mechanical engineer.

With guaranteed jobs for both brothers, the Canadian embassy in Paris granted them landed immigrant status. After that, George and Petko brought their families to Canada, including their wives, children, and their grandmother. But I wanted to do more for these families and provided them with housing in several of my rental properties to make their transition to their new country as smooth as possible, and continued to give them financial and moral support until they were truly established in Canada.

Today, the Rouskovs and Tsokovs flourish in their new land, contributing to Canada's beautiful mosaic of people. Emilia Rouskov currently works as the administrator of St. Dimitar Bulgarian Eastern Orthodox Church in Brampton, the house of worship whose creation I spearheaded and was gratified to see become a reality in 2005. Svet, Emilia's son, worked for years as a manager at the automobile parts supplier Magna International and is now a successful screenwriter in Los Angeles. Natalie, Emilia's daughter, came into the world in 1981 and was the first in the family to be born in Canada. She grew up with my daughters, Anna-Maria and Kristina Maria, and attended Sunday school with them at Sts. Cyril & Methody.

There were many other Bulgarians whom I met at Sts. Cyril & Methody, but Bill Evanov was not one of them, though he was a member of the church. Bill once worked for Johnny Lombardi's Toronto radio station CHIN, which is how I actually first encountered him when he approached me in the 1960s to buy ads. Eventually, he became vice-president of sales at CHIN, then went on to start his own company, Evanov Communications/Evanov Radio Group. Today he is still president of the firm, which now owns nineteen radio stations in Manitoba, Ontario, Quebec, and Nova Scotia. Evanov Communications celebrates its thirty-fifth year in business in 2019 — another huge success for Bulgarian Canadians!

My years at Sts. Cyril & Methody were rewarding ones during which I forged many valuable relationships and strong bonds with fellow Bulgarian immigrants. I started thinking about building a Bulgarian Eastern Orthodox church after years of travelling to downtown Toronto from Mississauga to attend Sts. Cyril & Methody every Sunday. It became more and more arduous, and parking on the street was a challenge. On many occasions, Bulgarian parishioners received parking tickets while attending Mass. Furthermore, Bulgarians were pitted in a minor rivalry with Macedonians for use of the church facilities. The situation was far from ideal, and it was clear something had to be done.

ST. DIMITAR BULGARIAN EASTERN ORTHODOX CHURCH

While attending Sts. Cyril & Methody, I met and became close friends with Dr. Konstantin Valtchev and his family, who were major contributors to the church. As our friendship developed, I shared my idea for a new, true Bulgarian church with Dr. Valtchev. Sts. Cyril & Methody and the other churches where Bulgarians worshipped in the Greater Toronto Area were all Macedono-Bulgarian. As early as the 1990s, I had started looking for a site to build our Bulgarian church. At the time, I was developing a subdivision in Brampton on Financial Drive. One day, while standing on the land at the southwest corner of Steeles Avenue West and Creditview Road, I glanced east and realized this was the perfect spot for the church, especially since in Bulgarian tradition the altar always faces east.

I was very excited with my discovery and immediately called Susan Fennell, Brampton's mayor at the time, to tell her about my idea to build a church. Right after that, I notified Dr. Valtchev. Mayor Fennell was quite receptive to the proposal, and soon, word spread to the Bulgarians in the area. Dr. Valtchev and I met with a few enthusiasts who loved our idea and were willing to serve on a committee to establish the church.

At that meeting, the first board of directors was selected as well as the name for the new church, which was easy. I had been baptized in Gorno Ablanovo in St. Dimitar, the local church. Also, my wife Didi's full name is Dimitrina, and we were married on October 26, the patron day for St. Dimitar. When I presented St. Dimitar as the name for our new church to the board, everyone voted with smiles on their faces and agreed unanimously. I was then appointed the first president of the church and was succeeded by Dr. Valtchev, who was instrumental in having our bylaws approved by the Bulgarian Eastern Orthodox Church and Industry Canada and subsequently adopted.

My family donated the land and the capital costs to build St. Dimitar. We paid all the expenses relating to the construction of the church and its establishment, and there is a plaque at the entrance that reads: "Built and Dedicated By the Kaneff Family, 2005."

Before we opened our church, our committee sought approval from His Eminence Metropolitan Neofit, bishop of Ruse, and His Eminence Metropolitan Joseph, bishop of New York City and head of the Church in Canada, the United States, and Australia. Both men travelled from Bulgaria and the United States, respectively, to consecrate our new church in May 2006. Today, His Holiness Patriarch Neofit is now the worldwide head of the Bulgarian Eastern Orthodox Church.

One of the biggest complaints from Bulgarian parishioners at the downtown church was a lack of parking. At St. Dimitar we have 150 parking spaces, more than enough. We also have ample amenities to accommodate weddings, christenings, and other cultural events. I am perhaps most proud of Bulgarian Sunday School Kaneff. Every year nearly eighty young Bulgarian-Canadian children are enrolled in the school at St. Dimitar to learn the Bulgarian language, our traditions, and the country's history. We now even have two affiliates of Bulgarian Sunday School Kaneff — one at St. John of Rila Bulgarian Orthodox Church in Niagara Falls and another in Mississauga. All told, 147 students attend the three schools. The current principal of the school is Stamena Dimova. She is a strong and dedicated leader with great enthusiasm who puts a lot of effort into teaching Bulgarian customs, traditions, and language to the children.

The only problem with St. Dimitar is that while most Bulgarians enjoy being part of a church community, we are generally not the most religiously oriented people. In fact, we are considerably less religious than, say, people from Poland or Croatia. Bulgarians were deprived of religious freedom for many years. The communists made it all but impossible to attend church. For instance, Didi was never allowed to attend Mass in her own city, Ruse.

If her mother wanted to take her to church for Communion, she had to do so at five o'clock in the morning. Didi had to wear a scarf over her head so that she would not be easily identified by people on the street.

While the communists were in control of Bulgaria from 1944 to 1990, many, if not all, of Bulgaria's beautiful churches were neglected. The Church had also been restricted in its activities while Bulgaria was under Ottoman rule from 1396 until 1878, a span of nearly five hundred years. Churches could be constructed but had height restrictions, making many of them underground structures. Bulgarians, therefore, endured centuries of religious restriction and repression.

Over many generations, Bulgarians became less committed to participating in church services for these reasons. Although we have some parishioners at St. Dimitar who attend church weekly, there are many others we only see at Christmas, Easter, or certain other holy days. For many Bulgarians, church has come to be about community as much as it is about religion.

To me, church is a discipline. I consider church attendance a part of my responsibility as the leader of our family. I also see religion as an important part of bringing up children; educating them in religion is just as important as teaching them how to read and write. Everybody needs to understand morality, and a church, mosque, or synagogue is the perfect place to learn these foundational lessons of life. Growing up in Bulgaria, I went to church every Sunday. Religion was a subject in school, just like arithmetic or history.

I am a strong believer in religion. I believe in it so strongly and I invested so much in our St. Dimitar church because, without religion in my life, I believe I am no different than an animal. To me, a person is simply not complete without a sense of religion or a strong feeling of spirituality that underpins his or her values. I see God not only in the traditional sense as our Creator but also as a symbol. God cannot get you home from work early or put you to sleep at night, but He can give you the ingredients needed to accomplish anything you desire. It is up to you to do what needs to be done. Throughout history, many people have tried to destroy religions and people's faith in their own Creator, but they will never succeed. I perceive our need for spirituality and faith to be a part of the human condition.

As a way of life, I follow the simple rules set out by God as they are broadly described in the Bible, and attribute the best parts of my life to Him. I contributed a great deal of my own effort in order to be successful, but I consider God to be my partner in every accomplishment. I listen to Him very closely; without God's help, I do not believe I would have become a somebody.

We finally finished building St. Dimitar Bulgarian Eastern Orthodox Church in March 2005. The windows were installed, the pews set up, and the altar put in place. Still, from the inside, it did not look complete. We lacked the religious icons that are traditionally painted on the walls; they are a staple of every fully established Eastern Orthodox church building.

Of course, we would have eventually paid for all of the icons ourselves, but we did not have to. Thankfully, a man we had never met would become a new benefactor of St. Dimitar.

A Bulgarian engineer named Lalio Metev invented a machine that made very fine silk fabric. Eventually, he sold the patent and became a wealthy man. Mr. Metev then wisely invested his money in high-yield Canadian bonds, which gave him 18.5 percent in interest at the time — a wise investment in a very unusual market, by Canadian standards. He nearly doubled his money every four years and did so for more than twenty-five years. After selling the patent, Mr. Metev travelled the world, eventually settling in Rio de Janeiro.

Shortly after St. Dimitar opened — without icons on the walls — Mr. Metev came to visit his family in Etobicoke. His niece is a member of the congregation, and we know his two brothers, who brought him by to see the church. As his brothers showed him around, Mr. Metev took one look at the walls and asked, "Don't Bulgarian churches usually have icons on the ceiling?"

We informed Mr. Metev that we had already purchased the icons for St. Dimitar's front foyer, altar, and walls. As for the cupola ceiling, we let him know we were still hoping someone else would donate the money.

"How much will it cost?" he asked.

We told Mr. Metev that we had priced the job at $175,000.

"I'll pay for it," he said matter-of-factly.

Of course, we did not believe him. We were no strangers to hearing empty promises. But Lalio Metev proved to be a man of his word: two days later, while I was enjoying a round of golf, I received a call from the bank.

"Mr. Kaneff," the bank manager whispered into the phone, "I have a transfer from Rio de Janeiro for $95,000. By law I have to report it to the RCMP."

The law stated that any transfer over $10,000 had to be reported by the bank. I told the banker to go ahead and disclose the information.

"Of course, it's all legal money," I told her. "A gentleman from Rio de Janeiro is paying for our church icons. Just report the money and don't worry about anything."

Soon after that, we received the remaining $80,000 and hired artists to hand-paint the icons. When they finished their job, the church looked fantastic. Several months later Mr. Metev came back to Canada to see what his money had paid for. He was rightly impressed. St. Dimitar will always remember Lalio Metev for his tremendous generosity. We are forever grateful.

In the months and years following its opening, I was deeply involved with the operation of St. Dimitar. Nowadays, Didi has taken on a volunteer role in its operations. There is also a church president whose work is essential, but Didi continues to assist with dedication. Kristina Maria now serves as president and donates many hours of her time representing the interests of St. Dimitar on a pro bono basis. More than ten years later we, as a family, are still St. Dimitar's greatest supporters and financial benefactors.

Dr. Valtchev, his wife, Kina, and daughters, Maria and Darina, are still important pillars of the church and are well respected and loved. Graduating from medical school in Plovdiv, Bulgaria, Dr. Valtchev specialized in obstetrics and gynecology in his native land for a dozen years before taking up a position in 1966 as chief of the Department of Obstetrics and Gynecology at Menelik II Hospital in Addis Ababa, Ethiopia. After three years, rather than return to Bulgaria due to the communist dictatorship, he and his family moved to South Africa, eventually immigrating to Canada in 1972. During his last year of residency at

Toronto's Mount Sinai Hospital, he invented an instrument, the Valtchev Uterine Mobilizer, which became a widely used surgical instrument around the world. Dr. Valtchev and his wife established a company — Conkin Surgical Instruments Ltd. — to manufacture the device, with Mrs. Valtchev serving as manager. Dr. Valtchev received an appointment as assistant professor and lecturer at the University of Toronto's School of Medicine, where he taught for many years, both at the undergraduate and graduate levels.

After more than a half century in medicine, Dr. Valtchev retired in 2006. One of his granddaughters, Christina, is now a doctor specializing in obstetrics and gynecology, while another granddaughter, Adriana, attends medical school at the University of Toronto.

Father Valeri Shumarov, the current parish priest at St. Dimitar, is a man with a big heart. He is tireless, he puts far more effort into his duties than required, and people love him.

Volunteers play a major role in the upkeep of St. Dimitar, and I am proud of them and the Bulgarian community as a whole. There are too many notable volunteers to list them all here, but one that should be mentioned is Dimitar Minkov. He is the well-respected founder, artistic director, principal dancer, and choreographer of the Bulgarian folk dance ensemble Dimitrovche, which was started in October 2010, and is his labour of love. It is an integral part of St. Dimitar's church activities and involves more than eighty dancers from ages five to sixty-five who dance in traditional costumes from all ethnic regions of Bulgaria. The ensemble has performed across North America as well as in Britain, Spain, and Bulgaria itself, preserving and popularizing Bulgarian dance and music while creating camaraderie, goodwill, and delight in the Greater Toronto Area's Bulgarian community. Kristina Maria is honorary godmother to the ensemble.

My mother-in-law, Ana, was a talented singer and part of the church choir at St. Dimitar. In the 1980s and 1990s, she was also a member of the church choir at Sts. Cyril & Methody and was a soprano with Bulgarka, a Bulgarian folk choir conducted and organized by Kina Valtchev. During that time, when Didi and I were members of Sts. Cyril & Methody, Anna-Maria and Kristina Maria attended the Bulgarian-language school there. I have cherished memories of their many performances at

Christmas and at the end of the school year and am proud to say that today my daughters can read and write Bulgarian fluently.

Ana provided a great deal of dedication, love, and support during our girls' growing years. She was not only their grandmother but also their confidante — a second mother to them in all respects. They probably spent more time with their beloved "Baba" than with me and Didi, especially when my wife started working in the mid-1980s. While Sunday school helped, it was thanks to the tireless dedication and teaching of Ana that the girls did more than merely learn basic Bulgarian expressions.

My mother-in-law was orphaned at age three and had a very difficult childhood and youth. In her twenties, she was a political convict, jailed for six months because she gave a loaf of bread to someone from her village who had escaped police arrest by the communists and was waiting on the outskirts to say goodbye to his family before beginning his journey to freedom.

Ana married Kosta Kolev, who had also been orphaned, in his case when he was only forty days old. Kosta, too, was jailed by the communists, who accused him of illegally profiting by selling kielbasa and salami to the Germans when they passed through Bulgaria during the Second World War. After Ana and Kosta started their family, they lived in one room for twenty years with Didi until my future wife graduated from high school.

My mother-in-law was always very supportive of me, voicing her happiness and satisfaction with me and bragging about how good a father and son-in-law I was. She was also instrumental in helping to raise our children in all aspects, speaking to them in Bulgarian and teaching them the language, traditions, and religion of Bulgaria, including baking and cooking, especially for Christmas and Easter. It is no wonder our girls were very attached to and affectionate with their Baba!

As for Christmas, we Bulgarians celebrate Christmas Eve in accordance with Eastern Orthodox tradition. In my family's case, we prepare seven meatless dishes, read the Bible, open gifts after midnight, and by 2:00 a.m. on Christmas Day, clean up. By 7:00 a.m., we are at the airport to fly off for our family vacation. After all these years, this is still what we do today. Sadly, we are no longer graced with Ana's company on such family get-togethers.

16

In Closing

As a man of ninety-three now, I am both surprised and amazed I have made it this far. I never dreamed my life would unfold in the ways that it has. I wanted to be a somebody, but I imagined that I might become a somebody like my father, a good man inclined to help others. To simply help my family, friends, community, and country was my true ambition.

When I think about everything I have accomplished, there is one key ingredient that made it all possible: drive. You have to want it, whatever it is. Mine was not a drive to be wealthy, nor was it an ambition to be powerful. I merely had a burning wish to prove to myself and to others that I had the ability to be successful. I always believed in myself, but I wanted to show the world what I could do, as well.

Upon arriving in Canada, I had no skills, no money, no friends, and worst of all, no ability to speak English. Through good luck, I earned a job with the Shipp Corporation, where I received the first opportunity to prove myself in this country. Given the chance, I knew I could succeed. At first I was only a general labourer, sweeping sawdust or hauling materials around a construction site. But I took real pride in my humble job because the opportunity was invaluable, and I wanted those who believed in me enough to hire me to know they had not made a mistake.

While others were eating lunch, I was working to improve my skills and get ahead. When my colleagues went home for the day, I stayed after hours and tidied the site. I did everything in my power to show I was worthy of my job and did anything I could think of to demonstrate I was capable of doing more. Even back then, I always wanted to keep moving forward.

During my time with the Shipp Corporation, I had my friend, Harry Beltz, show me how to cut a roof, and it happened while the other fellows were resting. I never even considered taking a break; I was always on the go. I would stand around with a sandwich or an apple in my hand while I learned on the job. I knew that nobody was going to force me to advance myself, nor would anybody else do it for me; I needed to be ambitious. I would not wait for others to bring the opportunities to me. I was always trying to make things happen.

The first house I built in Canada was a mere seven hundred and twenty square feet, small by any standard. But I built it myself, which is something most people cannot claim. I came from an agricultural background and had only a few months of experience in construction under my belt at the time, but I still did it. I was not afraid. I had the desire to prove I was worthy of Canada, and building a house was one way for me to show that an investment in Iggy Kaneff was a worthwhile one.

In a sense, I believe my relatively small stature — at five feet, five inches — made me more ambitious than the average man. I always saw myself as an underdog and used that as motivation. I was lacking some of the common characteristics one finds in a successful person. I was small, I was a foreigner, and I did not speak the language properly. I felt I was missing several key ingredients in the standard recipe for success. But I would not allow my deficiencies to hold me back. I knew I could overcome anything I might be missing through hard work and smart decisions. As long as I kept pushing, I always believed I would eventually break through to success.

Despite any shortcomings I might have had in the eyes of others, I never doubted myself, nor did I lack confidence. I always knew I would be successful and only required the opportunity to do it. Thankfully, Canada gave me the chance to show what I could do, and for that I will be forever grateful.

I was fearless when I needed to be, but there was still fear. I remember one time, while employed by Rex Heslop in Etobicoke, I was sent out to work on a very steep roof. I have always been afraid of heights and knew I would eventually be put to the test.

I stepped out onto that roof and worked the entire day, terrified of falling all the while. My fear never subsided, but I remember feeling proud that I had taken the risk. I had not allowed my actions to be ruled by fear, even though I was, in fact, petrified. I went out on the roof and did my job. Afterward, I asked the foreman to move me to another part of the job, and he complied with my request. Still, I was beaming with pride over the fact that I had faced my fear. Fear can be paralyzing, but I did not allow it to stop me from achieving my goals.

THE FUTURE OF THE BUSINESS

The Kaneff Group of Companies is the embodiment of my life's work; it has been a labour of love. I have put all my energy into growing a strong, reputable company known for doing good work while honouring its commitments, with employees who conduct business with integrity. These values underpin how we operate and manage relationships. I have full confidence that my company will continue to thrive for many more years because it has been built on a very solid foundation.

First and foremost, the company has been successful for long enough that we no longer require construction financing on all our projects. For most projects — except the very large ones — we can rely on the cash flows generated from our ongoing operations and properties to fund new construction work. We then have the option to take out financing against the property at a later date — if it is an income-producing project — or recoup our investment on the construction costs when we deliver the home to the client and the client pays for the balance of the home. Most importantly, it means we are not highly leveraged, which can be tremendously helpful in scaling growth but is a leading cause of bankruptcy and failure in down markets.

This provides us with an advantage in the marketplace. While many of our competitors are paying interest on their building loans, we are, for the most part, self-financed, which saves us money on every project. Equally significant, we have a good-sized property portfolio of diversified real estate holdings that includes land, apartment buildings, commercial space, and golf courses. Just as notable, we have a robust pipeline of new projects for future development. The Kaneff Group of Companies has not taken shortcuts. In fact, it is hard for me to envision ways in which we could be better organized. We are a very sound company, both now, and as I foresee it, for many years to come.

When I was just starting out with my business, I was intent on growing the company aggressively. I took a lot of chances because I did not have as much to lose. As I grew older, however, I became somewhat more cautious, and I consider that to be a positive. These days I have more experience and knowledge than ever before, and therefore I am more capable of avoiding unnecessary risks.

MY GIRLS

While building a golf business and continuing to operate a construction company, I was also involved, most importantly, in raising my two beautiful daughters, Anna-Maria and Kristina Maria.

Although it pains me to admit, raising natural children is somewhat different than raising adopted children, or at least it was in my case. Raising Danny and Heidi was often difficult for me. Sometimes it felt that the harder I tried to bond with them, the worse the results. But with Anna-Maria and Kristina Maria I never even had to try. They are my children, and they are just like me. I have always been able to understand them — ever since they were little girls — because we are so much alike.

I never had to push or motivate my daughters in any way. It appeared to me that they were self-motivated from a very young age. I never needed to stress the importance of their studies; they did that on their own with virtually no involvement or intervention from me. Right from kindergarten they were both very smart and driven.

My daughters are born workaholics, just like me. Still not yet in high school when we first opened the Lionhead golf course, at twelve and ten years old, respectively, Anna-Maria and Kristina Maria came to the course to work from 6:00 a.m. until 2:00 p.m. throughout their entire summer holidays. We offered a club-cleaning service to our Lionhead clients, and Kristina Maria would clean their clubs before they put them in their cars. She came home wet every day. Anna-Maria was in charge of vacuuming and cleaning the shelves in the pro shop and would comment on how many of them needed to be cleaned. They began taking golf lessons at this time, and I made sure they hit two buckets of balls each after work. Both of them often came home with blisters, but thanks to that early start, they are excellent golfers today.

Just as I had been while raising Danny and Heidi, I was still very busy with work while Anna-Maria and Kristina Maria were children. I might have been in my fifties, but I was still on the job site every morning before seven o'clock, ensuring that the thousands of Kaneff houses and apartments, along with our commercial plazas, were well built and made to last. I was regularly home for dinner at 6:30 p.m. with the girls — that was Didi's rule — after which I would go back to the construction site or my office or perhaps to attend a municipal council meeting.

Still, I always found time to spend with my daughters, mostly on the weekends. My wife was a tremendous help in this regard. She understood what I was trying to achieve and that I often had to work long hours to guarantee a job was completed properly.

Danny and Heidi, in many ways, had the same setup as Anna-Maria and Kristina Maria while growing up. In both cases, my mother-in-law lived in our house and helped raise the children. The daily routine was also nearly identical. Didi and her mother ran our household just as Katarina and her mother ran it before them. Personally, I was very busy when I had Danny and Heidi, I was very busy when Anna-Maria and Kristina Maria were young, and I am still very busy today. Nothing has changed in that regard.

When Katarina and I adopted Danny and Heidi in 1958 and 1959, I was busy with the construction business and the General Motors dealership. With Anna-Maria and Kristina Maria during the 1990s, my life was quite hectic with more housing developments, my expansion into commercial real estate development and property management, and of course, my foray into the golf course business. But I always made time for my children. Whenever they needed me, I was there. With Danny and Heidi, we had a cottage up north in the Muskoka Sands, where we often spent our weekends during the summer.

Both Heidi and Danny turned out to be very smart and accomplished people. Heidi excelled in academics and was an excellent student, while Danny blossomed when he was a little bit older. When he was a younger man, he had issues with punctuality and professionalism. But he grew to be a top-notch builder, and I respected his skills on the job. As he matured, Danny became one of the most skilled employees in my company. At his best, he was a brilliant construction manager.

Anna-Maria and Kristina Maria were both highly self-motivated from the very beginning, particularly in regard to academics. I always stressed the importance of education with my children, but Didi was the true scholar among us, herself a university graduate. She always helped the girls with their school work and encouraged them to learn and strive to do their best. Before long my daughters were fluent in English, French, Bulgarian, and even German. Along with their mother, Anna-Maria and Kristina Maria are true intellectuals.

Even as children, the girls were always busy. From the time of her first semester at Georgetown University, Anna-Maria always had one or two part-time jobs, along with an internship. She worked in the Economics and French Departments as a junior teaching assistant and grader, while also tutoring local children in French during her spare time. Additionally, Anna-Maria worked as a copy editor on a book being written by a local former diplomatic attaché while interning at the Center for Strategic and International Studies, a prominent Washington, D.C.–based non-profit organization, and for the U.S. House of Representatives minority leader. Not surprisingly, she paid for a portion of her undergraduate education, as did Kristina Maria.

After graduating, Anna-Maria worked at Morgan Stanley as an investment banker in New York City and San Francisco. By the time she completed her postgraduate work at Harvard University, my daughter had invested her money from Morgan Stanley and the World Bank and had made enough to support herself and pay for her postgraduate education. To say I was impressed would be an understatement.

Kristina Maria, too, made me proud again and again. She was accepted at Columbia University, where she chose to pursue her undergraduate studies. First, she co-led a one-on-one tutoring program for disenfranchised children from low-income areas of the Bronx and Queens in New York City. From there she was selected as a scheduling intern for former President Bill Clinton's non-profit organization during the fall of 2001. After serving as a research associate for Professor Henri Mitterand, Kristina Maria was voted class representative among the entire student body at Columbia College in 2003.

As anyone can see, our daughters are both bright, motivated, hard-working doers.

From the time they were babies, we wanted both Anna-Maria and Kristina Maria to receive the finest education. Since I was already more than fifty years old when they were born, I knew I would eventually want my daughters to take over the business. In order to do that to the best of their abilities, they would need to be properly educated.

Very early, I knew I wanted one of the girls to become a lawyer and the other to specialize in business. Luckily, their ambitions aligned with mine. When Anna-Maria was twelve years old, Didi and I figured out that she would be the businesswoman of the family. Whenever we brought her to Lionhead, she found her way to the cash register and tried to learn how to ring in transactions. During our family vacations, even in North America, she liked to take control of our negotiations for taxi rides and local souvenir purchases, along with any other bargaining opportunity that presented itself. Anna-Maria loved doing math in her head and competed with me regularly about who could correctly compute an arithmetic problem more quickly — it was a toss-up as to whether she or I won the challenge. She gravitated toward finance and money matters just like me.

While Anna-Maria was more hands-on, Kristina Maria was more laid-back, quieter, and more academically inclined. She was, and is, the family peacemaker, a quality Didi and I thought would lend itself well for her to become a lawyer or judge. But there has always been another side to Kristina Maria: she is the family comedian, always finding a way to see the silver lining in every dire situation. When she smiles, she makes the world smile, too. Her disposition and education have also made her a crafty and tough negotiator — skills I would like to think she got from me.

Didi and I began nudging the girls in those directions, but they actually required very little encouragement. Once the seed had been planted in their minds, our daughters devoted themselves to forging their own professional paths, and both have succeeded impressively. Most amazingly, they did it all with minimal help from us. They looked to Didi and me for guidance, but rarely for assistance. They were very proud from a young age and wanted to prove to themselves — and, I believe, also prove to me — that they were capable of achieving success on their own merits.

Kristina Maria and Anna-Maria collected degrees, along with honours, from their various institutions of higher learning. Great success was achieved by Kristina Maria at Columbia University and the University of Oxford, as well as at Osgoode Hall Law School in Toronto, while Anna-Maria earned honours at Georgetown University and graduated from Harvard Business School. In addition to their excellence in academics, my daughters were both incredibly well behaved. Never was there an act of rebellion or defiance toward their parents. Didi was an extraordinary mother to our daughters, always involved in their schooling and forever setting an outstanding example for the girls to follow. We have loved and continue to love our daughters, and they respect and love us, too.

Today, Kristina Maria makes a tremendous contribution to our community as a circle leader for an organization known as Peacebuilders International, which aims to help young people by keeping them in school and out of the criminal justice system. As far back as high school at the age of fourteen for a contest, she displayed a passion for contributing to peace in the world when she wrote and delivered a speech about the need for youth involvement in the struggle against violence. She won third prize for her speech in that provincial French-language competition. At the final round of the contest, which I attended, I could not understand a word Kristina Maria said, since I did not speak or comprehend French at all. Nevertheless, I was so overwhelmed by the moment that tears rolled down my cheeks uncontrollably and my chest swelled with pride when I heard my daughter talk.

Kristina Maria is a director of the NATO Association of Canada (formerly the Atlantic Council of Canada), is the president of the Ignat Kaneff Charitable Foundation, has served on the Peel Police Youth Services Committee, and has been an admissions interviewer for Columbia University. She is also on the golf tournament organizing committee for Community Living Mississauga, along with Anna-Maria, and is on that agency's board, as well. Previously, she was a member of the University of Toronto's board and was a Campus Council member at that university's Mississauga satellite.

Anna-Maria works with, and donates to, the Grassroots Reconciliation Group (grassrootsgroup.org), continues her involvement with United Way after being part of that charity's Women's Leadership Initiative, served on non-profit boards in Peel Region and Toronto, including the Credit Valley Hospital Foundation Board and the Royal Ontario Museum Board of Governors, and has been an admissions interviewer for Georgetown University.

Indeed, our girls have adopted my and Didi's views on charitable giving and community volunteerism, proving that charity does begin at home. There is no prouder father than me. When I look at my daughters, I see myself gazing back. They are like me, and we are the same.

For the past five years or so, in fact, my daughters have been running the company with Didi and me. These days I do nothing without discussing it with them, and I do not come to any final decisions without seeking their — and Didi's — input, understanding their concerns, and ultimately, obtaining their consent. This is the same dynamic we employ when one of my daughters has an idea to grow the company or start a new project. We are in a true partnership, though I am still the majority stakeholder. I continue to serve as the chairman and CEO of the Kaneff Group of Companies and retain the final say, but Anna-Maria and Kristina Maria are close to taking over fully.

At this time, Didi is the president of the Kaneff Group of Companies. Anna-Maria is now the executive vice-president, while Kristina Maria is our in-house counsel and vice-president. It is a family business in every sense, and with our various skills and specialties, we work together well.

In my heart, I hope my daughters continue to run the company together forever, succeeded by their children, and then by their children's children. I love the company because I built it from nothing, and I would like nothing more than to see it remain a family business.

BABA AND DYADO

For me, becoming a grandfather — or *dyado*, as we say in Bulgarian — has been the greatest joy of my life. It has been truly marvellous getting to know my granddaughters, Ignatia Anna — named after Didi's mother, Ana, and myself, and Emmanuelle Dimitrina Lynn — named after Didi and our son-in-law's mother. To describe it in words does not do justice to what it means to me.

I am also fortunate to have found in the girls' father, Michael, a wonderful son-in-law. He and Anna-Maria met at Harvard Business School, and I am told that it took Michael six years to get Anna-Maria to agree to see him for a second date. But once they reunited, the rest, as they say, is history. Michael is Australian, and we all enjoy spending time together with him. He is an accomplished and ambitious young man, and we are lucky to have him in our lives.

In my opinion, everyone should experience the joys of grandparenthood. When Ignatia, and later Emmanuelle — or "Little Iggy" and "Eddie," as they are known around our family — began speaking, and the words *dyado* and *baba* came out of their mouths, my heart melted. Being a grandparent has been the most fulfilling event of my life. It cannot be bought, and it cannot be replaced by anything.

Being a grandparent is an unusual feeling, different from raising children. Becoming grandparents has been wonderful and transformative for Didi and me. It has been like a rebirth. I would do anything for Little Iggy and Eddie. If I were starving and had just one piece of bread, I would give it to my granddaughters.

With the same devotion she showed as a mother, Didi has been helping in every possible way as a grandmother. Day and night, she would be there to help care for Ignatia and Emmanuelle if the need arose. We are a family in every sense of the word, and we would do anything for our granddaughters. My wife has been an incredible mother since the day our first daughter was born, and now she has reinvented herself as a truly remarkable grandmother.

From speaking to my own parents, I should have expected this great joy I am feeling from watching my granddaughters grow. Both my mother and father were overwhelmed by happiness whenever one of my siblings or I added a grandchild to our family. Even with that knowledge, however, I was not fully prepared for the beautiful feelings that came with becoming a grandfather. When I spend time with Ignatia and Emmanuelle, it is truly magical. To me, there is nothing better in the world.

THE MOST IMPORTANT THING IN THE WORLD

Without a doubt the most important thing in the world to me is my family. However, my family is followed by my community, which is closely trailed by my country.

I have always lived my life as if I were short on time, so the irony of living to be ninety-three is not lost on me. I have been driven by a sense of urgency ever since I saw my cousin, Bozin, drown in the Danube River as a ten-year-old boy. From that tragic event I came to understand that every new day is a gift from God.

Always rushing, I have felt that a lack of time has been my biggest problem. I want to do more than I possibly have time to do, and sometimes this results in frustration. I feel as though I have to do several things at once because of this time pressure. Even when I am on the golf course, I am always thinking about my work. I plan for what I can do next and then burst at the seams to work.

After thinking this matter through at length, I believe the key to a happy life is the health and well-being of the people you love. The happiness and health of your loved ones are simple yet important pleasures that should not be taken for granted.

At this point in my life the simplest things tend to bring me the most pleasure. I enjoy seeing beauty and prosperity in my community. I want to see everybody around me become successful, as long as they are willing to be honest, work hard, and endlessly strive to achieve their goals, whatever they might be.

I also work every day because I sincerely enjoy it even now. I still wake up every morning and thank God for giving me another day to enjoy His beautiful world. I have the same enthusiasm for life that I possessed as a ten-year-old boy. It has never been tempered, and I pray that it is never lost.

These days I find that I am just happy to still be making decisions. At my age I am delighted and proud to be handling the tough calls for my company. In fact, I believe that doing so every day is one of the things that keeps me sharp. If somebody disagrees with one of my decisions, I am always happy to debate the subject and come to a reasonable and fair conclusion. I am smart enough to realize I have very intelligent people around me, and that I am not infallible.

I am pleased to still be in a position to help others, maybe now more than ever. Although it may be difficult to believe, I really do not mind writing a cheque to the government to pay taxes. I am satisfied to know that the success of my family's company has enabled us to contribute a significant sum of money to help Canada and its citizens. Through taxation and donations, we are striving to help people who rely on our contributions and — to an even greater degree — on the government's support.

Be it my family, my community, or my country, I have found that the only true happiness in life comes from helping to create happiness for others.

HUMILIATION AND REDEMPTION

There is a simple little story that I have always felt perfectly encapsulates my experience in life, and I have told it often in the past. This story goes back to my first days in Canada during the early 1950s when I worked for Gordon Shipp in Toronto Township while still possessing only a rudimentary understanding of English.

Evidently, one of the foremen on the job, Johnny Morgan, believed I had absolutely no comprehension of English. He used a series of insulting and condescending words and terms to disparage me in front of the other men on the site.

"Look at that sucker," he would say about me as I walked past him carrying a load of building materials. "He's a swine, no better than a pig."

I did not possess the verbal dexterity to defend myself — nor was I in a financial position to risk my job by arguing with the foreman — but I understood what this man was saying, and I particularly comprehended his sentiment. Just as with German and Croatian, I was picking up English quicker than most. Certainly, I grasped more than Mr. Morgan believed I did at the time.

But, as much as I was hurt and upset, Gordon Shipp had provided me with a good-paying job and an opportunity to learn, and I could not throw it away in anger. Therefore, I stewed silently.

Although I continued to do my job for Mr. Shipp before moving on from his company several months later — improving my English all the while — I never forgot the humiliation I felt from Mr. Morgan's stinging remarks. He seemed to feel that just because I was a little immigrant from Bulgaria — a nobody in his eyes — he could treat me like a lesser person. He did not care, nor did he notice, that I was working harder than anyone else on the job site. He only saw me as an easy target for abuse. It hurt me deeply to be marginalized, but I saw no alternative other than to draw motivation from the incident before moving on.

The years passed, and by 1967 I found myself building the tallest apartment buildings in Toronto Township. They were far taller and bigger than anything Gordon Shipp's company had even attempted at that time. In fact, Mr. Shipp was still putting up one-storey and one-and-a-half-storey houses while I was building two twelve-storey apartment complexes that housed 240 units. Kaneff Construction was moving fast, and by this time my company had surpassed the Shipp Corporation in many ways.

Of course, Mr. Shipp was still my friend. He had given me my first real opportunity to work in Canada, and for that I would be grateful forever. Therefore, when he called me up one day and asked if he could send someone over to my job site to see how we were doing things, I happily consented. Truthfully, the area needed more apartment buildings than

I could provide; I felt that Mr. Shipp would be doing a service for the community if he, too, began constructing apartment buildings.

Unbeknownst to me, the individual Mr. Shipp chose to send as his emissary was none other than my old foreman, Johnny Morgan. More than fifteen years had passed, and in my heart I had forgiven Mr. Morgan for his hurtful comments. But I had never forgotten the humiliation, nor had I misplaced the mental image of his sneering face.

One morning Mr. Morgan appeared on the dusty construction site. He poked around for a few minutes before finally asking one of my men to point out the boss. My employee did so, and my former foreman headed toward me. From the corner of my eye, I caught Mr. Morgan's gaze as he approached me from a distance. I turned to greet him.

"Hello, Mr. Morgan," I said as he drew closer. I called him "Mr. Morgan" because he had been my foreman, and I chose to pay him that respect.

After so many years, our eyes finally met. Mr. Morgan recognized me instantly. I watched as the blood drained from his face, leaving him a pale white. I could tell that he recalled every bad word and insult he had sent my way, and from my expression he could see that I remembered them, too.

Mr. Morgan was stunned to see that I was doing so well, building the tallest apartment complexes in the area. To him, I had been nothing more than an unwelcome immigrant when I worked for Mr. Shipp, but I had become a somebody. He had assumed that I would always be nothing and had treated me as such.

Mr. Morgan never bothered to open his mouth that day. He lingered around the construction site and observed my operation for Mr. Shipp but did not speak to me.

At the end of the day I finally broke the silence. "Mr. Morgan," I addressed him, "how do you rate the work this sucker is doing?" The only reply to my question he could offer was a look of pure defeat. Turning around, he started walking away and left the construction site without a word.

A feeling came over me. It was not revenge; it was more like subtle satisfaction. I understood at that moment that I had truly become a somebody. I had done something worth doing, and Mr. Morgan's silence and subsequent disappearance from my construction site made that fact more apparent than ever before.

At that moment I knew I had done everything I believed I could do, and I knew that I was still capable of doing a whole lot more. I held my head a little bit higher because I finally recognized that I was Iggy Kaneff, the little Bulgarian who had made it big in Canada, and that sounded pretty good to me.

LESSONS I HAVE LEARNED

Oddly enough, the lessons I learned throughout my childhood in Bulgaria ended up serving me as well as anything I learned after leaving. First and foremost, one lesson has always stood out as most important: be honest with people, always.

I do my best to be honest at all times, and it has served me well. As I always say, if you cheat in golf, you will cheat in life and business. Most people will only give you one chance, so you have to make good on that chance with honesty and integrity. Anything less is not good enough. If you always tell the truth, you will never have a need for secrets or lies, nor will you have to keep track of the tales you tell others. Being honest consistently has proven to be a more valuable currency than any other, because honesty breeds trust, and trust creates lasting and successful relationships.

Furthermore, I believe it is important to help people whenever possible. That does not mean helping those you hope will somehow help you in the future. It is critical to help people who really need it. Nobody in our community should be forgotten or left behind; we need to help those who cannot help themselves.

I have always treated people with respect, and in turn they have done the same for me. You cannot expect to receive respect without first offering it. If you do not respect people, your career will be short; this is true for any job. Once people start doubting you, there is nothing you can do to restore their faith. Therefore, you should never give anyone a reason to doubt you. If you are honest and respectful without fail, you will not be doubted. More importantly, you will have no reason to doubt yourself.

The opportunity to be deceitful in a deal might present itself, but that is no way to do business, and it is no way to live life. When I see somebody in a vulnerable business position, I do my best to help that person. I do not want to be the only one around who is doing well; I want everybody in my community to experience success and happiness.

I have respect for those who try their best according to their knowledge and their means. Life is not easy, but you always have to keep trying, especially during the hard times. I believe that if you keep trying to help others while continuing to be of value to the community, good things will eventually happen. In fact, I am living proof of this guiding principle. I have not always made the right decision or the best decision, but I have always tried to be as thoughtful and fair as possible.

I cannot say with certainty that my advice will help every reader of this book. I suppose it depends on what somebody is looking for from life. But if it is your desire to be successful, maybe what I have said can help you. My hope is that people recognize that this book is a sincere and candid narration of my story; I never tried to paint an unrealistically rosy portrait of my life. Every part of this story has been faithful to the truth, and every word of it has come from my heart.

In my life, hard work, along with dedication to my community, has given me rewards beyond my wildest dreams. In fact, I have been rewarded many times over. When I sit in my house or walk around one of my golf courses, I continue to be in awe. I still cannot believe I have lived this life.

Of course, I never claimed to have achieved my successes alone; I had quite a bit of help along the way. However, those who helped me were also well rewarded themselves. The people who contributed to my success — among them, Grace Bridges, Eric McKnight, Gabriella Favero, Tracey McMahon, George Berzins, Crystal Frail, Brian Williams, Luis Martins, Grace Keegan, Beppi Paron, and Nick Doncheff — did not do it for nothing, and their work was not in vain.

There are a few guidelines I have always followed when it comes to business and life. They might seem simple, but they have proven essential to my success. First of all, when you make a deal — be it to build someone a house or to sell them a sandwich — it is of greatest importance to deliver on your end of the bargain. Your reputation and your character are more important than any deal. You can only fool people once. You will not get a chance to fool them a second time. With my company, a big part of our success can be attributed to people recognizing that we always do the job we say we will do. Every time and without fail.

It is the same way with a job. To be successful, you have to love your work and perform well consistently. Even if you feel overqualified for the position, you still have to love the job you have. If you can find a superior means of employment, then by all means take it. But until you get a better job, you should treat your current one as if it is the best. Through toil, your "bad" job will eventually bring you to a better one, as long as you treat it with respect.

As I learned from experience, you can only build a house one brick at a time. Similarly, everything worth doing requires time and care, and that includes your job. When I first started working in Canada, I made $1.10 per hour and was happy to be doing so. It was no fortune, but it was a lot of money to me. I valued the job I had, but I was looking to go from $1.10 to $1.20, then $1.30, and so on. However, if I had expected to go from making $1.10 straight to $5 — or $100,000 per year, or whatever the number — I would have been sorely disappointed when it did not happen, a victim of unrealistic expectations. You have to be grateful for what you have while constantly striving for more. Keep working and working. Eventually, you will be rewarded.

I often return to my roots in farming to illustrate what I have learned in life. When I received an honorary doctorate from the University of Toronto in 1994, I gave a speech that included this excerpt:

> In my modest country of Bulgaria, agriculture played a major and important role in people's lives. Let me tell you a story about three farmers who had gathered to celebrate Thanksgiving.
>
> The first farmer said, "It has been such a drought that I didn't bother seeding the fields."
>
> The second farmer said, "Yes, I agree. It was a bad year, and I seeded the fields but didn't bother to harvest them. It wasn't worth the effort."
>
> The third farmer said, "It was a bad year, but I seeded, cultivated, and then harvested. It wasn't much, but I

have enough to feed my family through the winter and I also have some seeds left over to plant next year."

The third farmer knew that if you don't seed, you can't harvest. The crop only grows if you plant the seed and cultivate it. I hope, my dear graduates, that you will remember this simple story, which has great meaning.

For every endeavour you undertake in life, you have to put the seeds in the ground, and with effort, love, patience, and persistence, you will see the fruits of your labour. It is particularly heartwarming to me that my daughter Anna-Maria took inspiration from my speech and used the story of the three farmers in her own valedictorian address when she graduated from Neuchâtel Junior College in Switzerland in 1997.

So, in summing up, here are some of the lessons I have learned in life and business:

- Always be honest with other people. Honesty builds trust, and trust forges sturdy bonds that stand the test of time.
- Help people as much as you can, especially those with challenges that make it difficult for them to help themselves.
- Treat people with respect and they will repay you in kind.
- Be a productive member of your community, giving your time, energy, and resources for the betterment of those you live and work with.
- In everything you do, always deliver on what you promise.

I am also known for my sayings and expressions, many of which have been influenced by my Bulgarian roots, while others have sprung from my experiences in business. A few have been touched on here and there elsewhere in this book. Most are translated from Bulgarian, so some impact has been lost because of that.

- If you have hair, you can always find a comb.
- Some good always comes from bad situations.
- When you have meat and vegetables, you have everything.

- A bird should never be ashamed of its nest. Any bird ashamed of its nest does not deserve to be from there.
- The fish always smells from the head first.
- Do not worry about the flag when the ship is sinking.
- Let us try to save the lamb and feed the wolf.
- I am only as good as my worst trade.
- The customer is the most important part of business.
- Without workers, we do not have anything.
- You can catch more bees with honey.
- Never before better (when I am asked how I am doing).
- Do not fix something that is not broken.
- God gives and God takes.
- Do not regret losing something you never had.
- If it is rainy today, do not despair. Tomorrow will be sunny.

These lessons are the culmination of my experience, and I know each of them to be true. It is my hope to pass them on to others so that those interested in my story can achieve success in their own way. This book was written so that others can benefit from my experiences, learn from my mistakes, and perhaps avoid some of the pitfalls that made my path more difficult than it had to be.

EPILOGUE

On Being Honoured

Over the years, I have received numerous honours and deeply appreciate each and every one of them, but there are a few I particularly cherish. Two of these have been given to me by my adopted country.

On January 27, 2011, Ontario Lieutenant Governor David Onley invested me with the Order of Ontario, the province's highest honour, which is given to Ontarians for their contributions to the arts, justice, science, medicine, history, politics, philanthropy, and the environment. The ceremony, held at Queen's Park, Ontario's legislature, was one of the most memorable days of my life. But more was to come.

When I was first notified about the Order of Ontario, it came as a complete surprise. Candidates for this honour are chosen after recommendations by distinguished citizens and organizations. The same is the case for the Order of Canada. Just before Christmas 2016, I was informed that I had been selected for induction as a Member of the Order of Canada. The ceremony was slated for January 2017, but I was unable to travel to Ottawa at that time, so I was invested with forty-four other people on May 12 of the same year.

This Order of Canada ceremony was particularly exceptional because it featured the premiere of the "Recipients' March," a processional commissioned to mark the order's fiftieth anniversary. The event took place in the Ballroom at Rideau Hall in the nation's capital and was presided over by Governor General David Johnston.

Equally unforgettable for me was receiving the Stara Planina First Degree, Bulgaria's highest civilian honour, in 2002. My homeland also appointed me the honorary consul for Bulgaria in Canada.

In the past twenty-five years, three honorary doctors of laws have been conferred on me from universities — the University of Toronto, York University's Osgoode Hall Law School, and the University of Ruse in Bulgaria. And there have been dozens of other distinctions accorded me, including recent ones such as the Building Industry and Land Development (BILD) Association's Lifetime Achievement Award, the Federation of Rental Housing Providers of Ontario Lifetime Achievement Award, the Bulgarian Ministry of Foreign Affairs' Golden Laurel Bough for my charitable works, and Community Living's Lifetime Achievement Award, all in 2016.

My life has been graced with a great number of things, but becoming acquainted with many of the prime ministers of my adopted country and several premiers of my home province has been especially rewarding for a little guy from Bulgaria. I have exchanged words and much else with Prime Ministers Pierre and Justin Trudeau, John Turner, Brian Mulroney, Kim Campbell, Jean Chrétien, Paul Martin, and Stephen Harper, while doing likewise with Ontario Premiers John Robarts, Bill Davis, David Peterson, Mike Harris, Dalton McGuinty, and Kathleen Wynne.

Once, when I was playing golf in Scotland, I asked a fellow golfer, who was a Scot, "How did a sport invented by a country with so few people spread all over the world the way it has?"

The Scottish golfer grinned and replied, "We may be only five million, but there are at least a hundred and fifty million of us around the world. That's why."

He had a point. At least thirty-three U.S. presidents out of a total of forty-five had Scottish or Ulster-Scots ancestry, and in Canada there have been thirteen out of twenty-two prime ministers with some Scottish ancestry.

The reason I mention this is that perhaps one day Canada might see a prime minister or a premier of Bulgarian descent!

APPENDIX

Anecdotes and Reminiscences

TED BAKER (LANDSCAPE ARCHITECT)

A guy walks up to the bar at the Credit Valley Golf and Country Club. The stranger beside him says, "You're Ted Baker. I'm Iggy Kaneff. Come to my office on Monday morning."

Now I had been trying to meet Iggy for months, only to be told by those around him that his company didn't need a landscape architect. So we met, discussed a new commercial project, and as I left, Iggy requested that his secretary, Mrs. Grace Bridges, give me a cheque, telling her, "Mr. Baker will be doing many projects with Kaneff."

That was in 1978. Hundreds of projects later, countless games of golf, lunches, and dinners later, Iggy became my mentor and one of my best friends. He is a loyal supporter of my work and my harshest critic. When we disagree, he is invariably correct.

In 1988, he stopped me as I passed by his lunch table and told me he wanted to build a golf course, not any course but the best one, and asked me to design it. Glen Schnarr found the property and secured the approvals, and Lionhead Golf Club & Conference Centre was born, followed by more courses: Streetsville Glen, Carlisle, Century Pines, Royal Niagara, and Royal Ontario.

Unlike many others who were building courses in the early 1990s, Iggy was the first to embrace public golf. He wrote the book on the management of high-quality courses open to everyone. His successful model is still being copied.

As impressive as all this is, there is another side of Iggy I'd like to share. Shortly after our initial meeting and during an Ontario provincial election, I mentioned to him that I thought rent controls were totally unfair. Iggy had thousands of apartments he had built with his own sweat and money and was continuing to take all the risks. Here, paraphrased, was his reply: "Teddy [I always knew I was in trouble when he called me Teddy], I came from a part of the world where even rudimentary shelter and food was not available for large segments of the population. Eventually, riots and wars took place. I can accept rent controls so that everyone has a roof over their head and can provide for their family. In such a country — Canada — I can work hard and prosper."

In doing so, Iggy has help thousands of people, including this "displaced person" from Port Credit. I will be eternally grateful.

MILA BULATOVIC

My relationship with Mr. Kaneff started in 1994 and has spanned almost twenty-five years. With Mr. Kaneff's assistance, I was able to start my own business providing cleaning services to multiple Kaneff locations. The Kaneffs have become so much more than just my employer; they are my friends and they treat my family as part of their extended family. I have a deep admiration for Mr. Kaneff and his many accomplishments and will always have a special place in my heart for the Kaneff family.

GRANT CARSON

After twenty-five years of working for Mr. Kaneff, I can still remember the first day I met him. I was just hired as executive sous-chef at the Lionhead

Golf & Country Club. When we were introduced, Mr. Kaneff welcomed me to the company and was excited for the upcoming season. He didn't call me by my given name but addressed me as "Chef" instead. That caught me a little off guard, and I looked behind me to see who he was talking to, then realized he was speaking to me. It was the first time I was called "Chef." To this very day, he calls me "Chef." After many golf seasons, menu changes, and meetings, I'm sure he finally knows my given name!

In preparation for my first season, I began menu-testing and presented my suggested items to Mr. Kaneff for his opinion. I set before him a beautiful steak with a Périgueux sauce and truffled compound butter. I must say I was very impressed with my selection and its flavour. Mr. Kaneff looked at it and said, "That's not a steak. I'll show you how to cook a steak."

I quickly ran back into the kitchen and prepared a minestrone soup and wild smoked salmon plate. Shortly afterward, I went out to the table to ask how his meal was.

"It was so good I forgot to taste it," he replied.

Phew! It wasn't until years later that I had the pleasure of Mr. Kaneff actually preparing me a steak. He was right. He cooks a fabulous one!

It's remarkable that after almost every single conversation I've had with Mr. Kaneff over the years that I've always walked away feeling I've learned something. Mr. Kaneff's energy and pursuit of perfection are truly inspiring.

BILL DAVIS (FORMER PREMIER OF ONTARIO)

Many years ago, I met Iggy Kaneff, who was known first by my late father, A. Grenville Davis. It was in the years when Iggy started out in business in Ontario. Since those early days, Iggy has built his way up and prospered. He is a great family man and has been most generous to various organizations in his community and beyond.

When Iggy met my father, Iggy was a member of the Liberal Party. I realize that he remains philosophically misguided after all these decades. Nevertheless, I admire him for all that he has accomplished and am pleased to call him a friend.

CRYSTAL FRAIL

I started working for the Kaneff Group of Companies when I was thirteen years old, helping out at reception and in whatever department needed assistance in filing or typing. At twenty years old, I began working full-time, first as a receptionist and then in accounts receivable. For the past twenty years, I have been in accounts payable. All told, I've worked for Mr. Kaneff for more than forty years. He is not just a leader to me but an inspiration, as well. He is one of the reasons why I'm always trying to be better. I appreciate him in so many ways.

VESSELIN GUEORGUIEV

I met Mr. Kaneff for the first time in 1994. I don't think he remembered me the next year when I went to his head office with my wife, Maria, to talk to him about jobs. We were recent immigrants to Canada and had heard that Mr. Kaneff was a kind and generous man. He said he wasn't sure if there were any jobs for us but that we should leave our phone numbers with him just in case. Twenty minutes later he called us, offering us both jobs. For the past twenty-four years now, I've worked for Mr. Kaneff in various capacities, currently as golf superintendent for Lionhead Golf Club & Conference Centre.

Mr. Kaneff is extremely benevolent and is the most hard-working man I've ever met. I'm thankful for having met him, worked for him, and for being his friend for almost a quarter century.

HAZEL MCCALLION (FORMER MAYOR OF MISSISSAUGA)

I have known Ignat (Iggy) Kaneff since 1969. Over the years, we have built a friendship grounded in respect and mutual admiration. Iggy has grown his business from that of a small homebuilder to running one of the largest real estate development and construction companies in Ontario. It has been a pleasure to have him build his business in Mississauga, and for me to preside over Mississauga as its mayor during the time in which his business flourished. His integrity and community-mindedness, including supporting the Mississauga and Credit Valley hospitals, Community Living Mississauga, the University of Toronto, and York University, are unmatched, but above all, he is a family man. These qualities make me proud to have known him for more than forty years.

TRACEY MCMAHON

I first met Mr. Kaneff when I started working for the Kaneff Group of Companies in 1976. I was just sixteen years old, had just graduated from high school, and was looking for my first job.

There was an advertisement in a local newspaper for a receptionist at Kaneff Properties, and with no job experience, I applied for the position. To the amazement of many, I was hired, and shortly thereafter was promoted to administrative assistant to the residential property manager, where I stayed for several years before another promotion to executive assistant to the senior executive vice-president. For the past five years, I have held the position of executive assistant to Mr. and Mrs. Kaneff.

To this day, I believe that Mr. Kaneff saw a very young girl at his door, reflected on his past as a very young boy who had himself been given an opportunity at the market garden in Germany, and decided to do the same for me. He took a chance on me that others were not willing to do. That's just the kind of person he is — always ready and willing to help people, which is evident in his lifetime of outstanding philanthropy.

J. ROBERT S. PRICHARD
(PRESIDENT EMERITUS, UNIVERSITY OF TORONTO)

Iggy Kaneff is a remarkable Canadian and one of my favourite people. His story is the best of our country, and it is Canadians like Iggy who have made Canada the envy of the world. From his earliest days after arriving in Canada in 1951 with $5 in his pocket, Iggy has built a great company, a great community, a great family, and a great legacy. He is a good and generous man.

I first met Iggy after I became president of the University of Toronto and he was a well-known developer in Mississauga and a generous supporter of the Mississauga campus of the university. Iggy led the development of both the Kaneff Centre and the Student Centre, helping to transform the campus from a suburban outpost of the university into a major university with more than fifteen thousand students. We recognized Iggy with an honorary doctor of laws degree for his leadership, and he was later recognized with the Order of Ontario and Order of Canada — all richly deserved celebrations of this remarkable man.

Iggy went from being a benefactor to being a dear friend. Iggy and Didi are fabulous parents. Our families became close, and we watched in awe as Kristina Maria and Anna-Maria emerged as outstanding young women prepared to take Iggy's business into the next generation.

My best times with Iggy are on his golf courses. No matter how I play — good, bad, or ugly — Iggy always wins and I always owe him money at the end. He changes the rules, bets, side bets, and all else, claiming he can do whatever he wants on his own courses. And always with a smile and a laugh. While he doesn't hit the ball long, he hits it straight and knows every inch of every green, making him formidable with a putter in his hand. We have played together, laughed together, and made great plans together on his golf courses.

I so admire Iggy for all he has accomplished and contributed to making Canada a better place and raising a beautiful family that will extend his legacy for generations to come. He is in every way a great Canadian and a great friend.

RUMEN RADEV, PRESIDENT OF THE REPUBLIC OF BULGARIA

As translated from Bulgarian to English.

In September 2017, I had the pleasure to welcome and personally thank Ignat Kaneff, Bulgaria's honorary consul in Mississauga, for his dedicated contributions to the preservation of the cultural and spiritual traditions of the Bulgarian community in Canada as well as for his implementation of a number of education and health-care projects in Bulgaria itself.

The Stara Planina Order First Degree awarded to Mr. Kaneff in 2002 and the Honorary Sign of the President he received in 2016 epitomize the high recognition and gratitude of Bulgaria for this emblematic Bulgarian entrepreneur, social activist, and philanthropist.

Mr. Kaneff's charity activity compels admiration and thanks for its scale and consistency as do the projects financed by the charitable Kaneff Foundation that meet the real needs of people. Regarding the latter, I was truly touched to receive as a gift the national flag that once waved above St. Dimitar Bulgarian Eastern Orthodox Church in Brampton, Ontario. This church, whose chief sponsor is Mr. Kaneff, is a spiritual, cultural, and educational centre for Bulgarians who live in the Greater Toronto Area.

In May 2018, we chose the Kaneff Centre, constructed with funds donated by Mr. Kaneff on the territory of "Angel Kanchev" University of Ruse, to be the site of the high-level Sustainable Development of the Danube Region conference held during the Bulgarian chairing of the Council of the European Union. At the conference, we discussed with the presidents of Austria and Romania ways to revive the Danube as a river that would truly connect European citizens and create new economic opportunities for them.

Mr. Kaneff's name symbolizes success, but more importantly, he is an example of how success is achieved through perseverance, tenacity, and honest work. I strongly hope that many Bulgarians will follow Mr. Kaneff's lead and adopt his corporate and social responsibility practices.

GLEN SCHNARR (URBAN PLANNER)

Iggy and I first met in 1979 when I moved to Mississauga for the position of general manager with the Credit Valley Conservation Authority. I recall telling my father-in-law at a Sunday dinner that I was playing golf with Iggy Kaneff the following week. He told me that Iggy had personally built his home on Enniskillen Circle in the Credit Woodlands over twenty years ago. I had to ask Iggy to confirm this, since it was hard for me to believe that the owner of a major land development company was a framing carpenter such a short time ago. Iggy not only confirmed that he personally built the house with his own hands but remembered the house number and that three little girls, including my wife-to-be, moved in upon completion.

Our friendship continued, and seven years later I started an urban planning and development consulting company that has worked with Iggy for thirty-two years since then. In the early 1990s, I remember suggesting to Iggy that he walk away from a mortgage on a hundred acres of property in West Oak Trails in Oakville, since the mortgage had a higher value than the property. Lots of developers were abandoning their raw land mortgages at that time. But not Iggy! He told me, "I wouldn't feel right if I did." He has always been a principled gentleman with high moral standards.

One of the first projects I ever did for Iggy was Lionhead Golf Club & Conference Centre. Ted Baker and I approached Iggy with a pro forma for a golf course development. Iggy advised us that for him "Golf was about fun, not about money." A few weeks later we were back in his boardroom, and KaneffGolf was born!

Years ago I recall stopping by Iggy's new house to attend to a few business matters. When I got there, he said, "Glen, before we get started ..." Then he called upstairs, "Anna-Maria, Kristina, come down and play a sonata for your future father-in-law." Iggy and the Kaneffs always treated us like family.

Iggy and I like to tell people that we both came to Canada in the same year — 1951. The difference is: Iggy arrived by ship and I arrived courtesy of my dear mother.

Not many people can say in their lifetime that one person was like their second father, one of their best friends, and their most important business associate. Forty years later I know that Iggy and I are most proud of this and our many accomplishments and countless memorable times together.

MAMDOUH SHOUKRI
(FORMER PRESIDENT OF YORK UNIVERSITY)

I first met Iggy Kaneff more than ten years ago when York University celebrated the naming of the new Osgoode Hall Law School's building after him. I was excited to meet the legend who transformed the city in which I live. It did not take us long to become close family friends.

I am sure that Iggy's remarkable life, incredible contributions to Canada and his fellow Canadians, and the many prestigious accolades and awards he has received will be covered appropriately in his biography. However, it is the remarkable human being behind all that success whom I call my friend.

He is a man of integrity whose actions and behaviour are guided by clear moral convictions, a quality that made him one of the most trustworthy people in the business community and among his friends. His modesty and friendly demeanour bring out the best in people. He is a very proud Canadian who continues to praise his adopted country and what it stands for. His dedication to his family is reflected in every conversation I have had with him. He also has a great sense of humour that reflects his positive spirit and love of people.

I was privileged to note Iggy's attributes in a few circumstances. I recall his reaction to knowing that he had received an honorary doctorate from York University for his contributions to Canada. His emotional reaction reflected a sense of pride and gratitude. His humanity and modesty were evident when he shed a few tears acknowledging the accolade.

In his daily golf game, Iggy shows a lot of his competitiveness, kindness, and sense of humour. Golfing with him is a lot of fun where I — a terrible golfer — was the recipient of his kindness, encouragement, and valuable advice. His sense of humour was demonstrated when we golfed with my son, a strong, athletic young man but not necessarily a great golfer. It appears that Iggy decided to get under the young man's skin. When my son was later asked about the game, he smiled and said, "I was not only beaten by a man three times my age but he also trash-talked me for eighteen holes."

I am pleased to see a biography of this remarkable man. It will be of great benefit to young people, demonstrating the value of hard work, integrity, and empathy. The book is a tribute to both the man and to the country he loved and that opened its arms to him.

DR. KONSTANTIN L. VALTCHEV (ASSISTANT PROFESSOR, UNIVERSITY OF TORONTO)

I have known Ignat Kaneff personally for more than forty years. Twenty years ago he had the desire to build a Bulgarian Eastern Orthodox church and invited me to join him in this project. We searched for suitable land on which to build, and when we didn't have any luck finding it, Iggy and his family graciously donated land in Brampton, Ontario. During that time, I became a member of his church planning and construction committee. In 2005, we opened the doors of St. Dimitar Bulgarian Eastern Orthodox Church, a gift from Iggy's family to the Bulgarian community in Brampton, Mississauga, and beyond.

For me, Iggy is a person with iron discipline, kind and humble. He hasn't wasted a minute of his life. He has been constantly building, selling, donating, and helping thousands of people with jobs and opportunities. He became the wealthiest and most philanthropic Bulgarian in Canada. He was awarded with many honours, among them the Order of Ontario and the Order of Canada. As a Bulgarian, I am very proud of his great achievements and the right to say that he is my friend. On a few occasions, I told him, "Iggy, God has given you many other gifts, but two of them are the most important ones — how to deal with money and people."

I wish Iggy many more years of health and happiness.

BRIAN WILLIAMS

One of my first experiences years ago as a junior accountant was when Mr. Kaneff approached me in the office hallway. He had watched a news cast the previous night and wanted me to explain the tax rebates and incentives the government had just announced for operators of gas stations.

I wasn't aware of the program but said I would look into it. When I went back to my desk, I did the research and returned to his office, feeling a bit nervous yet very proud that I had all the answers. After I explained the new incentive program, he asked, "How do we apply for this program?"

I was lost.

The moral of this story is not only is it good to have answers to Mr. Kaneff's initial questions, but you should also anticipate his subsequent questions before approaching him again.

Mr. Kaneff has not only been my employer but also my mentor and teacher over the past twenty-plus years of working alongside him. He has truly inspired me.

Acknowledgements

First, thank you to Steven Nyczyk for having the patience to work with me and my family over the past four years to tell my story. Your questions, diligence, and thoughtfulness have helped me share my story in a way no other writer or journalist to date has been able to do.

Thanks also to freelance editors Cy Strom and Michael Carroll, to Kathryn Lane and the rest of the staff at Dundurn Press, and to Steven Woods for his help organizing the book's photographs and captions.

Without the aid of my executive assistant, Tracey McMahon, helping me to keep on track and on schedule, I would have missed many sessions with our biographer, Steven. Tracey, thank you for also reading through the final draft to ensure that, like my schedule, everything was in order. You have been a constant in our family's life, and helped our company in innumerable ways over the past forty-three years — we are forever grateful for your dedication to and support of the Kaneff family and the Kaneff Group of Companies.

Importantly, I owe many thanks and a deep gratitude to my supportive family for their involvement in making this book project a reality.

ACKNOWLEDGEMENTS

Without the women in my life pushing me to share my stories and my life's reflections, this book would not have come to fruition. Thank you, Anna-Maria, Didi, and Kristina Maria — without your dedication to sharing my story, it never would have found its way into a book.

Index